STEPHEN DECATUR

ROBERT J. ALLISON

STEPHEN DECATUR

American Naval Hero, 1779-1820

University of Massachusetts Press
Amherst and Boston

Copyright © 2005 by the University of Massachusetts Press
All rights reserved
Printed in the United States of America

LC 2005005402
ISBN 1-55849-492-8

Designed by Dennis Anderson
Set in New Baskerville
Printed and bound by The Maple-Vail Book Manufacturing Group

Library of Congress Cataloging-in-Publication Data

Allison, Robert J.
    Stephen Decatur : American naval hero, 1779–1820 / Robert J. Allison.
        p. cm.
    Includes bibliographical references and index.
    ISBN 1-55849-492-8 (cloth : alk. paper)
    1. Decatur, Stephen, 1779–1820.   2. Admirals—United States—Biography.   3.
United States. Navy—Biography.   4. United States—History—War of 1812—Naval
operations.   5. United States—History, Naval—To 1900.   I. Title.
    E353.1.D29A69 2005
    359'.0092—dc22

                                                                    2005005402

British Library Cataloguing in Publication data are available.

For

John Robert and Philip

Two bold sailors

CONTENTS

STEPHEN DECATUR

"The navy has lost its mainmast"

T
HE PEACH blossoms were early in 1820. Just three days after spring began, Friday, March 24, the buds opened, weeks before their usual time. Washington sorely needed spring.

January had been the coldest in eight years. February brought snow. March had been cold, rainy, and raw. Emotionally and politically it had also been a hard winter. The economy staggered under an economic depression, while Congress considered the fate of the nation itself. The question of Missouri— should it be admitted as a slave state, or could Congress prohibit slavery in this new member of the Union?—had exploded into a question of the country's future. Anxious men and women, black and white, crowded the galleries to hear Congress debate their future. A Virginia senator, representing the home state of George Washington and James Madison, proposed to senators from Massachusetts, home of John Adams, that the states begin discussing ways to dissolve the Union.

It was a union that had lasted forty-four years, though its life seemed to be ebbing. Its past was slipping away. On March 14, receiving the news that George III had died at the end of January, John Quincy Adams reflected that the old king had reigned for sixty years, and that perhaps half a million Americans, including himself, had once been his subjects. Of the fifty-six men who had signed the Declaration of Independence, "only four are at this day numbered among the living. John Adams of Massachusetts, my father. Thomas Jefferson of Virginia, William Floyd of New York and Charles Carroll of Carrollton, Maryland."[1] With these patriarchs would go the memory of the past; America's future seemed very much in doubt.

At the other end of Pennsylvania Avenue, President James Monroe found himself at the center of an etiquette war, which had erupted over the question of whether his wife and daughters should call on the wives of ambassadors. Not as explosive as the prospect of the Union shattering, this social impasse at the White House nevertheless prevented the personal social encounters that enabled the political process to work smoothly. Even his daughter Maria's wedding, to her cousin Samuel Gouverneur of New York, had escalated the tension. Monroe's eldest daughter, Eliza Monroe Hay, had forbidden the ambassadors' wives to call on her younger sister, as they had not previously called on her. So the first White House wedding, on March 9, of these two cousins separated, north and south, by geography, was a private affair.

Washington came together that month not in celebration but in sorrow when illness struck the Calhoun household. Floride and John Calhoun's young daughter, Elizabeth, took sick in March, and the Washington ladies, still feuding over etiquette, joined together to nurse the girl and give her anxious parents a rest. President Monroe called every day, and his imperious daughter Eliza Hay sat up night after night with little Elizabeth. Even on the Saturday evening when Commodore and Mrs. Stephen Decatur were holding an elegant ball in honor of her sister's wedding, Eliza sat up with the Calhouns. Floride protested that Eliza's place was with her sister, but she was rebuffed. President Monroe himself insisted that Eliza, "the best nurse in the world," should spend the evening by Elizabeth's bedside. Louisa Catherine Adams, wife of the secretary of state, and other Washington women faithfully ministered at the Calhoun home, not because the brilliant and handsome John Calhoun was secretary of war, and possibly a future president, but because he and Floride were "really beloved."[2]

To relieve the atmosphere of gloom, Commodore and Mrs. Decatur planned an elegant ball at their mansion on Lafayette Square. With the White House no longer Washington's social center, the Decaturs had made their home, designed by Benjamin Latrobe and built with Decatur's prize money won by capturing the British frigate *Macedonian* in 1812, the heart of Washington society. None who had been in the capital eight years earlier could forget the night that the navy secretary's son, Lieutenant Archibald Hamilton, had arrived with the captured *Macedonian*'s flag at a Washington party at Tomlinson's Hotel in honor of other naval heroes: Isaac Hull of the *Constitution*, Charles Stewart of the *Constellation*, Jacob Jones of the *Wasp*. At nine the doors had opened suddenly, and in came young Hamilton, who had ridden nonstop from Connecticut, carrying the trophy. His father and the other captains took up the flag like a tent, parading around it around the room, then laying it at Dolley Madison's feet. This moment of dramatic triumph had become Decatur's signature, and now, in 1820, living in Washington as a naval commissioner, the gallant commodore and his beautiful and intelligent wife, Susan, opened their home to celebrate Maria Monroe Gouverneur's marriage. Those present at the Decaturs' would later recall the commodore's "devotion to his wife and her music, as she played upon the harp, the company forming a semicircle in front of her, Decatur himself, in uniform, the center of the semicircle, his eyes riveted upon his wife."[3]

Others planned parties for this festive week. On Tuesday, more than one hundred guests danced until after midnight at the home of Secretary of State John Quincy Adams and his charming wife, Louisa Catherine. General Van Ness, commander of Washington's militia, and Commodore David Porter, a fellow naval commissioner with Decatur, planned their own elegant balls for later in the week. In the midst of the revelry at Decatur's home, the host told Porter cryptically, "I may spoil your party."[4]

On the morning after the gathering at the Adamses' home, the secretary of state left for his office. He was stopped in his tracks by stunning news. Stephen Decatur had been "mortally wounded in a duel with Commodore James Barron." Adams "went immediately to Decatur's house," meeting on the way Captain Thomas Macdonough, the hero of the battle of Lake Champlain. Macdonough had just left Decatur, with news that was "discouraging but not decisive." Attending Decatur, the surgeon general issued a vague prognosis, humanely trying to keep Susan Decatur and her father "in suspense as long as possible."[5]

For Decatur, there was little suspense. From the moment he felt the ball tear through his intestines, he knew he could not survive. Carried home in agony, he forbade his wife to enter the room where he lay vomiting blood. As the house crowded with anxious well-wishers, Susan and her father spent the day in seclusion. Decatur still lived, General Solomon Van Renssalaer wrote his wife, "but will never see another sun."[6] Curious citizens filled the street outside. They honored Decatur as a "hero and a patriot" but, more important, loved him as a "citizen and neighbor."[7] Stephen Decatur, struggling against the inevitable, died after twelve excruciating hours at 10:30 in the evening.

Elizabeth Calhoun had died that afternoon.

Decatur's death was a "national affliction."[8] "Mourn Columbia! For one of thy brightest stars is set!" a Washington editor wrote when he heard the news.[9] "Our City is more deeply envelopped in gloom," Louisa Catherine Adams wrote to her father-in-law, the former president, "and every moment seems to teem with new trouble."[10] "Decaturs fall is an awfull event," John Adams wrote back, "if there is anything awful in this lower World. I have read Ivanhoe and there is nothing much more awfull in that."[11] Rumors of more duels swirled through Washington: Barron and John Rodgers had exchanged harsh words on the dueling ground, and Porter had castigated Barron's second, Jesse Elliot. These survivors, all except Barron captains in the navy, now would have to face off on the field of honor.

Business in Washington ceased. In the House of Representatives, the Speaker could hardly keep the members in order, "so anxious do they seem to ascertain the particulars," and so generally was "commodore Decatur beloved by the members."[12] Monroe canceled his afternoon reception—some recalled that in 1812 President Madison had not canceled his afternoon reception when Vice President George Clinton died—and all of the parties others were holding for his daughter and son-in-law were called off.[13] "From the moment Decatur fell, nothing else was thought of."[14]

On Thursday afternoon an unusually long procession of carriages followed the Calhouns as they laid their daughter in her grave. For the Calhouns, this tragedy was made more bitter by the memories of their daughter Floride's death five years earlier, when both parents had been struck down by grief. This time John could not bring himself to make the funeral arrangements, delegating the task to a friend while he buried himself in his work.

That evening, Congressman John Sergeant of Philadelphia "could not resist the inclination to take a last look at what remains of the gallant soldier." He went, alone, to Decatur's house, and for some minutes stood silently by the body. "Very little change had taken place," Sergeant wrote his wife. "I almost fancied I saw him breathe." But "alas, the breath of life had departed, and he lay in quiet and solemn stillness, as if he had died in peace with all the world. And so I believe he did." All had heard by this time of the scene on the dueling ground, as Decatur and Barron, both thinking they were dying, had forgiven each other. For Sergeant, this "generous forgiveness of his antagonist" was a final sign of Decatur's "magnanimity," the "great spirit that conducted him through life," which had made him the nation's hero. As he prepared to see Decatur to his grave, Sergeant told his wife to "kiss our dear children for me."[15]

Friday was a day of public mourning. A mass at St. Patrick's Church that morning for the assassinated duc de Berri drew all of official Washington. After the three-hour-long solemnities, thousands of mourners—most of the population of Washington, Georgetown, and Alexandria—thronged to the Decatur house.

The papers had published the order of procession. After the marine honor guard would come the navy officers, marine officers, clergy, and the hearse. On either side of the hearse would walk the pallbearers: Captain Thomas Tingey, commandant of the Washington Navy Yard; Captain John Rodgers, chairman of the Board of Navy commissioners; Macdonough, who had been with Decatur when he destroyed the *Philadelphia*; Porter, who had been a prisoner in Tripoli and captain of the first American warship to venture into the Pacific; General Thomas Sidney Jesup, who had raised a regiment in Hartford, bastion of antiwar feeling, while Decatur defended New London, in 1814; General Jacob Brown, son of Quaker Pennsylvanians, who had commanded the armies along the Canadian frontier, and would soon become general-in-chief of the United States Army; Captain Henry Ballard, who had been first lieutenant on the *Constitution*; Captain Stephen Cassin, a midshipman under Edward Preble against Tripoli and recipient of a gold medal for his own heroic command of the *Ticonderoga*; Lieutenant Joseph McPherson, who had commanded the *Hamilton* on the Niagara frontier; and Captain Isaac Chauncey, with Decatur a veteran of the French and Tripolitan wars, and in 1812 commander of the American forces on the Great Lakes. To these eight officers, and to the one whose remains they escorted, Americans owed their nation's survival. After the hearse would come family members, followed by President Monroe and members of the cabinet, senators and representatives, judges, army officers, the mayor and other District officials, foreign ministers, and then finally citizens.

But when it was time to start the procession, the Decatur house was so packed it was impossible to move. The funeral director came to the door, telling all who were not either members of Congress or officers in the military, to back away and clear a path for the mourners with official rank. A sailor standing outside answered back: "I tell you what mister. There's other people here besides officers and members of Congress that respect Commodore Decatur; and I say by G——, they shall go in." He turned to the crowd pressing at the door. "Come, anybody that wants to go in, I'll clear the way for him."[16]

The directors gave up on their order of march and reversed it: the citizens would lead and the dignitaries would follow. "Since the foundations of this city were laid," read one newspaper report, "no such assemblage of citizens and strangers, on such an occasion, has been seen."[17] The procession's pace was set by the guns fired at intervals of one minute from the navy yard, their sound growing more distant as the thousands of citizens walked from President's Square (now Lafayette Square) to Joel Barlow's old estate, Kalorama, on Rock Creek. Echoing over the somber town, the guns recalled with their steady, ordered firing the more lethal cannon fired by the privateer that Decatur's father had commanded in the Revolution, and the French war of 1798, when young Decatur had sailed as a midshipman under John Barry; the guns recalled the Tripolitan war, when Stephen Decatur had performed the most celebrated acts of naval heroism of the age by burning the *Philadelphia* and tracking down his brother's killer in the harbor of Tripoli, and had become the youngest man ever to be promoted to captain in the United States Navy; and they recalled also the humiliation of the *Chesapeake*, which Barron surrendered to the British in 1807, and how the nation had turned to Decatur to prepare its defenses; how, in 1812, Decatur had captured the *Macedonian* and redeemed the nation's honor, then lost the *President*, surrendering only when surrounded by an entire British fleet; and the brief Algerian war of 1815, when Decatur defeated the greatest Algerian admiral since Barbarossa.

The minute guns marked Decatur's way to his tomb, reminding all of the victories he had won for them, and seeming to sound a knell for the nation and its future. On Decatur's oak casket an engraved silver plate gave voice to a similar sentiment, that in Decatur "every virtue" of the "human character" had been "carried to its highest perfection!—Columbia mourn!! For time which soothes the grief of individuals will only render you more sensible of the irreparable loss you have here sustained!!!"[18] As Sarah Gales Seaton wrote, "In the event of another war, *he* would have been the first one to whom his country would have turned."[19]

And now he was gone. "Our gaiety is indeed turned to mourning and it is impossible to imagine a greater contrast in so short a time," wrote Louisa Adams, who had ridden behind the procession in a carriage.[20] Her husband, the secretary of state, walking with Secretary of the Treasury William Crawford (who had come within ten votes of beating Monroe for the presidential nomination four years earlier), had noticed John Randolph of Roanoke, the brilliant but erratic congressman from Virginia, "first walking, then backing his horse, then calling for his phaeton, and lastly crowding up to the vault as the coffin was removed into it," all the while, as another observer recalled, talking "wildly of his readiness to resent an insult in the same way."[21]

The procession halted at the vault. Dr. Andrew Hunter, the navy's chaplain, read a brief prayer. As Decatur's body, in a cedar-lined casket of oak, was placed inside, the marine guard fired a volley, announcing "the consignment of the Hero's Remains to the tomb" and sounding "as the knell of departed chivalry."[22]

Seeing a sailor overcome with grief, Judge Henry Baldwin, who would later sit on the Supreme Court, asked if he had served under Decatur. No, the man answered, he had never had that good fortune. But from shipmates who had, he'd learned to revere Decatur as "the friend of the flag, the sailor's friend." He told Baldwin, "The navy has lost its mainmast."[23]

Decatur, wrote John Quincy Adams, was "warm-hearted, cheerful, unassuming, gentle in deportment, friendly and hospitable." The "Nation has lost . . . one of its heroes—One who has illustrated its History and given grace and dignity to its character in the eyes of the world." The musket volley, Adams wrote, closed the tomb "over the earthly remains of a Spirit, as kindly, as generous, and as dauntless, as breathed in this Nation or on this Earth."[24]

"We have lost a hero," agreed Richard Rush, U.S. ambassador to England. Decatur had been "a man of ten thousand; great resources of native intelligence and propriety upon all subjects; as a companion delightful; formed for the highest ranges of action, no matter in what sphere; prudent, and I will say even forbearing, whatever he may have been in earlier days." The loss to the nation was grievous now but would be even more so in the coming years. "A man fit for any thing, and destined, as I think, to have achieved the greatest things; far greater perhaps than all he had achieved."[25]

Emotionally exhausted, Louisa Adams went to bed at eight that night. The week had begun in joy, but had plunged all to the depths of sorrow. In one twenty-four-hour span she had helped her friends bury their daughter, mourned the assassination of France's next king, and seen the gallant young Decatur to his grave. Her husband noted that the peach blossoms had appeared that day. But this sign of early spring did little to lift the mood. Louisa thought Decatur's final "parade" not appropriate to the occasion. Gallant he had been, a gentle man and a hero, but she feared these final honors would encourage others to seek revenge on the dueling field rather than staying to serve their nation in its time of need. A hero in his forty-one years, he could yet have been even more.

"Surely," Louisa Catherine Adams wrote her father-in-law, "this man threw his life away."[26]

CHAPTER I

"*To raise his voice to defend the right*"

ÉTIENNE DECATUR'S fever was a stroke of fortune for the U.S. Navy. A lieutenant in the French navy, Étienne nearly died in the West Indies. Too ill to cross the Atlantic, he was fortunate that his fever came during a brief interlude of peace between the French and British empires. His ship dropped him ashore in a British colony—Newport, in Rhode Island—and sailed home without him. Étienne Decatur's career in the French navy had ended.

A local family named Hill took in the nearly dead French lieutenant. He recovered sufficiently by September 1751 to marry their daughter Priscilla in Newport's Trinity Church. By this time Étienne was calling himself Stephen; he gave his birthplace as Genoa. He and Priscilla baptized their only son— named Stephen for his father—at Trinity Church in June 1752. The family then moved to Philadelphia, where Stephen Sr. found work on American merchant ships.[1]

Philadelphia was the British Empire's second-largest city. People from all over the world came to Philadelphia—from Germany and Sweden, from Africa and Ireland. It was home to St. Joseph's, the only Roman Catholic church in Britain's American empire. Immigrants arrived to farm in the rich countryside or to work in the busy seaport. From Philadelphia's docks were shipped wheat and meat to feed the labor force of the West Indies, and wood and iron to make barrels and ships to carry the empire's goods. Philadelphia owed its broad streets to the vision of its Quaker founders, and its dynamic energy to the men and women who came there to work.

Stephen was dead within a year of reaching Philadelphia. It is unknown whether Priscilla and her baby stayed on or returned to Newport. She may have kept boarders, or she may have been provided for by the merchants who had employed her husband. We do know that by the time the American-born Stephen Decatur turned twenty-one, he was already captain of a Philadelphia merchant ship. His earliest surviving letter reveals that at twenty-two he had little education but did have the judgment, character, and experience to command a ship. On "February the 27th, 1774," he wrote to the ship's owner, Joseph Cowperthwait, "sorre to in form" him that the "ise in the Rever" had caused "a grate Deel of trubel" and done great "Damedg" to the ship. He asked Cowperthwait to come as soon as possible, though Decatur had already begun making repairs on the "advice of a Carphinder."[2]

Decatur could not spell, but he knew what needed to be done. Presumably he was able to repair the ship. He continued in the merchant service until 1775, the year the strained relationship between Britain and its American colonies snapped. American merchants had a choice: remain loyal to their king and empire and continue receiving the benefits of British trade in the West Indies and protection by the British fleet around the world, or support an uncertain rebellion against that empire. Decatur sided with the rebels. His merchant backers supplied him with a privateer, the *Royal Louis*, named in hope of winning support from the French Crown; the following year he was given command of the *Fair American*. Decatur used these ships to attack British merchant vessels. Under the rules of war a successful privateer captain and his crew would have shared the spoils of victory over these merchant ships. Stephen Decatur was a successful captain.

At some point in this lucrative but dangerous period Stephen married Ann Pine, from one of Philadelphia's Irish families, and in early 1777 their first child, a daughter, was born. The child, named Ann Pine Decatur, was still an infant when they had to flee Philadelphia as the British army occupied it. Stephen probably took his two Anns, wife and daughter, by sea to a temporary home, a two-room cabin on the coast at Sinepuxent (now Berlin), Maryland. Ann stayed in Sinepuxent even after the British left Philadelphia in the summer of 1778. She was now pregnant with her second child; her husband was at sea when she gave birth to a son in January 1779. She named the boy Stephen, for his father and grandfather.

Captain Decatur was still at sea harassing British merchant ships when Ann and her two children returned to Philadelphia that spring. Now that the city was again in American hands, Decatur could visit more frequently. He and Ann bought a house on Front Street, near the river, where she and the children settled while he went back to sea. A granddaughter remembered Ann Decatur as "a woman of great spirit, firm in her convictions and not afraid of speaking her mind freely." A family story tells of the time she happened to be among a group that included British officers, while she held her one-year-old son in her lap. "The conversation turned upon the then absorbing topic of the day," and Ann Decatur "spoke boldly for what she felt the just cause." A British officer cautioned her, "Mistress Decatur you exercise your womans privilege to speak your mind but when that fine boy of your grows up you will have to teach him to exercise more caution." According to the family legend her fine brown eyes flashed with anger as she said, "Sir, I shall teach him ever to raise his voice to defend the right, and if need be to protect it with his hearts blood."[3]

Ann Decatur was a formidable woman. Sometime in 1781 her husband sought permission from the American authorities to have his mother, Priscilla, come down from New York to join his family. It is a mystery why Priscilla Decatur was in British-occupied New York City, but by August 1781 she was on hand for the birth of her third grandchild, John Bines Decatur. She was also on hand sixteen days later when the infant was buried in St. Peter's churchyard.

Ann would have three more children: another daughter, Elizabeth, who lived for nine months in 1785, and two more sons, James and John P. Decatur. Her husband had by now resumed his career as a merchant captain. Ann and her mother-in-law raised the children, teaching all of them to defend "the right" with their heart's blood. The British officer saw only an American woman with a child; he could not look into the future and see that three of this woman's children and three of her grandchildren would serve in the U.S. Navy, and that the baby she held in her lap would one day bring home a British frigate as a trophy.

What was the family like? While we can get closer to the family life of this generation than the previous one, much still remains shrouded in mystery. We know that the Decaturs lived on Front Street, facing the waterfront; we know that their neighbors included merchants, a tailor, a barber, clerks, another sea captain, and a doctor. It was not Philadelphia's most elegant neighborhood, nor was it the worst. It was a busy place: most of the commerce of the United States was loaded and unloaded at their front door.

Captain Decatur was at sea during most of the 1780s on merchant voyages to France and the West Indies. His son Stephen became an excellent swimmer, sailor, and fisherman. He was not big, but his quick mind and devastating wit made him a leader among the neighborhood boys, who called him "Captain Dick," short for "Decatur." His physical courage also impressed his peers. Years later one of his friends remembered how the neighborhood boys would swim in the Delaware, near where the Philadelphia Navy Yard is today. A few of the braver boys dared to swim out to a merchant ship moored in the channel and dive off its terrifyingly high sides. "One of them ran up the bowsprit quite out to the tip end of the jib-boom, from which he instantly plunged head foremost into the stream. It was Decatur."[4]

His mother sent him to a school kept by a woman named Mrs. Gordon. Like Priscilla Decatur, Mrs. Gordon was the widow of a sea captain; she supported herself by keeping school after her husband was lost at sea. Stephen was not a keen student—he was more interested in swimming and sailing than in study—but he developed a lifelong affection for his first teacher. Later his parents sent him to the Episcopal Academy on Fourth Street, which boasted a distinguished roster of students, including Richard Rush, son of Dr.

Benjamin Rush, signer of the Declaration of Independence, and friend of Franklin, Adams, and Jefferson. Stephen and Richard Rush did not become close friends as children, but Stephen did form a bond with Richard Somers and Charles Stewart, who would later serve with him in the navy. Stewart's most vivid memories of their schooldays at the Episcopal Academy were of their fistfights across the street in the Quaker burying ground. Rush would look back on those days, too, when he was attorney general of the United States and ambassador to England, and marvel that the pugnacious and hot-tempered Stephen Decatur had grown up to be an articulate and thoughtful leader of men.

Stephen was eight when his father decided to give him an education he could not get in a schoolroom. He was taking a cargo to France and decided to take his son along. One version of the story says that the trip was to benefit young Stephen's health; reportedly he had nearly died from whooping cough. Others say the trip was to benefit the boy's mother, who found Stephen more than she could handle. This voyage to France in the summer of 1787 was Stephen's first time at sea, and his first extended time with his father. Had he stayed in Philadelphia, he might have seen the delegates to the federal convention meeting to draw up a new Constitution for the United States; he definitely would have noticed John Fitch's experimental steamboat moving up the Delaware River against the current. Both of these events of 1787 would become important to Decatur's later life, though not as important as his first sea voyage. It would be eleven years, though, before he took another.

Stephen's parents did not intend to apprentice him to a merchant captain. He would be educated. When the academy closed briefly in 1790, perhaps because the students spent most of their time fighting across the street, Stephen's parents sent him to the College of Pennsylvania's grammar school. He did not graduate. Instead, after a year or two he went to work for his father's employers, the merchant firm of Gurney and Smith. One of Stephen's best friends at the time was Francis Gurney Smith, son of one of the partners; young Smith and Stephen's other friends stayed in school while Stephen became a clerk in Gurney and Smith's countinghouse. Keeping the books on Gurney and Smith's international trade would be as close as Stephen would come to the sea at this time.

Stephen's parents did not want to send him away while his father was also gone so much. A boyhood friend, James K. Hamilton, remembered coming home from fishing with Stephen when the two were about fourteen. In front of the Decatur house one of their neighbors—a young man known for his drinking—was shouting at Stephen's mother. Stephen's younger brother

John stood by crying. John had imitated the man's drunken walk, and the man had knocked him to the ground. Now as the "dissipated" neighbor be-rated Ann Decatur, Stephen stepped between them, saying, "Do you know who that lady is, Sir? That is my mother; she must be treated with respect." The man shouted back that he did not know or care who that lady was; and he complained that the boy, John, had not treated him with respect. "If you have any complaint to make against my brother, Sir," Stephen said, "make it to me." The man tried to make his complaint to Stephen in the same way he had complained to John, by knocking him down. As he raised his arm, Ste-phen hit him so hard he fell to the ground and needed to be helped up by strangers.[5]

A boy might encounter a drunk in any city; Philadelphia was also the nation's capital and so had its share of political belligerents. The 1790s were a particularly contentious time. The French Revolution, with its ringing call to abolish all monarchy and aristocracy, had divided Americans. Some called for the nation to support the French people as their allies in and heirs to their own Revolution; others saw the French Revolution as creating anarchy and terror. The United States was at a relatively safe distance from the turmoil of Europe, and Americans were able to argue and agitate without risk of losing their heads. But in 1793 France and England went to war, and the French Republic sent an ambassador to America. Citizen Edmond Genêt had come to demand that the United States honor its 1778 treaty with France and join the war against England. The Washington administration proclaimed U.S. neutrality in the war, which infuriated Genet as well as the Americans who backed the Revolution.

Supporters of the French cause wore "liberty caps" or decorated their tricornered hats with French cockades. Supporters of Washington wore blue cockades in their hats. Men wearing their political opinions on their hats could easily spot one another; if their colors differed, they might start a fight. Stephen and his friends were coming home from fishing one day when they passed the Buck's Head Tavern. The boys were all wearing blue cockades, showing their support for the president. A group of men outside the tavern— all wearing "liberty caps"—told the boys to take off their blue cockades and join the "lovers of liberty." When Stephen refused, one of the men tried to tear off his blue cockade. Stephen resisted. In an instant Stephen's friends and the "liberty" men were engaged in a free-for-all in front of the tavern. Fortunately for the boys, some sailors from Captain Decatur's ship arrived on the scene, joining the fight against the men. They won, and carried home their captain's son, still wearing his now battered blue cockade.[6]

During this period of international crisis, Congress in 1794 voted to create a navy. Republicans opposed this naval expansion, fearing that it would get the United States embroiled in a war with France. The administration's justification was that in 1793 Algiers had seized a dozen American merchant ships; the nation needed to protect American commerce in the Mediterranean. Led by James Madison, the Republicans argued that building frigates would be too expensive, that it would be cheaper to subsidize Portugal's navy (which then patrolled the Straits of Gibraltar) than to build one from scratch. Despite these objections Congress authorized a navy. The firm of Gurney and Smith was awarded a contract for one of the frigates, the *United States*. Legend has it that young Decatur was sent to New Jersey to supervise cutting timber for the ship. He may have done so; or the legend may simply have grown because he was working for Gurney and Smith while the *United States* was being built within sight of his boyhood home, and he later began his naval career as a midshipman on the frigate. In 1812 he would command it to victory over the *Macedonian*.

Regardless of the opportunity to cut timber in New Jersey, working in a countinghouse would not have been the most exciting occupation for young Stephen. He continued to sail and fish—and to fight. To escape the political violence of Philadelphia and the horrific yellow fever outbreaks, his parents bought a farm ten miles outside the city, at Mount Airy in Byberry County. His father was not giving up the sea; he continued to captain ships for Gurney and Smith, and he also manufactured gunpowder on the farm.

In 1795 Stephen's sister Ann married a marine lieutenant, James McKnight. Stephen had attended the University of Pennsylvania, though by 1796 he was working full-time for Gurney and Smith. Virtually nothing is known about his personal life during these years. One source has him courting Senator Rufus King's granddaughter, which is impossible (King had only been married since 1786, and his eldest child, a son, was just ten years old when Stephen Decatur joined the navy).[7]

When the United States and Algiers made peace in 1795, the Republicans tried to stop construction of all six frigates Congress had authorized. President Washington insisted that three, including the *United States*, be finished, which it was by February 1797. On February 22 Washington commissioned John Barry to serve as captain of the *United States*. Barry, a friend and colleague of the senior Stephen Decatur, was now the first captain in the U.S. Navy. By 1797 French warships were attacking American merchant ships; although the administration cited the need to protect American merchants from the French, its Republican critics charged that the administration wanted the frigates in order to wage war against France. The Republican newspaper editor Benjamin Franklin Bache visited the shipyard in April

1797; when the workers saw their most vociferous critic inspecting their work, they attacked him.[8]

Barry was careful in selecting his officers and midshipmen, conscious that he was creating a navy for the new nation. He asked young Stephen Decatur to be a midshipman, but Ann Decatur did not want her son to go to sea. When Barry presented his list of officers to Secretary of the Navy James McHenry in July, Decatur's name was on it, but he would not serve. Barry also would not get the first lieutenant he had wanted—Richard O'Brien, a merchant captain just returned from ten years' captivity in Algiers. Instead of becoming an officer in the new navy, O'Brien would become the nation's consul general in Algiers.[9]

Finding men to serve and supplying the ship with provisions and adequate weapons would continue to be a problem for Barry and others in the early navy. With the nation divided on whether there needed to be a navy at all, Barry found that he had to fight for every scrap of wood to build his ship and every piece of hardtack to feed his crew. He was hard-pressed to cajole men into serving in the navy when they could earn better money on a merchant ship. Work on the ship nearly stopped that fall when another epidemic of yellow fever struck Philadelphia. The disease ravaged the ship and the city, killing a marine on board as well as Bache, the newspaper editor. Surgeon's mate John Bullus, a friend of young Decatur's who had studied under Benjamin Rush, attended to the sick when the ship's surgeon was stricken.[10]

As Barry pressed ahead to finish his ship, another political uproar gripped Philadelphia in the spring of 1798. President Adams had sent three negotiators to resolve the problems with France, but no accord had been reached. The Republicans charged Adams and his diplomats with alienating the French. The arrival of dispatches from Adams's envoys sparked a debate. Republicans asked why Adams would not release the dispatches. Could it be because they revealed his envoys' ineptitude? Could it be that they showed that the French were eager to make peace but were being stymied by Adams's warmongering? The Republican press kept up a steady stream of invective against the president.

When Adams released the dispatches in April 1798, even the Republicans were stunned. The three diplomats had failed. They had got nowhere with the French foreign ministry because the first three minor bureaucrats they had encountered (the Americans called them "X, Y, and Z") had demanded a hefty bribe before the Americans could get to see anyone else. The French had rebuffed the Americans not because Adams was a belligerent warmonger but because the French government was utterly corrupt. Adams sent the damning dispatches to Congress vowing that he would never send another envoy to France unless he were treated as the representative of an independent republic. He proposed an immediate expansion of the navy—and the creation of a separate Department of the Navy—to protect American interests abroad.

Congress voted to spend $950,000 on expanding the navy and, on the last day of April 1798, created the Navy Department. That day President Adams signed a midshipman's warrant for Stephen Decatur Jr. John Barry and young Stephen had reached an agreement that Decatur would serve. The family story has it that neither man asked Ann Decatur's permission in advance, but when Captain Barry presented her with the president's warrant, she could not refuse. Stephen Sr. would take a leave of absence from Gurney and Smith to captain the twenty-gun sloop *Delaware;* Stephen Jr. would sail under Barry on the frigate *United States.* Barely half a century after Étienne Decatur had been put to shore from a French warship in Newport, his son and grandson set out from Philadelphia to make war against the French navy.

CHAPTER 2

"You knew the French Republic were at war"

C APTAIN JOHN BARRY came aboard the *United States* at New Castle, Delaware, on the afternoon of July 4, 1798. Secretary of the Navy Benjamin Stoddert wanted Barry to cruise between Cape Henry and Nantucket to protect American merchant ships and, if necessary, "to defend this Extent of Coast against the Depredations of the Vessels . . . from the French Republic."[1] Stoddert would be disappointed in Barry's cruise. The *United States* did not stay long at sea and did not attack any French ships. But the cruise began Stephen Decatur's lifetime in the navy.

Barry had taken great care in selecting his junior officers and midshipmen. Fighting the French was only part of his mission: his grander goal was to develop the United States Navy. Barry's lieutenants—David Ross, John Mullowny, James Barron, and Stephen's old schoolmate Charles Stewart—were responsible for running the ship and for direct supervision of the midshipmen, younger men in training themselves to become lieutenants. There was no naval academy to train officers; instead, officers were trained directly by senior captains and lieutenants on board fighting ships. The *United States*'s midshipmen—Freeborn Banning, James Caldwell, Edward Dyer, Jacob Jones, and the two schoolmates Richard Somers and Decatur—lodged on the berthing deck, just forward of the lieutenants' wardroom. These young "gentlemen," as midshipmen were called, were responsible for ensuring that orders were carried out and for directing the furling and unfurling of sails.

Each night Barry dined alone with one of his lieutenants, getting to know each one, and giving each the benefit of his own knowledge. Barry took his role as their mentor seriously. The officers responded to his instruction and engaged their midshipmen with the same care.

For Stephen this was a new experience. He had sailed under only one other captain—his father. Barry was different; though he and Stephen's father were old friends, they were not equals in ability. Barry, after all, had been given command of a frigate, while Stephen's father commanded a more humble sloop. According to one of the navy's other frigate captains, Thomas Truxtun, Stephen's father was not qualified to be more than a boatswain or a sailing master.[2] Young Stephen certainly recognized his own limited experience. He sought out a former British naval officer, Talbot Hamilton, to tutor him in navigation, and when he finally set foot on his new ship, he penciled in the name of each line on the rail behind it in case his memory failed. Years later he would encourage his own midshipmen and lieutenants to do the same.[3]

Decatur had not applied himself to his formal studies at the Episcopal Academy or at the University of Pennsylvania, but he now threw himself into learning navigation and ship handling. He was commencing a new part of his education—more practical and more engaging to him than his formal studies on land. Perhaps he sensed this change, but also thought back on the course of his life up to this point, when he gave his first month's pay as a midshipman—nineteen dollars—to his first schoolteacher, the widow Gordon.[4]

As Barry began to drop the *United States* farther down the Delaware on the morning of July 8, two ships coming upstream hailed him. Stephen's father commanded one, the sloop *Delaware*. The other was a French privateer, *Le Croyable*, that he had captured off Egg Harbor, New Jersey. The senior Decatur continued on to Philadelphia with his prize, the first American capture of the war. *Le Croyable* would be rechristened *Retaliation* and added to the American fleet, commanded by Lieutenant William Bainbridge.

Four days later Decatur and the *Delaware* rejoined Barry with new instructions from Stoddert. The sloop and the frigate would sail together to Boston, where two new ships, the *Herald* and the *Pickering*, were under construction. Barry would then lead this squadron to the West Indies, where they were to capture French ships and redeem captured American prizes. "It is Time We should establish an American Character," Stoddert wrote. "Let that Character be a Love of Country and Jealousy of it's honor."[5]

Barry and Decatur sailed for Boston. It was not easy to keep the ships together. "Capt. Decatur thought he could sail with anything," Barry wrote Secretary Stoddert, but "he never saw a vessel he could not come up with or leave with ease, untill he got alongside of the United States."[6] The *United States* was a fast sailer, designed to combine speed with firepower. They did not meet any French ships on their way to Boston, but they did meet the British warship *Assistance*, also out cruising against the French. British Captain Thomas Hardy had his first look at the *United States*, which he would encounter again fifteen years later.[7]

Boston received the captains and crews of the *United States* and the *Delaware* "as the brave and patriotic defenders of our country's rights."[8] Although the *Pickering* and the *Herald* were not quite ready, the visit to Boston was a tremendous success. While there had been opposition in Philadelphia to the military buildup, New England staunchly supported the war against France. Barry and Captain Decatur visited the Boston Exchange, whose merchants depended on international trade, and the next day the captains joined a delegation of congressmen calling on Governor Increase Sumner at his home in Roxbury.

After nearly a week in Boston, the *Pickering* and the *Herald* were ready. Barry led his squadron out of Boston harbor for the West Indies. The voyage was uneventful except for a near-battle with an English frigate. The British captain had hoped to decoy unwary French vessels by flying the French flag. When Barry saw the French colors, he ordered his own men to raise the French flag to decoy the ship, then steered toward the presumed enemy. As the *United States* closed in and prepared to fight, Barry ordered the French flag taken down and raised the American colors. Almost at the same instant the British captain ordered his own French flag taken down and the British standard raised. After a moment the British captain, Thomas Cochran, invited Barry to come aboard his ship, the *Thetis*. Cochran gave Barry the British signals to avoid future cases of mistaken identity, and Barry invited Cochran and his officers to dine with him aboard the *United States*. Cochran, who fifteen years later would command the British fleet off the American coast and keep the frigate *United States* bottled up in New London, on this day was impressed with the new American ship.[9]

The squadron did its best to stay together, Barry lunching with the elder Decatur on board the *Delaware* when possible, and by the twenty-first of August they had anchored off Bridgetown, Barbados.[10] After learning of French movements in the area, Barry sailed off, saluted by two American privateers as he departed Bridgetown. The next morning the *United States* spied a sail. The stranger tried to escape through the narrow passage between Dominica and Martinique, but Barry pursued under full sail, drawing on his years as a merchant captain in these same waters. As darkness fell, Barry drew close enough to fire two warning shots. The stranger stopped. It was the French privateer *Sans Pareil* out of Guadeloupe. *Sans Pareil* surrendered, and Barry put the prize under the charge of the senior Decatur and the *Delaware* while the *United States* sailed off after more prizes among the islands. After two weeks' sailing between Guadeloupe, Dominica, Montserrat, St. Eustatia, and Antigua, Barry and Decatur rendezvoused at the Swedish colony of St. Bartholomew. From here they sailed for Puerto Rico, where the French had put ashore American prisoners and sent the merchant vessel *New Jersey* to be redeemed.

Barry was about to enter San Juan harbor when a strange sail appeared on the horizon. The *United States* came about and gave chase. After five hours in pursuit, Barry was close enough to identify the mystery sloop as the French privateer *Jalouse*. For the next seven hours *Jalouse* evaded his cannon but finally surrendered. Barry secured *Jalouse*'s sixty-seven crewmen in the *United States*'s hold, sent a prize crew to take the captured ship into San Juan, and again set sail for Puerto Rico. Realizing that hurricane season was approaching, when few vessels would venture out and his own would be in jeopardy, Barry decided to head for home. He was disappointed with the few prizes he had taken.

Barry and the *United States* reached Philadelphia on September 21. Three days later the *Delaware* landed its prisoners at New Castle, Delaware, and Captain Decatur and his son-in-law James McKnight boarded a pilot boat to take them to Philadelphia. Ann Decatur's joy at the return of her husband, son, and son-in-law was tempered by the anxiety she had felt while they were gone. In late August she had been so ill that she required a doctor's care. While the *United States* and the *Delaware* had been reprovisioning at St. Bartholomew, Ann had been writing to Dr. Benjamin Rush, complaining that she had "Been Indisposed for some time, and find myself growg worse"; the illness had "Settle[d] on my lungs." After listening to her mother cough, daughter Ann had become "very unhappy" and told her mother it was "high time [she] Should apply to a physician." Mrs. Decatur asked Rush to come to the family home at Mount Airy. She hoped he could "Spare time to come out in the morning if you will Ride out in the evening and you can Return in morning as early as you think proper." That is, he could either come in the morning or he could come in the evening and stay overnight. Rush did attend to Mrs. Decatur; many years later when he reviewed his patient records he found this letter and preserved it to show the "sort of letter the Mother of a hero writes."[11] Of course, neither Rush nor Mrs. Decatur knew in 1798 that she would be the mother of a hero; she knew only that her son had come home bearing gifts. She did not record what he brought for the family, but he did bring his old teacher Mrs. Gordon a barrel of sugar and a bag of coffee.[12]

Secretary Stoddert was not interested in family reunions or teachers' gifts. "Barry returned too soon," he wrote to President Adams. Stoddert wanted French prizes, and he was furious that Barry and Decatur had come back so early with so few; he had suggested a two-month cruise. Stoddert predicted, and fervently hoped, that his other squadron, under Alexander Murray, would "return with more brilliancy." President Adams suggested that Barry go out again to "sweep the West Indies seas and get as many French seamen as they are called, whether they are Italians, Spaniards, Germans or negroes, as we can." Stoddert knew, though, that a Caribbean cruise in hurricane season would be unnecessarily dangerous. Barry's next cruise, beginning on October 8, was to patrol between New York and New Hampshire; the senior Decatur on the *Delaware* would cruise between New York and the Chesapeake.[13]

The *United States*'s second cruise would also be too short. Stoddert had assured Barry that there was no danger of hurricanes this late in the year. The first night out a gale blew up. Barry tried all night to run the *United States* ahead of the storm, but the next day the storm broke on the ship. Waves crashed over the deck, the wind tore the foresail apart, and ballast shifting in the hold crushed a marine to death. The ship was blown south. Barry reckoned they were about 250 miles east of Cape Hatteras when the bowsprit cracked, leaving the forward rigging hanging slack and useless. Without a functioning foremast, Barry could not keep the ship running before the wind; the added stress on the other masts would snap them as well. Already the *United States* was rolling uncontrollably. He knew that unless the rigging could be secured, the ship would be lost.

Lieutenant James Barron volunteered to climb the foremast rigging to secure the line and sails. It seemed impossible, but it was the only way to save the ship. Barry would not suggest that any man risk his life—death seemed almost certain—but he and Barron both knew that the entire ship and all the men would be lost unless someone could secure the rigging. In the violent storm Barron climbed the mast and "got the purchases on the shrouds," another lieutenant wrote in his journal; he "succeeded in getting the rigging taut, and the lanyards secured without accident."[14]

Barron's courage allowed Barry to keep the ship from foundering on the voyage home. Secretary Stoddert was not angry that Barry had returned so soon this time. Instead he took advantage of the fact that Barry and four of his other captains—Decatur, Truxtun, Richard Dale, and Thomas Tingey—happened to be in Philadelphia at the same time for a conference on the state of the navy. The five captains got together and made recommendations for deployment. They knew that although their fleet was relatively small, by using their resources judiciously, they could protect American trade in the Caribbean. Stoddert approved their plan for sending a larger number of ships into the West Indies now that hurricane season was definitely over.

Barry left Philadelphia once again on December 18, 1798. He now had more than 400 men on the *United States* (Congress had authorized only 344) and nine more ships would joined his Caribbean squadron—the new forty-four-gun frigate *Constitution*, the twenty-four-gun *George Washington*, *Portsmouth*, and *Merrimack*, and five smaller vessels. Having more ships and more men would enable Barry to take more enemy prizes and to convoy more American merchant ships without losing all of his fighting force.

On February 3, 1799, the *United States* spied an armed French schooner between Martinique and Barbados. The American frigate began to chase the enemy. After five hours, reported Barry, "to the astonishment of all hands," the enemy "attempted by short stretches to get to windward of us directly under our battery."[15] What was the French schooner doing? It appeared to be attacking an American frigate. The *United States* opened fire and sent a shot through the enemy's hull.

Midshipman Decatur was sent to take command of the prize, a six-gun privateer *L'Amour de la Patrie*. As he drew near, he saw the crew in a panic stripping off their clothes and diving from their ship. *L'Amour de la Patrie* was sinking fast. Decatur noted that although the French Revolution had abolished all religion, the sailors were "imploring the protection of the omnipotent with gestures, professions and protestations." Seeing how quickly their ship was going down, knowing that the survivors would swamp his own boat, Decatur called to the Frenchmen remaining on *L'Amour de la Patrie* to put their helm up and try to steer for the *United States*. The French were able to do this, keeping their ship afloat until it was a cable length from the *United States*. As the American crew plucked the fifty-eight French sailors from the water, the French captain, Pierre Solimniac, looked with surprise from the American flag on the *United States* to Decatur in the boat. Decatur enjoyed telling the story. Solimniac, in his broken English, with "well-feigned surprise" asked, "Is that a ship of the United States?"

"It is," Decatur replied.

"I am very much astonished, Sir," Solimniac said. "I did not know the United States were at war with the French Republic."

"No, Sir," Decatur replied, "but you knew the French Republic were at war with the United States; that you were taking our merchant vessels every day, and crowding our countrymen into prison at Basseterre to die like sheep."[16]

After *L'Amour de la Patrie* sank into the Caribbean, Barry continued on to Barbados. There he met fourteen American and three British merchant ships waiting for an escort. He also learned that Truxtun on the *Constellation* had defeated the French frigate *L'Insurgente*. Barry continued his own cruise through the West Indies gathering merchant vessels to convoy home and unsuccessfully attempting to exchange his own fifty-eight French prisoners for Americans taken by the French. But he found no other French ships either to trade with or to capture. The French seemed to have gone to "some other part of the world."[17]

Although his cruise had not produced many French prizes, it had produced several worthy young officers. Barry wrote to Secretary Stoddert from Dominica's Prince Rupert Bay in mid-March 1799 recommending several for promotion. Two of his lieutenants, Ross and Mullowny, would make fine officers, but he thought the third lieutenant, James Barron, was "as good an Officer and as fit to command as any in the service." Barron's heroic climb into the rigging during a gale, and his service throughout the cruise, made him a man worthy of promotion. Barry also recommended three of his midshipmen for promotion to lieutenant: Banning, Somers, and Stephen Decatur. They were ready and able to be "good Lieutenants for small ships or Brigs."[18]

After nearly a month at Prince Rupert Bay gathering merchant vessels, the *United States* prepared to convoy them home. By the time Barry had escorted these twenty-five ships to Bermuda, they were beyond reach of any French squadron that might reappear, so Barry left the merchant ships and set his own course toward Philadelphia. By mid-May the *United States* had docked at Chester. On May 21, 1799, about a year after he had entered the navy as a midshipman, Stephen Decatur received his commission as a lieutenant. Barry asked to have Decatur and Somers assigned to his ship.[19]

Charles Stewart—now first lieutenant on the *United States*—took charge of the ship's refitting and recruiting of more men. He sent Decatur to open a recruiting station in Philadelphia. Decatur was doing well enlisting men until a merchant ship bound for the East Indies offered higher wages than the navy could pay. Some of the men Decatur had signed now jumped aboard for the East India voyage. Decatur walked across the dock to the East Indiaman. He mounted the deck and found his recruits. When the ship's mate saw Decatur and ordered him off the ship, Decatur produced the enlistment papers the men had signed. The mate screamed at Decatur to leave his ship, using the kind of language one would expect from an angry first mate on a merchant vessel. Decatur held his temper, ignoring the torrent of abuse as he calmly escorted his men back into the service of the U.S. Navy.

Decatur had won the skirmish. He had lost neither his temper nor a single recruit. Barry would have been pleased, but Stephen's father was not. Even though Stephen had prevailed, the Indiaman's mate had got the last word. The mate had insulted Stephen Decatur and the U.S. Navy; if the mate did not apologize, then the entire navy would be disgraced. Stephen turned to Somers for advice. Somers paid a call on the merchant ship and demanded that the mate apologize. The mate refused.

According to the senior Decatur's notion of honor, his son had no choice but to challenge the mate to a duel. When the East Indiaman anchored next to the *United States* off New Castle, the mate came aboard to tell Decatur that he was "ready to accept his invitation." Decatur had not yet offered an invitation, but did so now. He also told Charles Stewart, the senior lieutenant, that a duel was imminent. Decatur was not concerned for his own safety; he did not think that the mate was a very good shot. As he told Stewart, the duel was necessary to protect the navy's honor and dignity. Decatur did not intend to kill a man over harsh words. He would aim for the hip—to wound but not kill. With Somers as his second, the duel went as Decatur had predicted. The mate missed; Decatur nicked the man's hip. Then all parties went back to their ships. It would be twenty-one years before Stephen Decatur would fight another duel. In that one, too, he would aim at the hip, but his opponent would not miss. In the intervening years Decatur would act as second in three duels, one of them fatal. More often he would use his persuasive powers and his position to prevent disagreements from escalating to the dueling ground.[20]

With the *United States* fully manned and provisioned, Barry cruised south to the St. Marys River, then north to Cape Cod and back to Charleston and Norfolk before putting into Newport, Rhode Island, to await instructions. They finally came. President Adams had decided to send a new peace mission to the French, and the *United States* would carry the commissioners—Chief Justice Oliver Ellsworth and Governor W. R. Davie of North Carolina—to France. Barry would lead a small squadron of ships across the Atlantic on this mission. As "commodore" of the venture, he could leave the day-to-day operation of the *United States* to Captain Samuel Barron, James's elder brother. Barry sailed from Newport on December 3. The crossing was so rough that the two diplomats were thoroughly worn out by the time they reached Lisbon. It was even too rough to sail on to L'Orient, so after the diplomats and naval officers attended an elegant ball in Lisbon organized by the American consul, the *United States* left Ellsworth and Davie in La Coruña, Spain, to make their own way by land to Paris. The ship received needed repairs in La Coruña before sailing for home in February 1800.

Just a few days before the *United States* reached home, the elder Decatur had set sail from Philadelphia as captain of his own new frigate, named *Philadelphia* in honor of the city's merchants who had given it to the navy. Decatur's former employers Gurney and Smith had led a fund-raising campaign to pay for the frigate, which their firm had built. The navy reciprocated the generosity by putting Decatur, former partner at Gurney and Smith, in command of the ship. It would be his last command in the navy.

Meanwhile, the two Atlantic crossings had revealed more problems with the *United States*. The timbers had not been properly seasoned before construction, so the ship had to be taken apart and rebuilt with seasoned lumber. Stephen could have stayed with the ship and remained close to home in Philadelphia, but instead he signed on to the eighteen-gun brig *Norfolk*, bound for Santo Domingo. He spent the summer of 1800 on the *Norfolk*, doing convoy duty in the West Indies. By the time he returned home in the fall the *United States* was nearly finished, and by December was ready to sail for Guadeloupe.

By this time the peace envoys the *United States* had dropped off in Europe had settled the French crisis, but no official confirmation had reached the *United States* before it sailed. It would be a peaceful cruise, as French authorities in the West Indies had proclaimed that their privateers would no longer attack American ships, and Barry would not attack a French ship without provocation. Barry's cruise did not produce French prizes, but it did show the American flag in the West Indies and also provided experience for the junior officers, who learned to navigate the dangerous waters between islands, to command men, and to evaluate and work with one another.

Midshipman Robert Spence later recalled (after he had become a captain in the U.S. Navy) his first encounter with the *United States*'s lieutenants, men Barry had "selected from among the most promising in the navy."[21] These men stood "on the quarter deck, grouped, as is the custom in different places, conversing on the various subjects of their profession." The lieutenants were all "pleasing, gentlemanlike men, having the characteristic air and look of sailors." Spence noted that Decatur's "manner and appearance" were "calculated to rivet the eye and engross the attention." Spence had often tried to imagine what Homer's Odysseus would look like, to imagine the physical attributes of a classical hero; in Decatur on the *United States* quarterdeck, he wrote, "I saw it embodied." He felt himself under "a kind of spell" as Decatur "riveted my attention." Spence asked another officer what kind of man Decatur was. "Sir, Decatur is an officer of uncommon character, of rare promise, a man of an age, one perhaps not equaled in a million!"

Suddenly the cry of "Man overboard!" broke Spence's reverie. He heard orders called out from the foredeck and spar deck—"Second cutters away! Third cutters away!"—as crews prepared to launch rescue boats. Spence turned back—but Decatur was gone. Then Spence saw him "spring from the mizzen chains" over the ship's rail. Spence ran to the stern, searching the water. "In a few moments I saw a youth upheld above the surging wave by a buoyant and vigorous swimmer, and thus sustained" until the boats reached them. The man who had nearly drowned would live to see "his preserver the pride and glory of his country." In an instant, Decatur had transformed himself from a classical into a contemporary hero.

But even heroes can argue. One night in the crowded wardroom Decatur told Richard Somers—the ship's first lieutenant as well as his best friend— that the hat Somers was wearing made him look like a "fool." Somers, who knew Decatur's sense of humor, laughed, but six other officers were not amused. Where Somers had heard an old friend making a joke, they had seen a junior officer insulting a senior officer. Worse, the senior officer had laughed at the jest. By insulting Somers, the younger officers felt, Decatur had insulted every officer in the navy.

Somers called for wine, but when it came, he and Decatur were the only men to drink. The other officers refused to drink with Somers unless he demanded an apology from Decatur; if Decatur would not apologize, then Somers must challenge him to a duel. Somers and Decatur thought this was ridiculous. Decatur had no reason to apologize, and Somers had no reason to challenge him. Somers hated dueling; as Decatur's second in Chester, he had tried to negotiate a settlement. But he also saw six junior officers turning away from him, believing him a coward. If they thought Somers a coward, the ship's discipline and morale would collapse.

Still, Somers would not challenge his best friend to a duel merely to appease six junior officers. He knew Decatur did not think him either a fool or a coward. But as he and Decatur discussed the situation, it became clear that the junior officers had lost respect for him. Decatur proposed a way to end the problem peacefully, but Somers knew that he had too much to prove to his officers. They wanted him to assert his honor and bravery, and so he would do it. With Decatur acting as his second, Somers challenged each of the six junior officers to duel him.

Somers, Decatur, and the six officers set a day and terms for the encounter. One after another Somers would duel each of the junior officers until either he was dead or they were satisfied that he was a man of honor. On the appointed day Somers and Decatur set out to prove Somers's bravery. He may have resolved not to aim at any of the men; in any event, he missed the first man at whom he fired. The officer did not miss him; he hit Somers in the right arm. The doctor bandaged Somers's wound as the next opponent appeared. Somers missed again; his opponent hit him in the leg. As the doctor bandaged Somers's leg, Decatur offered to take his friend's place. Somers refused, though by now he could no longer stand. Too weak from loss of blood even to sit up, Somers needed Decatur to hold his firing arm. With Decatur propping him up and steadying his arm, Somers wounded his third opponent. Again Decatur offered to take his friend's place for the three remaining duels. Again Somers refused. At this point the other officers agreed that Somers was no coward. They all returned to the ship.[22]

The *United States* sailed back to Philadelphia in March 1801. This was an uncertain time for the new navy. In December the seat of the U.S. government had left Philadelphia for the newly built capital in Washington, D.C. Philadelphia would continue to be the nation's economic capital, but the government would no longer have daily reminders of the importance of international commerce. In March a new administration took over—Thomas

Jefferson had been elected president—and the Republicans, who for a decade had vociferously challenged the navy as an expensive luxury, controlled Congress. How long would the navy survive with the Republicans in power?

This anxiety was all the more acute since the commissioners had ended the French war. The U.S. Senate ratified the peace treaty with France in February, and Congress almost immediately reduced the size of the navy. Only seven of its ships would remain afloat; seven others would be dismantled and the rest sold. Nineteen of the navy's 28 captains and 74 of its 110 lieutenants would be discharged. The entire rank of commander—an intermediate step between lieutenant and captain—was eliminated.[23]

Stephen Decatur had earned enough of a reputation to stay in the service. His brother James received his midshipman's warrant, and their father was one of the nine captains to keep his commission. But the senior Decatur resigned from the navy and retired, first to Mount Airy, then to Frankford, outside Philadelphia, where he moved the family and set up a gunpowder works.

Dramatic sea battles stand out in the navy's history. But other issues emerge from the letters of captains such as Barry to the secretary of the navy. Where to find men to sail the ships? Where to get provisions to feed them? How to manufacture guns and ammunition? These problems of supply would continue to trouble the navy. Barry knew that his young officers had to be courageous heroes and also capable administrators. His young lieutenants—Barron, Stewart, Somers, Decatur—were both. The navy's other great problem was simply to justify its existence. Over strenuous Republican opposition the Adams administration had created the Navy Department in 1798. Now, as the Republicans took power in 1801, the captains needed to assure the nation that they posed no threat to the republic's survival but indeed were necessary to ensure it.

CHAPTER 3

"Those Yankees will never stand the smell of powder"

IEUTENANT DECATUR may have asked himself why he had so eagerly studied the arts of war and command. For years Thomas Jefferson's party had criticized the navy as a wasteful extravagance, and now the Republicans were determined to cut the federal deficit. They would dismantle and store the frigates and discharge most of the officers and men. Although Decatur would remain in the service, he must have wondered what role this smaller navy would have under the new administration.

Jefferson soon learned that he needed a navy after all. News came from the Mediterranean that Tripoli was threatening American merchant ships. Its ruler, Yusuf Pacha Qaramanli, had been promised annual tribute payments by the 1796 treaty. He was irritated that the tribute never seemed to arrive, and that the treaty spoke of him as a subsidiary of Algiers, which received more than he did. The United States had even built a beautiful frigate, the *Crescent,* for the Dey of Algiers. Yusuf was already at war with Sweden; he now threatened war against the United States. The war would be fought strictly against American merchant ships in the Mediterranean.

Jefferson responded quickly, but not forcefully, to these rumors of war. He ordered Commodore Richard Dale to sail to the Mediterranean on the frigate *President,* along with the *Philadelphia* and the *Essex,* there to cooperate with Sweden in blockading Tripoli. Samuel Barron would command the *Philadelphia,* and his brother James would be captain of Dale's flagship. William Bainbridge would be captain of the *Essex,* and Lieutenant Stephen Decatur would be his second in command. Dale was not to initiate hostilities. The administration assumed, and told Commodore Dale he was to assume, that the United States was at peace with all the world. The president did not know that on May 14 Tripoli had actually declared war against the United States.

The *Essex* had just returned from the Indian Ocean, where, under Edward Preble, it escorted American merchant ships from the East Indies. This made the *Essex* the first American warship to venture into the Indian Ocean; a dozen years later David Porter would take the *Essex* to the Pacific, the first American warship to sail there.

Bainbridge's Mediterranean cruise would be unremarkable. On the first of June the three frigates, along with the schooner *Enterprise,* sailed from the

Chesapeake, making a timely arrival in Gibraltar after a month at sea. They found two Tripolitan ships, the twenty-six-gun *Meshouda* and a sixteen-gun brig, in the harbor. But Dale had been instructed to preserve peace, not to make war. The Tripolitan admiral Murad Ra'is assured Dale that their two countries were at peace. When Dale decided to leave the *Philadelphia* to block-ade the Tripolitans in Gibraltar, Ra'is and his crews abandoned their ships, crossed over as passengers to Morocco, and made their way by land to Tripoli.

Unlike Yusuf Qaramanli, Murad Ra'is apparently did have a strong dislike for Americans. He had been born Peter Lisle in Scotland. As a sailor in Mediterranean ports he had learned Arabic, and in New England ports he had learned to detest the United States. Sailing out of Boston on the mer-chant brig *Betsey*, he had been captured in 1796 by a Tripolitan ship. Lisle the merchant sailor converted to Islam, became Tripoli's High Admiral, or Murad Ra'is, and married Yusuf's sister. In Tripoli he had found opportuni-ties which had eluded him in America. Now he made his way back to Tripoli to organize the war against the United States.

Dale, still not aware that his country was at war, visited Morocco and Al-giers, where it was reported that his arrival had put to rest any threat of hostilities from either state. He sent the *Essex* from Gibraltar to convoy an American ship to Sicily and to escort the *Grand Turk*, carrying American tribute to Algiers and Tunis. The *Essex* also escorted American merchant vessels from Algiers to Sicily, Sardinia, and Barcelona.

For Decatur, this routine cruise in convoy was a chance to observe William Bainbridge, another kind of military leader, at close hand. Bainbridge had come out of the merchant service, where the men were better paid than in the navy; consequently Bainbridge was used to men who would stand harsher treatment. Bainbridge was known as a stern officer and severe disciplinarian, referring to each sailor as a "damned rascal" as he punished him with the flat side of his sword. He had once broken two swords over a drunken sailor's head; on another occasion it was his sword that broke the sailor's head.

Bainbridge was young, only twenty-seven, and had been a captain just over a year. He had been six days shy of his twenty-sixth birthday when he was commissioned a captain, the youngest man yet to earn the rank. So far his naval career had not been brilliant. Perhaps because he was younger than some of his sailors, and barely older than his midshipmen, he felt a need to establish his authority absolutely. Early in the cruise he spent almost an entire day "disciplining" the crew, flogging out any problems before they arose. After this the *Essex* did not record any more punishments for nearly six months, and there are no accounts of Bainbridge breaking either heads or swords to discipline drunken sailors.

Bainbridge had become the first—and so far only—American captain to surrender to an enemy when the French captured his sloop *Retaliation* in 1798. Two years later he was commander of the USS *George Washington* when the Dey of Algiers commandeered it to carry tribute to Istanbul. Although he had the distinction of being the first American naval captain to visit the Ottoman capital, he did so at the command of a foreign ruler. Now he was determined not to suffer the same disgrace.[1]

Decatur, in his first position of authority, was beginning to develop a very different kind of reputation. He was "as proverbial, among sailors, for the good treatment of his men as he is for valor," his biographer wrote; and a marine recalled that "not a tar, who ever sailed with Decatur, but would almost sacrifice his life for him."[2] According to a biography written in the 1840s, during a national campaign against brutal punishments in the navy, Decatur had the "happy art of governing sailors rather by their affections than their fears"; one officer recalled that Decatur "seemed, as if by magic, to hold a boundless sway over the hearts of seamen at first sight."[3]

Meanwhile, the *Essex* nearly became embroiled in war in the Mediterranean. Although the squadron had been sent against Tripoli, the *Essex*'s first hostilities were with Spain.[4] On the day it arrived in Barcelona, the ship was crowded with visitors from shore and from a Spanish xebec in the harbor. Spanish civilians praised the *Essex*'s appearance, the "manly gentility" of the officers, and the crew's "clean and rugged vigour," contrasting all with the Spanish xebec and its officers and men. This was too much for the Spanish sailors. That evening, as Bainbridge was being rowed from shore back to the *Essex*, the xebec opened fire, forcing Bainbridge to board the Spanish vessel. The Spanish commander verbally insulted Bainbridge, who angrily returned to Barcelona to complain. The authorities there advised him to put his complaint in writing. Bainbridge was furious. The authorities were treating the incident as a simple misunderstanding, suggesting that the Spanish officers did not realize that Bainbridge was an American ally. Of course they knew he was an American, Bainbridge replied; they had all spoken English to him earlier in the day. They were now bent on humiliating him, and their government in Barcelona was cooperating.

Bainbridge was outraged but unsure how to handle this insult. He needed to stay in Barcelona to reprovision the *Essex* with food and water. He could not easily let the insult pass, nor could he respond without causing further damage. But while Bainbridge felt frustration, Decatur acted. The next evening Decatur and some junior officers were being rowed past the xebec when a Spanish officer called out to them "by the most provoking language." Decatur had the boat pull alongside the xebec and called for the commanding officer. He demanded an end to these insults. When the commander did not comply to his satisfaction, Decatur promised to return the next morning to discuss the matter further, and his boat shoved off. The next morning when Decatur came aboard the xebec asking to see the officer who had been in charge the previous evening, he was told, alas, that the officer had gone ashore. So there would be no mistake, Decatur left this message: "Well, then, tell him that Lieutenant Decatur, of the frigate *Essex*, pronounces him a cowardly scoundrel, and that, when they meet on shore, he will cut his ears off."[4]

This raised the stakes. Now the authorities in Barcelona, who had dismissed Bainbridge's complaint, hastily tried to prevent further trouble—either duels between American and Spanish officers or riots between the sailors. They called in the American consul and proposed a truce: they would restrict the Spanish officers to their xebec if the Americans agreed not to leave the *Essex*. Consul Nathaniel P. Willis could not accept this. The Americans were in port to buy provisions; if they could not go ashore, they could not set sail. Bainbridge and Willis realized that they had reached an impasse, which could not be resolved in Barcelona. Bainbridge then interceded with Decatur to prevent him from making good on his challenge to the Spanish officer, and forwarded all his correspondence to David Humphreys, the American minister in Madrid. Humphreys smoothed over the problem at the Spanish court, and the *Essex* was able to complete its reprovisioning peacefully.

Bainbridge and Decatur had nevertheless responded differently to the Spanish insults. The cautious and diplomatic Bainbridge, sensitive to his position, had sought relief from the officials in Barcelona. He knew that they would not want an international incident provoked by a loudmouthed Spaniard. Decatur, by contrast, went directly to the offending Spanish officer to put a stop to his insults, and backed up his demand with the threat of force. Humphreys was still resolving the problem in Madrid when the *Essex* sailed.

While the *Essex* was engaged in this Spanish crisis, the schooner *Enterprise* encountered a Tripolitan ship. Lieutenant Andrew Sterrett brought the *Enterprise* within pistol range alongside the Tripolitan, and for three hours the two ships fought. The Tripolitan captain, Mahomet Sous, struck his colors three times, but each time, as the Americans slackened their fire and prepared to accept his surrender, he raised his flag again and opened fire. American cannon and marine sharpshooters proved more effective than the enemy's. After three hours, fifty of the eighty Tripolitan crew were either dead or wounded; they would not raise the Tripolitan flag again.

Sterrett had not lost a single man, and had decisively won the battle. But he was still not sure if his country and Tripoli were at war. President Jefferson had not given Americans the power to capture enemy vessels, so Sterrett had the Tripolitan's masts cut down and its cannon and ammunition tossed into the sea. With one small sail remaining, the ship was allowed to make its way home. Jefferson seized upon this victory in his first annual message as a demonstration of both American skill and American reluctance to wage war: the Americans were committed to the increase of the human race, not to its destruction. Dale sailed home with the rest of the squadron, leaving the *Essex* to blockade the abandoned Tripolitan vessels in Gibraltar. Bainbridge kept the men in readiness to fight, drilling them at their guns.

With no enemies to engage, the Americans began to turn on one another. Decatur apparently did not realize when a party of midshipmen asked permission to go ashore on March 27, 1802, that it was so two of them, Thomas Swartwout and James Higginbotham, could fight a duel. Higginbotham put a bullet through Swartwout's heart. Later that day the midshipmen returned to the frigate with Swartwout's body.

Decatur notified Bainbridge, who had gone across the bay to Algeciras for the day. Bainbridge had Higginbotham arrested, and at dawn the next day sent a boat to Gibraltar to buy wood for Swartwout's coffin. He also requested that Consul John Gavino get permission to bury the midshipman in Gibraltar. British authorities refused to allow this, so the following day, Sunday, the American officers crossed the Bay of Gibraltar to Algeciras to bury Swartwout at the Spanish fort of St. Iago.

Swartwout's death shocked all the officers. Decatur learned from his own lapse: he had not known that his midshipmen were planning to duel. Midshipmen at the time were particularly prone to exaggerated feelings of honor, and were more ready than more mature officers to seek justice at the dueling ground. Of the eighty-two naval duels reported between 1798 and 1820, fifty-two involved midshipmen. Decatur would keep a closer watch over the midshipmen in the future, and as a captain in 1809 would require his midshipmen to sign a pledge promising to refer all disputes to him for settlement.[5]

Sterrett's victory was the only battle during the first year of the war. The squadron was limited to blockading Tripoli or Gibraltar, and convoying merchant ships. But on February 6, 1802, after news of Sterrett's victory reached America, Congress formally declared war against Tripoli and took action to make the fighting force more effective. American captains were now allowed to capture enemy ships, and the period of enlistment was extended from one year to two. The men sent out with Dale's squadron the previous year were now due to come home, and Congress wished to avoid a manpower shortage if the new squadron, scheduled to sail in the late spring of 1802, did not resolve the war within a year.

Jefferson's administration wanted this new and larger squadron to be commanded by the driven and forceful Thomas Truxtun. Truxtun, who had received a gold medal for his services in the French war, would command the fleet from his flagship, the *Chesapeake*. But before he sailed, Truxtun and the administration ran into problems. As commodore of the squadron, Truxtun hoped to be spared the day-to-day details of running his flagship so he could focus on the overall strategy against Tripoli. Just as Dale had been able to leave the *President*'s command to Barron, Truxtun asked to have a captain put in charge of the *Chesapeake*. This would free him to conduct the war, and also to train the men, whom he found to be "all young and very inexperienced"; though they might eventually "be clever they are deficient at present."[6]

Secretary of the Navy Robert Smith told Truxtun that he could not spare another captain to serve under him. Truxtun had accepted the command conditionally—meaning, Smith believed, that unless a captain was placed in charge of the *Chesapeake*, Truxtun would refuse the assignment. Assuming this to be the case, Smith informed Truxtun that the navy accepted his resignation.[7] Truxtun was stunned; he began to believe that the navy had not sincerely wanted his services. Back in January he had been traveling through Washington, on his way to take command of the *Chesapeake* in Norfolk, and was momentarily struck speechless when President Jefferson asked him at dinner if he was traveling north or south. Did Jefferson not know that Truxtun was on his way to Norfolk? Even if the president was not aware that Truxtun had come from New York, he surely knew that Norfolk was south of Washington. Or was the president indicating that he hoped Truxtun would refuse the assignment?[8]

Whatever the reason, Truxtun was out of the navy, and out as squadron commander. The navy turned to the next senior captain, Richard Valentine Morris, who had been assigned to the *Constitution*. Morris instead went to Norfolk to command both the *Chesapeake* and the squadron. Dale had assembled and sailed his squadron as a unit; Morris would dispatch his ships as each was ready. The *Enterprise* had already sailed, the *Constellation* would go in March, the *Chesapeake* in April, and the *Adams* in June, with two other ships sailing in the fall.[9] When Morris arrived in Gibraltar in May, Bainbridge welcomed him with a dinner aboard the *Essex*; on leaving the Mediterranean, Bainbridge pointed the *Essex*'s bow toward America.

The ship arrived in New York in July. Bainbridge and Decatur had a near-mutiny on their hands by the time they docked. Secretary Smith had ordered the ship to sail from New York to Washington and discharge its crew in the capital. It made administrative sense to have the *Essex* sail to Washington, which was becoming the center of the naval establishment. The frigate was due to come out of service, and would be anchored in the Potomac's eastern branch. But Smith also knew that sailors discharged in New York could easily sign aboard merchant ships; in Washington their options would be limited, and many would likely reenlist in the navy. When the sailors reached New York and were told that they were to sail on to Washington they protested being discharged "on a tobacco plantation in Virginia." At Bainbridge's order, the most vocal protesters made the voyage to Washington in chains.[10]

When the *Essex* reached the capital on August 9, Decatur was ordered to the frigate *New York*, which was about to sail under James Barron's command. Barron had been Decatur's first commanding officer on the *United States*; he had then been a lieutenant, Decatur a midshipman. Barron now appointed Decatur his first lieutenant, a sign that the navy's captains regarded Decatur as a capable young officer. The *New York* sailed on September 1, 1802, for Decatur's second cruise to the Mediterranean.

The passage was not smooth. Just a week out of port a snapped mast threw a sailor to his death and damaged the ship too severely to continue across the Atlantic. The *New York* returned to Norfolk for repairs. By early October the ship was again ready to sail, and reached Gibraltar safely by mid-November. Decatur had left Gibraltar just five months earlier, under the shadow of Swartwout's death. He now returned to the Mediterranean to find an even heavier burden, the news that his brother-in-law, Marine Captain James McKnight, had died in a duel in Livorno the previous month. The duel had begun in a long-standing quarrel between McKnight and Lieutenant R. H. L. Lawson of the *Constellation*. Lawson had accepted McKnight's challenge, but insisted that the men should stand three paces from each other. McKnight called Lawson a coward and "an Assassin for proposing so short a distance."[11] Lawson in turn accused McKnight of cowardice, and though other marines assured McKnight that neither he nor Lawson could be called a coward, the two resumed their quarrel. Their seconds—navy lieutenants Jacob Jones for Lawson and David Porter for McKnight—set new terms: six paces, two pistols (each with a single bullet), and once the pistols were fired, cutlasses. Neither man fired his second pistol; Lawson's first shot pierced McKnight's heart.

When the Americans carried McKnight's body to Livorno's American Hotel, they were ordered to take him to "a vault near the Burial ground" for the coroner's examination. The horror of McKnight's death was compounded by the laws of Livorno requiring the removal of the fatal bullet, which would be used as evidence in court. Captain Daniel Carmick "threatened to make a corpse of the Surgeon" who began to cut open the dead marine, accusing the coroner of "cutting up my friend for the experience of his Students," but he finally left the Italian doctors "up to their Armpitts in blood" so he could make funeral arrangements. He found an English burying ground in Livorno, where the novelist Tobias Smollett had found his final rest, and set about raising money to build an appropriate monument over his "brave and honourable" friend.[12]

But Captain Daniel Murray, so deaf he had no idea this trouble was brewing, forbade too much honor being paid to a duelist. He had both Lawson and Jones arrested, and reacted angrily when he heard that Carmick was raising funds for a monument. Murray, who refused to attend the funeral, thought the monument should say that McKnight "had fallen victim to a false idea of Honor." Murray mourned the loss of such a "worthy member of his family and country"; he had thought McKnight a "very deserving officer, though rather irritable." But he believed that dueling was wrong, and making too much of a show over dead duelists might encourage more duels. He therefore proposed that any officer who gave or received a challenge, or served as a second, should forfeit his commission. He was willing to extend the penalty to anyone who failed to inform the commanding officer, for Murray would certainly have tried to prevent the duel had he known about it.[13] The death of McKnight was a personal blow to the Decatur family, but through Murray's proposals, it bore fruit. Decatur, having lost one midshipman and now his brother-in-law, personally took steps to prevent a recurrence.

Back in Philadelphia, Stephen's sister Ann Decatur McKnight was left with four young children—Mary Hill McKnight, Stephen Decatur McKnight, Anna Pine McKnight, and the baby, Priscilla Decatur McKnight. They continued to live with her parents at the Frankford farm. Ann was eventually remarried, to Dr. William Hurst, with whom she would have another daughter, Catherine Louisa Hurst. The other children took to calling Dr. Hurst their father, and he proved a less irritable husband and parent than Captain McKnight.

Battles over private honor were practically all the fighting the American fleet would do under the command of Richard Valentine Morris. Nathaniel Willis, the American consul in Barcelona, regretted that Morris had not stopped there on his way from Gibraltar to Italy, as "a Tripoline Cruiser of About thirty Tons" had been off the coast just a few days before, and Morris could have sent the schooner *Enterprise* to capture it.[14] But Morris interpreted his orders as requiring him to preserve peace and protect American commerce, so the American fleet spent most of 1802 and early 1803 convoying merchant ships from one port to another.

Perhaps the fact that Morris had brought his wife and his young son, Gerard, along on the cruise was a factor in his failing to seek out the enemy.

As the *Chesapeake* sailed off Barcelona, Midshipman Henry Wadsworth recorded in his journal this scene of "domestic happiness":"The Comdr. Seated on a Match tub, his Lady in a chair by his side with a book, Gerard between them each having a hand, on each side them a nine pounder mounted with the implements of War; at their backs on the Bulwark are fixed battle axes in the form of a half moon & a row of shot in a shot Locker." And then there was also "black Sal (or brown) Sal the maid sitting perhaps on the Deck leaning against the Gun carriage."[15] Wadsworth noted in his journal, which he was keeping for his sister back in Portland, that Mrs. Morris was conspicuous for "virtues which constitute the chief loveliness of your sex," a passion for reading, and a knowledge of history and geography. Although "her person is not beautiful, or even handsome," Wadsworth thought she "looks very well in a veil."[16] Not that all was inaction for Mrs. Morris. In June 1803 she gave birth to a second son, though by then her husband had thoughtfully found her an apartment in Malta.

Mrs. Morris had an easier delivery than the wife of Forecastle Captain James Low, who gave birth in the boatswain's storeroom on February 22, just after the ship left Algiers. Midshipman Melancthon T. Woolsey hosted a christening in his apartment for the baby, christened Melancthon Woolsey Low. But this happy event did not bring harmony to the ship. While Mrs. Hays, the gunner's wife, officiated at the ceremony (Mrs. Low was still to unwell to attend), in the forward part of the berthing deck the wives of the boatswain, carpenter, and marine corporal "got drunk in their own quarters out of pure spite—not being invited to celebrate the Christening of Melancthon Woolsey Low."[17]

As President Jefferson had remarked in response to the victory of the *Enterprise* in 1801, the Americans were committed to the increase of the human race, not to its destruction. But the fact that the navy seemed to be busy making love, not war, led to some mocking of any Americans' pretensions to fight. The fleet happened to be in Malta in mid-June, after the birth of Morris's second son, when British vice admiral Horatio Lord Nelson, on the frigate *Amphion*, came into port. The American ships joined Malta's forts in saluting England's and the world's greatest naval hero. Nelson returned the salute, though some of the Americans felt unworthy of the honor. A few days earlier a Tripolitan xebec, mistaking the British war sloop *Termagent* for the American frigate *Adams*, had opened fire. The English captain called his men to quarters and opened fire, and "the Tripoline struck her colors." Sadly Wadsworth wrote, "I wish it had been the *Adams*."[18] He lamented, "Twelve months pass'd after I enter'd the Straits before I saw Tripoly."[19]

Having been at war for nearly two years without actually fighting, the

Americans were beginning to acquire a pacific reputation. "Those Yankees will never stand the smell of powder!" a British officer sneered at two of the *New York*'s midshipmen attending the theater in Malta.[20] One of the midshipmen was Joseph Bainbridge, the captain's younger brother. Bainbridge and his friend tried to escape the taunts in the lobby, but the British officers followed them. One of the officers bumped Bainbridge, accidentally, twice. When the British officer bumped him a third time, accidentally, Bainbridge knocked him to the floor. The management cleared the lobby, but the next morning the Englishman's second called on Bainbridge. Bainbridge, following the new protocol, reported the matter to his superior officer, Stephen Decatur.

Decatur learned that the challenger was James Cochran, secretary to Malta's governor, Sir Alexander Ball. He suspected that Cochran was an experienced duelist and had picked out Bainbridge as a likely mark. Cochran was expecting to face two young and inexperienced midshipmen on the dueling field. Instead, Decatur insisted that he be Bainbridge's second and set the terms. Cochran and Bainbridge would face off at four paces, or twelve yards.[21] Such close range made Bainbridge the equal of the more experienced Englishman. Cochran had wanted ten paces; his second complained that four paces "looks like murder."

"No, Sir," Decatur answered. "This looks like death, but not murder. Your friend is a professed duelist, mine is wholly inexperienced. I am no duelist, but I am acquainted with the use of the pistol. If you insist upon ten paces, I will fight your friend at that distance."

When they met on the morning of February 14, 1803, Cochran's second continued to press for ten paces. Decatur would agree only if Cochran agreed to face him rather than Bainbridge. "We have no quarrel with you, Sir," the second told Decatur. Decatur made it clear that if they were challenging an American midshipman, they did have a quarrel with him.

Cochran had apparently become unnerved by this exchange. Now Decatur began the procedure of the duel.

"Take aim!" he ordered. And then he paused. Cochran seemed nervous, unsure of what else Decatur and Bainbridge might have planned. When he saw Cochran's hand tremble, Decatur ordered, "Fire!" Cochran's hat flew from his head as Bainbridge's shot carried it off; Cochran's shot disappeared harmlessly wide of Bainbridge. Decatur asked if Cochran was satisfied. He was not, and insisted on another round. Decatur advised Bainbridge to fire lower this time if he wanted to live. Cochran had missed once; he probably would not miss again.

Decatur again called, "Take aim!" paused more briefly this time, then

"Fire!" Bainbridge's shot hit Cochran just below his eye, killing him instantly. Decatur and Bainbridge, miraculously unhurt, quickly returned to their ship. Governor Ball demanded that the two be charged with murder. Although ordered to hold them, Barron took them aboard the *Chesapeake*. He was sailing back to the United States and turning the *New York* over to Morris. Despite Lieutenant Isaac Chauncey's request to have Decatur remain aboard the *New York* as his second lieutenant (Morris would have command of the squadron as well as the ship, while Chauncey would handle the daily operations), Decatur returned home with Barron on the *Chesapeake*.[22]

Decatur now had completed two cruises in the Mediterranean as part of the American war against Tripoli. He had done convoy and blockade duty, though he had yet to face an enemy other than Spanish or English duelists. He left Malta under a cloud, threatened with arrest, to return to a country that doubted the value of a navy—and now, thanks to Morris's incompetence, had reason to question its effectiveness.

CHAPTER *4*

"If it had not been for the Capture of the Philadelphia"

W HEN THE *Chesapeake* reached Washington at the end of May 1803, Decatur was ordered to Boston to oversee construction of the sixteen-gun brig *Argus*. He was to complete the task quickly, enlist a crew of seventy men, and sail to the Mediterranean. There he would deliver the *Argus* to Isaac Hull and take command of Hull's schooner, the *Enterprise*. It would be Decatur's first command.

First, though, Secretary Smith, recognizing that Decatur had been "almost constantly in service" for five years, allowed him to spend two weeks "with your friends in Phila." before proceeding to Boston.[1] Over the five years of his service, Decatur had spent perhaps five months in Philadelphia. Whenever he could, he had found opportunities to sail away from home. Now, as he had for the past five years, he would pass only briefly through Philadelphia.

His assignment to Boston introduced Decatur to Captain Edward Preble, who was already there refitting the USS *Constitution*. Decatur would complete the *Argus* under Preble's supervision, and Preble would take charge of the American forces against Tripoli. Preble was not an easy man to work for. Like Decatur, Preble seemed impatient, but for different reasons. His health was failing—he had never fully recovered from his daring voyage to the East Indies during the French war—and his doctor had already forbidden him to take command of a ship in the war against Tripoli. Preble now, in this brief moment of relatively stable health, pushed himself and those under him to work quickly and efficiently. Decatur, who had already heard about Preble's reputation as a strict disciplinarian with clear ideas of order, saw this at work at Boston.

Preble was now determined to finish the task President Jefferson had entrusted to him. He would arrive in the Mediterranean with an expanded fleet: while Decatur was building the *Argus* in Boston, Charles Stewart was in Philadelphia building the *Siren*, John Smith was building the *Vixen* in Baltimore, and Richard Somers in Norfolk was refitting the *Nautilus* as a schooner. This new force and new commander marked a revised strategy for the war. Morris had been a disaster. Not only had he failed to fight Tripoli, but also his feeble attempts to enforce the blockade had led to his arrest in Tunis. His utter powerlessness had contributed to a breakdown in discipline; his men had exchanged fire only with one another, in duels or drunken brawls.

Preble would be a different kind of commander. He was in Boston overseeing extensive repairs to the *Constitution*, which was slowly rotting away in the Charles River, where it had been anchored since the end of the French war. Preble had also begun construction on the *Argus* (which he had wanted to call the *Merrimack*, after the New England river; Secretary Smith and President Jefferson named it instead for the adventurous ship that sought the golden fleece). He was determined to move quickly. Within two weeks of laying the *Argus*'s keel at Harrtt's shipyard in Boston, Preble predicted that it would be finished ahead of schedule. Secretary Smith wrote that he would be pleased "if the Brig building under your superintendency, being the last ordered, shall be the first ready for sea."[2] Decatur, arriving on July 9, reported to Smith that he was sorry "to find the *Argus* not in that state of forwardness I am induced to believe you expected she would be in at this period." Still, the ship was "planked up & sealed, & her bottom is now preparing for coppering," and "her spar's rigging, sails & boats are nearly completed." Furthermore, he wrote, "the builders assure me she will be launched this month."[3]

To meet this schedule Decatur had to compete with Preble, who had assigned all available workers and material to his flagship rather than to Decatur's brig. Decatur also had to compete with Preble for sailors, and for both sailors and workmen he was competing not just with Preble but with Boston's merchant fleet as well. The *Argus* would not be the first ship launched; at the end of July, by which time Decatur had hoped to be under way, Somers and the *Nautilus* had already reached Gibraltar.[4]

While twelve days of "almost incessant rains" in Boston set back Decatur's construction schedule, he moved ahead to find a crew. Unable to enlist enough men there, he persuaded Preble to release Lieutenant Joseph Blake from the *Constitution* to the *Argus*, and then dispatched Blake to New York, "where we can get men without difficulty."[5] Although Blake was able to enlist nearly a full crew in New York, "a cantageous disorder" raging there killed four of the recruits and threatened all the rest.[6] Finding men was in any event easier than finding capable men. Preble had recommended that his boatswain William Moshier be "dismissed from the service—he is not capable of filling the station." Instead Moshier was assigned to the *Argus*, where Decatur also had "a great deal of trouble with him without being able to procure the smallest service from him." Ultimately Moshier was dismissed from the navy.[7]

Preble finally sailed in the middle of August, and one week later Decatur had the *Argus* ready to launch. He was chagrined at having told Secretary Smith that "we should be able to launch much earlier than we have," but he had "had the assurances of the builders to that effect & trust no censure will be attached to me for the delay." He was prepared for the launch on August 20, but there was a further delay: the descent from the shipyard to the harbor had not been built at a steep enough angle. At last on August 21 the *Argus* was in the water. The rigging and final finish work could not be completed until the ship was afloat, but Decatur promised Secretary Smith that the *Argus* "should be ready for sea in ten days after launching, which time I shall not exceed," and he hoped to have the vessel ready even earlier. But then he learned that Preble "had contracted with the riggers & other workmen that they should have fourteen days after launching to compleat their work in," and they would not do the work in any less.[8]

Finally, on September 5, the *Argus* was ready for its maiden voyage. It was Stephen Decatur's first ship, and he would sail it, loaded with $30,000 in gold and silver for Preble's fleet, to Gibraltar. But now a sudden gale blew up and kept the ship in Boston harbor until September 8, when Decatur was happy to report to Smith that "the Argus sails well."[9] For two days the *Argus* sailed with "fresh breezes" from the north and east. On their third day out the crew entered the Gulf Stream as the fresh breezes turned to a heavy gale "from the NE with a remarkable heavy sea going." Decatur had the main topsail, foresail, and "storm main staysail" reefed and the jib boom rigged in. But still the bowsprit "sprung," cracking under pressure from the stress of wind on the rigging and sails and endangering the masts. As was his duty, Decatur delegated his first lieutenant, along with the boatswain, sailing master, and carpenter, to inspect the damage. They concluded that with its bowsprit snapped, the *Argus* would not be fit to cross the Atlantic; in fact, it could not even sail "in a common Wind & Sea." Decatur turned his wounded brig toward Newport. There he reported his first impressions to Secretary Smith. Before the bowsprit snapped, he had noted that the *Argus* "sails fast. is very stiff & scuds well, but in lying to she pitches remarkably heavy."[10]

Newport's naval agent promised a new bowsprit in four days. On close inspection Decatur found four large knots in the snapped one, two of them rotted through to the center. Preble had objected to this flawed bowsprit "before I joined the Argus," but finally "concluded it might do."[11] Decatur learned otherwise. The repairs complete, he brought the *Argus* to sea again on September 27, and this time successfully crossed the Atlantic, reaching Gibraltar on the first of November.

Preble was already there. For an awkward moment on his arrival, Richard Valentine Morris was also in port on the *New York* and William Bainbridge on the *Philadelphia*, each captain flying the commodore's pennant and claiming to be commander of the entire operation. Preble did not stay to sort out this difficulty. Morris eventually sailed home to the United States, where he would be cashiered by President Jefferson, while Bainbridge sailed to Tripoli. Preble took the *Constitution* to Tangier, where he and Isaac Hull on the *Enterprise* sorted out a problem with a rebellious governor who was threatening to attack American ships. Preble's arrival resulted in the emperor's reaffirming Morocco's peace with the United States. When Preble returned to Gibraltar, Hull and Decatur exchanged commands, and Preble outlined to his subordinates the new American strategy in the Mediterranean. Decatur and the *Enterprise* would convoy the supply ship *Traveler* to Syracuse, where Preble would establish his naval base. Preble thought the Sicilian port a better place to base his fleet than Malta, where there were too many British sailors with whom his Americans were likely to fight.

From Syracuse Decatur would sail on to Tripoli to join Bainbridge and the *Philadelphia* in their blockade. Lest there be any misunderstanding, Preble sent a circular letter to American diplomats throughout Europe announcing to all nations that the United States and Tripoli were at war and that the U.S. fleet was blockading Tripoli.[12] Preble hoped to rendezvous with his entire fleet in Syracuse by December, but told Decatur he was not to wait. "Even in the worst season" Decatur should "shew yourself off Tripoly . . . if only for a day or two at a time" to convince the Tripolitans that "there Vessels is not safe, in leaving port at any season of the year."[13]

This would not be the fair weather cruising of Morris, who never actually reached Tripoli. Preble would keep pressure on the enemy, forcing Tripoli to make peace. With the *Philadelphia*, the *Constitution*, and the five smaller vessels relieving one another from their base at Syracuse, the Americans could maintain a constant presence off the coast of Tripoli. Preble was confident that by this show of force the United States could secure peace by spring.

Southwest of Sardinia on November 24, Preble encountered the British frigate *Amazon*. It delivered stunning news. The *Philadelphia* had run aground off Tripoli and now was in Tripoli harbor, its crew taken prisoner, the ship itself being transformed into a Tripolitan warship.

The *Philadelphia*'s loss "deranges my plans of operations for the present," Preble wrote, a setback both for its strategic result—Tripoli's harbor now was defended by a forty-gun American frigate—and for its emotional impact. "Our national character will sustain an injury with the Barbarians," he wrote the secretary of the navy. And while Preble tried to reassure Bainbridge, now in captivity in Tripoli, to others he showed his fury. He was astonished that the *Philadelphia* had put up no resistance. Not a single man, Tripolitan or American, had been wounded in the attack. "Would to God," he raged, "that the Officers and crew of the Philadelphia had one and all, determined to prefer death to slavery; it is possible such a determination might have saved them from either."[14] Instead, Tripoli now held three hundred American hostages. "If it had not been for the Capture of the Philadelphia, I have no doubt, but we should have had peace with Tripoly in the Spring."[15]

Preble's major problem—winning the war—had just become more difficult. He found Decatur waiting for him off Sicily, and the captain and lieutenant sailed into the harbor at Syracuse together. Preble would have to devise a new strategy; he might even have to request new forces. He also needed to move quickly to train the men still under his command into an effective fighting force.

Preble could not have been optimistic about turning these men, under these officers, into the warriors he needed. On the first of December he informed Decatur that the sailors the young lieutenant had sent ashore to fit rigging "were this Afternoon most of them drunk." Preble had locked one of the drunken sailors "in Irons" aboard the *Constitution* "for impertinence to me." He blamed the drunkenness not so much on the men as on "the negligence of the Officers in charge of them," and told Decatur to find out who was responsible. Preble promised that he would "certainly take notice of it." He did not need to say that the ultimate responsibility rested with Decatur.[16]

Known as a hard officer, Preble was not pleased with Decatur's apparently lax discipline. Decatur, only twenty-four years old and in command just a few months, had much to learn about controlling sailors. A captain like Preble could command respect through his reputation for previous deeds and through a fierce countenance; a young man like Decatur, younger than many of his own sailors, had not yet earned the reputation, and if he tried to assume the ferocity, he might overplay it into sadistic brutality or farce. Bainbridge, the youngest man to be commissioned a captain in the U.S. Navy, was known for using merciless floggings early in a cruise to set the proper tone of discipline. Decatur wanted to avoid this kind of savagery, preferring instead to keep order through gentler coercion—withholding rum rations or other alternatives to flogging. Such measures might have worked on the *Argus*'s crew, men signed on to a new ship under a new commander. But the *Enterprise* crew, trained under Hull, tested the new lieutenant and found his limits.

The day after Preble's reprimand, *Enterprise* midshipman Walter Boyd went on a roaring drunk in Syracuse. When Boyd started abusing the Syracusans, Lieutenant Jonathan Thorn tried to restrain him and ordered Boyd back to the *Enterprise*. Boyd then turned his drunken anger on Thorn. When Lieutenant James Lawrence took Boyd by the arm to return him to the ship, Boyd "collered him & at the same time drew his dirk." Lawrence disarmed the drunken Boyd and forced him back to the ship, where Decatur put Boyd under arrest and gave him three days to sober up before telling Preble about the episode. Lawrence and Thorn forgave Boyd, who wrote a contrite note to Preble begging the commodore to do the same. Accordingly, Preble declared himself "unwilling to condemn to destruction a young man whom I am informed has promising talents for the first offence that has come to my knowledge." Since "the officers who were insulted" had been generous enough to pardon Boyd, Preble agreed to "grant him mine in hopes he may learn prudence and merit the indulgence"[17]

Despite his apparently lax discipline, Decatur seemed to be an officer in Preble's mold—eager for action, meticulous in preparation. Preble ignored the news that the British government wanted Decatur, along with Midshipman Joseph Bainbridge, arrested for their roles in the death of James Cochran in Malta. Preble regarded dueling as yet another sign of failed discipline, but he would not sacrifice an officer and a midshipman to atone for duels under previous commanders.

Syracuse presented its own share of hazards. When Preble's ships had first arrived, "it was dangerous for the Americans to walk the streets at night," recalled the novelist Washington Irving, who passed through a year or so later. But the Sicilians "soon found that they came off the worst in those encounters."[18] Late one night Decatur and Midshipman Thomas Macdonough were returning to their launch when three armed "ruffians" jumped them. Backed against a wall by the surprise attack, Decatur and Macdonough drew their swords and fought back. As two of the robbers lay bleeding in the street, Macdonough chased the third, who had run into a house, racing after him through the tiny rooms and up the stairs to the roof. Cornered, the robber jumped to his death. Decatur and Macdonough returned unhurt to the *Enterprise*.[19] By the time Irving visited in February 1805, a year after the Americans had first arrived, he found that "any one who talks english may walk the streets at any time of night in perfect security."[20]

Preble, though, had not come to Syracuse to make the streets safe. His sole object was to fight Tripoli. He and Decatur set sail for Tripoli in December, leaving Lieutenant John Smith and the *Vixen* in Syracuse. On the morning of December 23, the *Constitution* and the *Enterprise* were in sight of Tripoli's coast when they spotted a sail approaching from the shore. At 8:30 the *Enterprise* turned to chase the stranger and forced it to stop two miles from the *Constitution*. Both American vessels were flying British flags to confuse the stranger, a ketch sailing under the Ottoman flag. Preble sent a boat to bring the Ottoman captain, Mustapha Rais, to the *Constitution*. As he questioned the captain, he noticed that back on the Turkish ketch twenty officers were quietly conferring. Preble suspected that they were not Turkish but Tripolitan. He ordered the British flag lowered from the *Constitution*'s mast and the American flag raised, a signal that provoked "the greatest confusion" on the ketch, which Preble then ordered his men to seize.[21]

The ketch turned out to be the *Mastico*, bound for Bengazi and then Istanbul, where it was to present Tripoli's gifts to the Captain Pacha. Among these gifts were forty-two African men, women, and children. Preble sent these prisoners, and the *Mastico*, to Syracuse under Decatur's escort, while he took the rest of the crew—Mustapha Rais, seven Greek and four Turkish sailors, and ten Tripolitan soldiers and two Tripolitan officers—aboard the *Constitution*. The men were put "under the half deck," while Mustapha Rais and the two officers lodged in Preble's cabin.

Preble did not know how significant this capture had been. It was the *Mastico* that had led the attack on the *Philadelphia*, and Mustapha Rais "with great eagerness executed the removal of the People and himself conducted the American prisoners unto the Palace of the Bashaw."[22] Preble suspected the officers were part of the Tripolitan navy, but in Malta he discovered just how important a captive Mustapha Rais was. In Malta Preble was able to sign a new ship's physician, Dr. Pietro Francisco Crocillo, who had previously been physician to Yusuf Pacha Qaramanli. (When Crocillo left Tripoli, Yusuf turned to the *Philadelphia*'s Dr. Jonathan Cowdery for medical attention.) Crocillo recognized Mustapha Rais and confirmed that the *Mastico* was indeed a Tripolitan warship. Preble declared the *Mastico* a prize and brought the prisoners back to Syracuse. Among their personal effects he found watches and swords belonging to the *Philadelphia*'s officers. Mustapha Rais would spend the rest of the war in New York City.[23]

Back in Syracuse, Preble gathered his junior officers in the *Constitution*'s cabin to discuss their next step. He would maintain the blockade, but he recognized that the loss of the *Philadelphia* had given Yusuf Qaramanli the upper hand. If Preble could destroy the *Philadelphia*, it would shift the balance back in the Americans' favor. Decatur may have been the first to suggest the idea, though Charles Stewart also proposed it, and from Tripoli, William Bainbridge himself wrote to Preble, in lime juice so his captors could not read his message, proposing "the idea of destroying the Frigate (which lies in the harbour)." Bainbridge thought that it could be done "by sending a few boats prepared with combustable to burn her." If a vessel came "about sun-set so as to prevent her being seen from the shore, and then stand in for the Town, her boats might get into the harbour unnoticed" and destroy the ship before Tripoli could launch its gunboats.[24]

Preble, Decatur, and Stewart prepared to act. Tripoli's forces would easily spot an American ship sailing into the harbor, but the captured *Mastico* could be disguised as a Mediterranean trader. It was agreed that Decatur, with seventy volunteers, would sail the *Mastico*—which Preble had renamed *Intrepid*—into Tripoli, with Stewart on the *Siren* backing him up. The Americans would be dressed as Maltese sailors. None of them knew the harbor, but fortunately in Malta they had met another Italian, Salvatore Catalano of Palermo, who knew Tripoli well. He had been there when Bainbridge and his men were brought in. Now he would guide Decatur into Tripoli to destroy the *Philadelphia*.

On the last day of January 1804 Preble wrote out his orders. The weather was still so bad he did not deliver them to Decatur and Stewart until Friday, February 3. That afternoon Decatur mustered his crew on the *Enterprise* quarterdeck. Preble had told him to take seventy men, "if that number can be found ready to volunteer their services for boarding and burning the Philadelphia." Decatur explained briefly the nature of the mission, not revealing its details but emphasizing its danger. No man could be ordered to risk his life on such a perilous mission: sailing into the enemy's harbor to destroy a heavily armed and heavily guarded ship. Decatur asked for volunteers. Every man and boy stepped forward.[25]

CHAPTER 5

"The great smoke cloud spreads its wings"

A N HOUR after he received Preble's written orders, Decatur and his men were sailing for Tripoli aboard the *Intrepid*; Charles Stewart escorted them in the *Siren*. The men left behind in Syracuse knew only that the two ships were "bound on some Secret Expedition," though Midshipman Ralph Izard wrote his mother that "I am in hopes we shall have the happiness of seeing the Philadelphia in flames." All things considered, Izard would have preferred to be "a Soldier in these times in Louisana," where "there is a chance for distinguishing one's self" in an anticipated war against Spain. Little did he know what opportunity the men of the *Intrepid* were about to seize.[1]

The *Intrepid* was designed to carry only twenty or thirty men, but for this mission Decatur needed to pack seventy-five men aboard. He and the other lieutenants—James Lawrence, Joseph Bainbridge, and Jonathan Thorn— and Surgeon Lewis Heerman shared the tiny cabin. Pilot Salvatore Catalano and seven midshipmen slept on a platform laid atop the water casks, so close below the deck they could not sit up without bumping their heads.[2] Eight marines bunked down opposite the midshipmen, and down in the hold, on top of more casks, were the fifty sailors. Rats and lice did not distinguish between officers and men.

Wherever there weren't men, there were barrels. In the hold were the provisions, mostly left over from the *Intrepid*'s last cruise as a Tripolitan merchant ship, and by now rancid. There was enough food for two or three weeks at the most; the ship could carry no more. The main deck was packed with barrels, too—all filled with explosives. A stray spark or a dropped candle would blow up the ship.

Exactly a week after leaving Syracuse, the *Intrepid* drew in sight of Tripoli. Decatur sent Catalano and Midshipman Charles Morris to inspect the harbor. Catalano knew the harbor, but Decatur's men did not know Catalano, so Decatur sent Morris along to confirm the Italian's judgment. Morris and Catalano reported back that the west wind was driving the surf too high for a safe entry into Tripoli. The men grumbled, as Decatur anticipated they would, suspecting that the foreigner Catalano was intentionally delaying them. Morris, however, confirmed the necessity of waiting.

The men were even more miserable when Catalano's judgment was borne out. The surf stayed high, and on Sunday blew into a gale that battered and drenched *Intrepid* and *Siren* for the next three days. When the storm finally abated on Wednesday, February 15, Decatur sailed toward Tripoli. The next morning he and the men readied their ship for its mission.

The men had all been drilled in each step of their task. First, they would board the *Philadelphia* and take possession. Estimates varied on how many Tripolitan sailors were guarding the ship; there might be twenty or thirty, or there might be many more. The Americans would have to strike suddenly, and could not use their guns. Swords were more effective than pistols in this kind of close-range action. Gunshots also would alert Tripoli's other defenses. Three cruisers, two galleys, and nineteen gunboats, with more than 100 cannon, and the formidable land batteries with 115 guns guarded the captive *Philadelphia*. If these opened fire, Decatur would not have to carry out his mission; Tripoli would destroy the *Philadelphia* and *Intrepid* with it.

So the men were to board and do their work quietly, using the password "Philadelphia" to tell friend from foe in the dark. Once they had overcome the enemy, each lieutenant and midshipman would lead a team of sailors to a different part of the great ship. Some would go to the berthing deck and some to the gun deck, while others would take parts of the main deck. Each man would carry a candle and a bundle of kindling. Men remaining on board *Intrepid* would pass over the igniting agent from the barrels on the deck as others in smaller boats circled to fight off Tripolitans coming to retake their prize. The *Siren* would support the attack, and when necessary take off the *Intrepid*'s crew—or its survivors.

Intrepid made its way slowly toward Tripoli on February 16. In sight of the harbor, Decatur's ship appeared to be struggling to make and by nightfall. From the shore it looked to be heavily laden, as well as damaged by the recent storm. This was a trick. Decatur had had the men rig heavy lumber, doors, and pieces of wood behind the ship to slow it down. The men remained crammed in the hold, coming up on deck only six at a time, to maintain the pretence that it was a trading ketch. The officers covered their uniforms' elegant golden braid, and all wore the clothing of Maltese merchant sailors. Flying the British flag, rigged like a Mediterranean trading vessel, the *Intrepid* neared Tripoli's harbor. Would the enemy suspect? Decatur was relieved to see the British consulate raise the Union Jack in welcome, a sign that at least the British consul believed him to be a friendly trader.

Both ships—*Intrepid* and *Siren*—were to enter the harbor's westernmost point, beneath the mole and the Seteef shoals, at seven in the evening. They would make their way to the *Philadelphia* and then join together to attack at ten. But the wind died as the sun set, and though *Intrepid* was by now in the harbor, Stewart and the *Siren* had fallen too far behind to come in. Decatur could not ask Stewart—his friend and senior officer—for advice. Should he wait for *Siren*? Should he turn back and try again the next day? Any delay might jeopardize the whole plan by giving the Tripolitans more time to see through the deception. What should he do? It was now his mission. Should he wait, so it could go off as planned? Would it be possible with one ship to do what had seemed nearly impossible with two?

If Decatur did not go ahead, the whole scheme might fail. *Intrepid* was nearly out of provisions; the men had been crowded below for two weeks. There might never be another chance. Decatur told his men to prepare to enter Tripoli's harbor without the *Siren*, remarking, "The fewer the number the greater the honor."[3] And, he need not tell them, the greater the risk.

Then came another change in plans. The surf was still too strong at the harbor's westernmost entrance, so *Intrepid* had to pass through the main channel, to the east of Shineel. Decatur ordered silence as the ship entered the harbor, an order that Midshipman Morris thought "appeared to be unnecessary." As *Intrepid* passed the first fortification, each man sat alone with his silent thoughts, knowing that they were within range of the "white walls of the city and its batteries."[4] The wind, still very light coming from the northwest, shifted to the northeast, bringing *Intrepid* to within two hundred yards of the *Philadelphia*. By 9:30 the wind had shifted again and was now coming off the land. This caused the frigate's bow to turn, leaving the *Intrepid* becalmed in *Philadelphia*'s lee. The two ships were parallel, the *Intrepid* twenty yards from the captive ship's larboard (port side) gangway. Decatur and Catalano stood alone at the wheel, the men hiding beneath the *Intrepid*'s bulwarks. Above the gunwales of *Philadelphia*, by the light of the crescent moon, they could see a dozen Tripolitan sailors watching them drift closer. According to the plan, the men in *Intrepid*'s launch, which had been towed behind, quietly rowed toward the *Philadelphia* to attach a line and draw the two ships closer together.

The Tripolitan captain called out to the *Intrepid*, ordering the stranger to keep away. Catalano replied that they had lost their anchor in the storm and asked permission to tie up next to the frigate. Catalano and Decatur and the crew now were within a few yards of *Philadelphia*'s cannon, with no wind to move them out of range. *Philadelphia* lowered a boat to help pass the line to the *Intrepid*. The Tripolitan asked what was that other ship—the *Siren*—he had seen off the harbor. Catalano replied that it was the *Transfer*, a welcome bit of news for the Tripolitans, who had purchased the British man-of-war at Malta.

The men in the two boats exchanged their lines and passed them to the crews on the *Intrepid* and *Philadelphia*. Men still hidden beneath the *Intrepid*'s bulwarks, lying on deck, pulled the rope to bring their ship beside the *Philadelphia*. A glimpse of officer's brocade here, the glint of a saber there, the shadows of men beneath the bulwarks raised the Tripolitans' suspicions. From the boat and the *Philadelphia*'s deck came the shout, "Americanos!" "Board now Captain!" Catalano shouted. Decatur, in *Intrepid*'s bow, commanded, "No order to be obeyed but that of the commanding officer." As he saw the *Philadelphia*'s gun crew remove the tompions from the frigate's cannon, he sprang for the *Philadelphia*'s main chain plates shouting, "BOARD!"[5]

Midshipman Morris, fearing he would not hear Decatur's command, had taken up a position next to the lieutenant. As Decatur jumped he followed, and as the command was being given, Morris was already on the frigate's deck. Decatur caught his balance on the railing, and as he jumped down to the deck, Morris rose up. Instantly Decatur prepared to strike him with his sword. "Philadelphia!" Morris shouted, stopping Decatur's raised right arm from striking him down. Behind them the men "hung on the ship's side like cluster bees," and within an "instant, every man was on board the frigate."[6]

To the few dozen Tripolitans on board, this sudden appearance of fifty armed men springing out of a ketch that a moment earlier had seemed to hold fewer than eight was enough to cause panic. Decatur and his men drew their swords as they formed in a great arc and swept across the main deck, forcing some Tripolitans overboard, fighting those who stood their ground. While the Americans on the frigate fought to get possession of *Philadelphia*, others in the *Intrepid*'s boat tried to intercept swimmers who might alert other Tripolitan ships. Within minutes the Americans had possession of the *Philadelphia*. All the Tripolitans but one were forced overboard—dead or alive. One Tripolitan remained on board, a wounded prisoner who was taken to *Intrepid*.

From the *Intrepid*, Surgeon Heerman recalled how the "gun deck was all of a sudden beautifully illuminated by the numerous candles of the crew," who set out in their teams, each man carrying a three-inch candle lit from the lanterns carried aboard in canvas sacks slung over their shoulders. The assigned crews scattered to their stations as Decatur paced the upper deck, calling through each hatchway to ask if all was ready. When each crew reported yes, he returned to each, working from bow to stern, "giving the word succinctly at each, 'Fire!'—in order of insuring the simultaneousness of setting fire to every part of the ship alike."[7] Perhaps as Decatur strode *Philadelphia*'s deck he recalled that his father had first commanded this ship after it had been purchased for the United States by the citizens of his nation's largest city. Perhaps he toyed with the idea, as Catalano and others would suggest after Decatur was dead, of raising the sails and bringing the frigate out of the harbor. Or perhaps his mind was simply focused on his mission, which was to destroy the ship, and on accomplishing the mission without losing any of his men's lives.

The men now ran through the ship with their candles as the igniting agents were passed aboard from the *Intrepid*. Midshipman Morris, waiting anxiously for his crew in the ship's cockpit on the berthing deck, could already smell the smoke from the gun deck above. Finally his crew arrived, set their fires, and made it safely through the burning gun deck to the main deck, and back to the *Intrepid*. Decatur stood on the *Philadelphia*'s railing, counting as his men jumped back onto the *Intrepid*. Finally all seventy-four, plus the Tripolitan prisoner, were aboard, and Decatur followed, the last man off the *Philadelphia*. Within twenty minutes of Decatur's order to board, all of the *Intrepid*'s men were off *Philadelphia* and the ship was in flames. As tongues of flame shot from the *Philadelphia*'s gunports, licking the *Intrepid*'s cotton sails and the barrels of flammable tar on deck, Surgeon Heerman noted that the *Intrepid* was being drawn closer to the burning ship as the fire sucked in all the available oxygen. Decatur ordered his men to push away with the spars and then man the sweeps to row clear. Finally, the attached boats towed *Intrepid* farther from the flames.

Just as it was pulled away, the *Intrepid* caught the land breeze which the *Philadelphia* had blocked and absorbed. The breeze carried *Intrepid* away from the blazing frigate but not out of danger. Burning embers from the ship showered down on the *Intrepid*, threatening to ignite the combustibles on deck. As the brilliant light from the fire illuminated the entire harbor, Decatur's men suddenly realized that they had accomplished their mission. All the tension of the last two weeks was released, and they stood "looking and laughing and casting their jokes" at the blaze. But Decatur knew that the mission was not yet accomplished. As his men's concentration and discipline slackened, he "leapt upon the companion[way], and, flourishing his sword, threatened to cut down the first man that was noisy after that."[8]

Now the Tripolitans on their ships and on land opened fire. For half an hour as the *Intrepid*'s men pulled at their oars, the Tripolitans kept up a heavy but ineffectual bombardment. One shot tore through the topgallant sail, but otherwise the shots fell short. As the Tripolitans opened fire, so did the *Philadelphia*. Its loaded cannon, heated by the flames, went off, those on the starboard side bombarding Tripoli, the larboard guns falling just short of the *Intrepid*. The sailors towing *Intrepid* commented "upon the beauty of the spray thrown up by the shot between us and the brilliant light of the ship," which appeared "magnificent," as flames inside, "illuminating her ports, and, ascending her rigging and masts, formed columns of fire, which, meeting the tops, were reflected into beautiful capitals," with the "occasional discharge of her guns" giving the appearance of "some directing spirit within her." Midshipman Morris recalled the sublime background formed by the "walls of the city and its batteries, and the masts and rigging of cruisers at anchor, brilliantly illuminated" by the blazing ship.[9]

Watching his ship burn from the Pacha's palace, Bainbridge found it a "most sublime sight, and very gratifying to us."[10] Just that morning he had written in lime juice to Preble, again proposing the "idea *of destroying the Frigate*," and was much pleased by the result, even though Yusuf Qaramanli increased guards on his prisoners after the attack.[11]

The *Philadelphia*'s surgeon, Jonathan Cowdery, now tending to the Pacha's family, had spent the day treating Yusuf's daughter, whose husband had entertained the doctor hospitably. At five, Cowdery heard reports that two English merchant vessels were approaching the harbor. He thought no more of it until about eleven o'clock, when "we were alarmed by a most hideous yelling and screaming from one end of the town to the other, and a firing of cannon from the castle. On getting up and opening the window which faced the harbour, we saw the frigate *Philadelphia* in flames."[12]

Yusuf watched "the whole business with his own Eyes," the Danish consul reported, but the "fire ship was beyond reach before they could give orders," and the frigate was completely destroyed.[13] The destruction of the frigate was a double blow to the Pacha, who had secretly sold it to Tunis. Ironically, that same day his plans to sell the ship had been squelched when Lieutenant Richard Somers on the *Nautilus* captured the Maltese brig *St. Crucifisso*, bound for Tripoli. The *St. Crucifisso* claimed to be sailing to Tripoli to pick up cattle—Preble had given the governor of Malta permission to transport cargo ordered before the American blockade—but Somers found it carrying not only Tripolitans but goods bound for Tripoli as well. The story was even more intriguing than this, as the ship's owner, Gaetano Andre Schembri Count de Gallino, was Tripoli's agent at Malta, and had his own scheme to sell the *Philadelphia* to Tunis. Somers's capture of the *St. Crucifisso*, and Decatur's destruction of the *Philadelphia*, ruined the plan.[14]

When they heard the cannon firing and saw the flames rising Arabs from the countryside thought that the city was under attack. They raced into Tripoli, only to witness the spectacle of the *Philadelphia* burning. A century later a very old man, Hadji Mohammad Gabroom, described the scene as his father, a guard in 1804, had related it to him: "The great smoke cloud spreads its wings like some evil bird over the harbor and soars to the upper regions of the darkness, its red talons always taking something from the face of the earth, which it carries toward the outer sea. . . . Soon the red devil tongues make the harbor light as the day and redder than the sands of the Sahk-ra when the sun is low in the west. When the breath of Allah blows back now and again, the big tongues change their course and lick out at the castle. They make its walls and ramparts red like blood and like some monster dragon as it spits back its fire guns."[15]

By one in the morning on February 17, Decatur and his men reached the rocky islands separating Tripoli's harbor from the open sea. The *Siren*'s boats met them, and as they steered toward Syracuse, they could still see *Philadelphia* blazing. Its mooring lines had burned, and the great frigate had drifted to the edge of the harbor. By dawn the *Intrepid* and *Siren* were forty miles out to sea, but they could still see the burning hulk of the *Philadelphia*.[16] "These Americans have wise heads," Hadji Mohammad Gabroom's father had told him. "When they lose their ship, they lose it to everybody."[17]

By ten in the morning on February 19, the two ships were in sight of Syracuse. An anxious Preble ordered the *Constitution* to signal *Intrepid* and *Siren*, "Business, have you completed, that you was sent on?" From *Intrepid*, Decatur ordered back the reply, "Business, I have completed, that I was sent on."[18] Preble dispatched boats to tow the returning ships into port. At half past ten the *Siren* and *Intrepid*, gone for more than two weeks, sailed "in triumph" through the squadron—*Constitution*, *Vixen*, and *Enterprise*—"receiving three cheers from each as the[y] pass'd."[19]

Stewart and Decatur presented Preble with their written reports and gave their verbal accounts of the expedition. News of the *Philadelphia*'s destruction circulated throughout the Mediterranean, and Decatur became nearly an instant hero. Robert Spence, a midshipman left behind at Livorno, recalled later that Decatur was soon known as "'*the terror of the foe.*' It was an achievement admired as *unexampled*. At Naples you could hear of nothing but the '*brave Decatur*'—and all foreign officers with whom I conversed, spoke of it as a most brilliant affair, managed with the greatest address and intrepidity—an intrepidity which nothing but success could rescue from the imputation of rashness."[20]

Years later, as the story was retold, it would be reported that Lord Nelson, blockading the French fleet at Toulon, called it the boldest act of naval heroism of the age. Although it is quite unlikely that Nelson did say this—there is no contemporary reference, and the first published account appeared in Alexander Slidell Mackenzie's biography of Decatur, forty years after the event—it is also possible that Mackenzie heard of it from a sailor who had been in the Mediterranean at the time. The destruction of the *Philadelphia* would leave a lasting impression throughout the Mediterranean, and would secure Decatur's reputation for dashing courage.

Preble's official report arrived back in Washington shortly after the news that the *Philadelphia* had been captured. Throughout the nation, Decatur's heroism revived spirits. Preble reported to President Jefferson that "Lieutenant Decatur is an officer of too much value to be neglected." He was impressed not only by Decatur's feat of "destroying an enemy's frigate of forty guns," but also by "the gallant manner in which he performed it," sailing "in a small vessel of only sixty tons and four guns, under the enemy's batteries, surrounded by their corsairs and armed boats, the crews of which stood appalled at his intrepidity and daring." In any European navy this gallantry would earn a lieutenant "instantaneous promotion to the rank of post captain," and Preble asked the president to promote Decatur immediately "as a stimulus" to other junior officers. "It would eventually be of real service to our navy." Jefferson agreed, and though word of Decatur's promotion did not reach the Mediterranean until September, Preble immediately began treating Decatur as a captain.[21]

CHAPTER 6

"I find hand to hand is not child's play"

THE NEW HERO would have little time to rest on earned laurels. Preble had only a few men, and he needed to use them effectively. The day after Decatur returned to Syracuse, Preble ordered him to sail for Messina to oversee the *Enterprise*'s refitting. "It is expected that not a moment of time will be lost," Preble warned, as "in the latter part of March I shall sail with the Squadron on an important expedition, where I shall want your services." Preble also warned Decatur to stay within a budget: "You are not to expend any money in Ornamenting the Schooner Enterprize—I expect One thousand dollars will pay the expences necessary."[1] Perhaps Preble recalled that Charles Stewart had tried to get the government to pay for furnishings for the lieutenants and midshipmen and wanted to make sure that Decatur did not develop extravagant tastes at government expense.[2]

Strong west winds forced Decatur off course from Messina, and he put in at Malta. Although he was still wanted by the British as an accomplice to murder, he was not arrested when he anchored, but was instead invited to dine with the governor. The governor was still without a secretary, though the replacement for the one Decatur had helped to kill was on his way. On a return visit to Malta, Decatur would get to know the new secretary, Samuel Taylor Coleridge, who reached Malta sometime in July 1804. Decatur made a vivid impression on Coleridge, not as a military hero but as a political thinker.

In addition to Mediterranean politics, the conversation between Decatur and Coleridge focused on the unfolding drama in Louisiana. Would the United States wrest it from Spain? Would the United States buy it from France? Although Americans today might regard the Louisiana Purchase as having sealed the nation's greatness, the sudden expansion of the republic troubled Decatur. "I remember Commodore Decatur saying to me at Malta, that he deplored the occupation of Louisiana by the United States," Coleridge later recalled, "and wished that province had been possessed by England. He thought that, if the United States got hold of Canada by conquest or cession, the last chance of the United States becoming a great compact nation would be lost."[3] It is not clear how much Decatur's words have been filtered through Coleridge's own ideological prism. Coleridge recalled Decatur's sentiment because it very nearly coincided with his own belief that a nation would become great if it were challenged by its neighbors, looking to history for examples such as Greece being challenged by Persia or Rome by Tuscany and Carthage. What is clear is that with the purchase of Louisiana, the destiny of the United States took a different path, and that the nation would ultimately look inward, to develop its own continent, rather than outward, to engage with the rest of the world.

Coleridge closed his 1818 essay "On the Law of Nations" with an extended paraphrase of Decatur's dinner table conversation:

> "An American commander, who has deserved and received the highest honours which his grateful country, through her assembled Representatives, could bestow upon him, once said to me with a sigh: in an evil hour for my country did the French and Spaniards abandon Louisiana to the United States. We were not sufficiently a country before: and should we ever be mad enough to drive the English from Canada and her other North American Provinces, we shall soon cease to be a country at all. Without local attachment, without national honour, we shall resemble a swarm of insects that settle on the fruits of the earth to corrupt and consume them, rather than men who love and cleave to the land of their forefathers. After a shapeless anarchy, and a series of civil wars, we shall at last be formed into many countries; unless the vices engendered in the process should demand further punishment, and we should previously fall beneath the despotism of some military adventurer, like a lion, consumed by an inward disease, prostrate and helpless, beneath the beak and talons of a vulture, or yet meaner bird of prey."[4]

All this was conjecture about the future; the war and its complications were in the here and now. The wind had carried Decatur away from Messina, and now instead of sailing on to repair the *Enterprise*, he set his course for Tunis. As he sailed into port, he met a twelve-gun Tripolitan ship sailing out. The Tripolitan followed him back in.

Just a year earlier, Commodore Morris had been arrested in Tunis; Decatur might suffer the same fate. The Bey of Tunis had purchased the *Philadelphia* through his agents in Malta, but Decatur had destroyed his property. The Bey summoned U.S. consul George Davis to the palace. Pleading illness, Davis declined, and warned Decatur to leave port by morning.

Davis feared for Decatur's arrest, which Decatur could prevent by slipping out under cover of darkness. But the fact that Decatur had arrived so suddenly in Tunis and then disappeared in the night provoked a different reaction. Bey Hamouda Pacha was wary of this American commander who had destroyed the *Philadelphia*. "Each wandering Bedouin," Davis reported, "details the daring action, and augurs something dreadful to our enemy from this event." Americans had been easy targets for humiliation. Decatur's raid, said Davis, was "the only occurrence, which has forced them to view the

American character with proper respect." When the *Enterprise* had suddenly reappeared in Tunis, the "sight of her gave a general panic" to the Tripolitans, "who took baggage and abandoned their Corsair the same evening."[5] The Tripolitans had no wish to encounter Decatur at sea. He sailed on for Sicily.

When Decatur finally reached Messina, he reported, the *Enterprise* was "in a much worse state, than I had any idea of." It would be, he informed Preble, "a lengthy and expensive Job" to repair the ship fully, so he would "only do what she cannot do without to make her safe in any season." The carpenter estimated that he could finish the job in twelve days; Decatur "urge[d] him to effect it in less." While in Messina, Decatur would also inspect gunboats that Preble hoped to borrow from the king of Naples. Needing more ships for his blockade and attack on Tripoli, Preble knew that it made more sense to borrow or buy them in the Mediterranean than wait for them to be built in America and sailed across the Atlantic. Decatur found that of the twenty gunboats available in Messina, "there are Six equipt and in good order."[6] The king agreed to lend Preble these six boats and two bombards, along with ninety-six sailors.

In the meantime, Decatur's own sailors were growing restive. The crew wrote to Preble from Messina, reminding the commodore that they had now been in the service beyond their term of enlistment. Were they volunteers, the men asked, or had they been "impressed in a service, whose liberty and independence our fathers fought and bled to establish and defend—against tyranny and oppression?" They demanded, "Can we then call ourselves Men, if we do not cast our thoughts on our families" back home in "that Country that we have risked our lives to defend and protect?"[7] Despite the fact that his men were eager to return home, Decatur managed to persuade all but fourteen of them to sign on for another tour, and many volunteered to serve in the borrowed gunboats.

Preble knew how rare it was to get men to stay beyond their enlistments. Decatur had a special gift for persuasion. He nevertheless anxiously awaited the arrival of the frigate *John Adams*, coming to replace the *Philadelphia* and, more important, to bring new men. The crew waited, too, as Preble expected the *John Adams* to arrive every day, and every day they were disappointed. While he could keep the men busy enough to avoid duels or courts-martial, he could not stop them from deserting. Preble had chosen Syracuse over Malta, a port busy with British ships, to reduce opportunities for desertion. When the *Constitution* visited Malta in March, Preble had to keep two midshipmen and four sailors patrolling in a boat every night to prevent his men from jumping ship.

While Preble was in Malta, and Decatur in Messina, a French privateer put in at Syracuse. An American sailor slipped off his ship and joined the privateer's crew. The French ignored Lieutenant John Smith, the senior American officer in Syracuse, when he demanded the American's return. Smith then asked the governor, Marcello DeGregorio, to intervene. DeGregorio neither agreed nor refused. Smith put his request in writing. DeGregorio ignored it. The French privateer sailed. In April the American returned to Syracuse aboard a Maltese vessel the French had captured at sea. By this time Decatur had come back to Syracuse. Rather than going through the proper and ineffective channels, or appealing to DeGregorio, Decatur sent a party of men to the Maltese prize, where they seized the deserter and brought him back to the *Enterprise.*

The French were furious and demanded that DeGregorio help recover the man. The governor ordered the city gates shut, imprisoning Richard Somers and eight other Americans who were ashore at the time. The men would be his prisoners until Decatur released the deserter. DeGregorio sent a few of his officers to convey this message to Preble, who was not moved. "You know he is not a man who commands his temper," Henry Wadsworth wrote of the meeting on the *Constitution* between Preble and DeGregorio's officers. "So in the rage the tables and chairs and Neapolitan officers hats flew about in the cabin, and when the light was again brought in it was some time before these unfortunate messengers could be found."[8] Preble's response to Governor DeGregorio was equally blunt: the arrest of Somers and the other men "was rash and improper, and an insult to our Flag, which I would not submit to." In response, Preble would hold DeGregorio's messengers as his prisoners until the governor released all of the Americans.[9] If DeGregorio did not return Preble's men, then Preble "would do as he pleased about it," and "would knock the town down about there ears."[10]

DeGregorio was caught in a bad situation. Rumors were flying that the French were about to occupy Syracuse, and now his failure to return the deserter, whom the French claimed as one of their own, would give them the pretext they needed. France was a much more powerful enemy than the Americans.[11] Preble's fleet, however—nearly the entire U.S. Navy—was in his harbor, and DeGregorio hoped to preserve good relations. He sought out a neutral intermediary. Frances Leckie, the wife of a British merchant in Syracuse, knew the governor and had become friendly with Preble. Mrs. Leckie wrote to Preble at the governor's request to say "that the situation of his Court with the French Government is such, that without disobeying the orders recd. he could not act otherwise than he has done," though it would always be his wish to promote the interests of "the American nation." She went on to tell

Preble that DeGregorio's "weakness" made him susceptible to the "bad advice" of those around him.[12] The governor himself wrote Preble to pledge his loyalty and friendship, hoping for an opportunity "to embrace you at any place you may Judge most fit," and adding a postscript: "What pleasure it would give me if you would honor me with your Company tomorrow to Dine in Company with Mr. Decatur."[13]

It is not known if Decatur and Preble accepted the governor's invitation. In any event, it is doubtful that Preble allowed DeGregorio to embrace him. But Preble did not follow through on his threat to take the matter up with the king of Naples, and two days after this episode, when Preble notified the governor that a Syracusan deserter had swum to the *Constitution* but was refused entry into the U.S. service, DeGregorio sent both an officer to retrieve the deserter and a letter of thanks to Preble.[14]

The episode reveals a number of things. First, Preble and Decatur were determined to make their flag respected in the Mediterranean. Second, Preble's biographer, Christopher McKee, speculates that this incident made Preble realize the importance of having American naval bases in the Mediterranean to spare the fleet the necessity of relying on the vagaries of local or global politics. Finally, Preble felt that the United States "must either abandon foreign commerce to more enterprising nations and become simply an agricultural state like the Chinese," or else become a mercantile power like the British or the Dutch with outposts throughout the world.[15]

Preble was interested in Syracusan politics only as far as they advanced his main goal, winning the war against Tripoli. He maintained a tight blockade of Tripoli, but knew that he needed to make a more direct attack. Rather than continue to wait for the *John Adams* to arrive, he set sail for the coast of Africa. He hoped that his continuing blockade would have weakened Tripoli's economy enough to force Yusuf Pacha to negotiate. Tobias Lear, the American consul in Algiers, suggested offering $600 for each prisoner Yusuf held. But Preble wanted to reduce this figure, which would amount to $180,000, a sum the Pacha would certainly accept. He sent Richard O'Brien, former captive in Algiers and American consul general to the Barbary States—and, like Preble, a native of Maine—ashore to offer $60,000 ($50,000 in ransom, $10,000 as a gift to the Pacha). Tripoli's prime minister, Mohammed D'Ghies, angrily rejected the deal.[16]

O'Brien left clothing and supplies for the American prisoners, and then with Preble sailed for Tunis. Preble ordered Decatur to prepare the borrowed gunboats for his next assault on Tripoli. By the end of July, Preble's squadron was again off Tripoli, waiting for the right wind to attack. Preble needed every advantage he could get. His entire fleet—the frigate *Constitution*, the *Argus*,

Enterprise, Nautilus, Siren, and *Vixen,* six gunboats, and two bomb ketches—
had less than half the firepower of Tripoli's land batteries and fleet. Tripoli's
nineteen gunboats formed an outer line of defense in the harbor; and inside
were two galleys, two schooners, and a brig. On shore Tripoli had 115 cannon
and a new encampment of 25,000 soldiers.[17]

A sudden Mediterreanean gale blew up, forcing Preble's squadron off
station, tearing the *Constitution*'s foresail and maintop "to ribbons," and
threatening to sink the smaller gunboats, flat-bottomed craft that rowed
poorly and sailed worse. The gale finally subsided on the first of August, and
the squadron again approached the coast of Tripoli. By noon on August 3,
with Preble and his fleet two or three miles from Tripoli's outer batteries, the
enemy's gunboats began to advance. Preble gave the order for an attack.

Under Preble's plan the American ships had to turn about and tack to get
into battle formation. Yusuf Pacha watched the fleet maneuver from his palace. The Americans had been approaching the city, but now they seemed to
withdraw without firing a shot. "They will mark their distance for tacking,"
Yusuf said. "They are a sort of Jews, who have no notion of fighting."[18] But by
half past one the American ships again faced Tripoli, and Preble gave the
order for his commanders to man the gunboats. The larger ships could not
approach the shallow rocky coast. They would cover the two bomb ketches
and the six gunboats, which would do the bulk of the fighting. The ketches,
under Lieutenant Commander John Dent and Lieutenant Thomas Robinson, would throw their shells into the town. The six gunboats, each manned
by two dozen Americans and a dozen Italians, arranged themselves in two
divisions of three boats each. Somers commanded the western line, on
Preble's right, and Decatur the line on Preble's left. These six gunboats would
take on Tripoli's nineteen. At a quarter to three the bomb ketches began to
fire, and according to John Darby on the *John Adams,* "the enemy's shipping
and batteries opened a tremendous fire," which Preble's larger vessels vigor-
ously returned.[19]

Somers's gunboat sailed poorly, and his entire division had problems. His
own boat was driven leeward, behind the line of Tripolitan boats he was to
attack. Lieutenant Joseph Blake, third boat in Somers's division, misread the
Constitution's signals, and instead of advancing he held back, missing the
battle entirely. Blake later would be "publickly caled a cowerd" and forced to
resign from the navy.[20] James Decatur, Stephen's younger brother, commanded Somers's other gunboat. When James realized how far off course
Somers was drifting, he moved to join his brother's squadron. Somers, left
practically alone against five Tripolitan gunboats, managed to sail back into
the action and drove the enemy onto the rocks.

Stephen Decatur's squadron had more success. The Tripolitans shot off the lateen yard on Joseph Bainbridge's gunboat, leaving it adrift and astern of the others. But as he drifted, Bainbridge maintained a steady fire to cover the other American boats. He eventually ran aground under the batteries of Tripoli, but Bainbridge and his men got free from the rocks and returned to the battle.

The gunboat strategy was to close in with the enemy, then open fire with grapeshot to wound the crew and cover the action in a dense cloud of smoke. Then the Americans would leave their own boat under the control of the Italian sailors, board the enemy, and fight with "pistol, sabre, pike, and tomahawk" on the enemy's ship. Two dozen Americans would face thirty-six to fifty Tripolitans, on their own vessels. The men fought mainly with their boarding pikes or sabers. Pistols took precious seconds to aim, and even longer to reload; once fired, the pistol was most effective as a club or a boomerang, or a shield to ward off sword blows. "I find hand to hand is not childs play," Decatur wrote, " 'tis kill or be killed." This was the way Tripolitans fought, and Decatur had come to believe that "we could lick them in their own way and give them two to one." The Italians, he would later recall, "claimed the honor of the day, while we fought they prayed."[21]

Decatur boarded the first of the Tripolitan gunboats. An open hatchway divided the boat along its length from bow to stern, forming a trench down middle. As he and his men boarded on one side, the Tripolitan crew fled to the other, some continuing over the side. Decatur and his men had a moment to gather their thoughts as the smoke cleared, then he led his men around the bow and stern ends of the hatchway. Fighting with their swords, pikes, and hatchets against odds of perhaps two to one, Decatur and his men took control of the enemy gunboat within ten minutes. Decatur personally snatched down the Tripolitan flag as his men tied the prize to Gunboat Number 4.

On Gunboat Number 6, Lieutenant John Trippe had run alongside a Tripolitan, fired his guns, and then begun boarding. But Trippe, only nineteen years old, plus Midshipman John Henley and nine sailors were stranded on the enemy boat when their own gunboat moved off. These eleven Americans were trapped on a gunboat manned by thirty-six Tripolitans, who knew they were stranded. Trippe and Henley charged the Tripolitan captain—an athletic man, twenty-five years old and more than six feet tall—who slashed Trippe at least eleven times with his saber. But Trippe and his men fought back bravely and effectively, gradually disabling the Tripolitan crew and shifting the odds in their own favor. When Trippe signaled his opponent to surrender, the Tripolitan, now bleeding as freely as Trippe, refused. Reluctantly,

Trippe struck a fatal blow at the Tripolitan captain, who fell to the deck. To the end of his own short life (he died of yellow fever in 1810), Trippe regretted having to kill this formidable and worthy opponent. Trippe's own heroism, fighting on against overwhelming odds, became legendary in the U.S. Navy.[22]

James Decatur on Gunboat Number 2 found the largest of Tripoli's gunboats, and closed in and opened fire. As he prepared to board the enemy, the Tripolitan struck his colors in surrender. When James Decatur stepped onto the Tripolitan's rail to take possession of the prize, a Tripolitan shot him in the head. The Tripolitan boat sailed off, leaving the stunned Americans to pull their dying lieutenant out of the water. Midshipman Thomas Brown took command of Gunboat Number 2. He got close enough to Stephen Decatur's boat to shout that they had captured the largest of Tripoli's gunboats but had been tricked. James had been mortally wounded. With his own prize in tow, Stephen Decatur turned back to find the Tripolitan gunboat.

Decatur and his men once more closed with the enemy, and again they boarded. He was even more outnumbered now, with seven of his men wounded and others left manning the prize and guarding prisoners. Wounded or not, all of Decatur's men were prepared to fight. He, Midshipman James Macdonough, and eight sailors boarded the enemy boat. For twenty desperate minutes they fought. Decatur and Macdonough picked out the captain and went for him. With his saber Decatur tried to strike him, but the captain deflected the blow with his boarding pike and snapped Decatur's sword. With Decatur for an instant disarmed, the captain thrust his pike at Decatur's heart. Decatur blocked with his arm, which absorbed most of the blow as the pike's tip pierced his chest. Pulling the weapon from his flesh, Decatur gripped it and with a sudden jerk wrested it from his enemy. The Tripolitan captain lunged, and the two men fell to the deck, wrestling and straining to reach their other weapons.

American and Tripolitan sailors rushed to help their captains in this desperate fight. A Tripolitan sailor waited for a moment when Decatur was on top to come from behind and raise his own sword over Decatur's head. An American named Daniel Frazier, already wounded in both arms from the day's first battle, saw his captain about to lose his head and instantly threw himself between Decatur and the Tripolitan's sword. Frazier was badly wounded, but Decatur was spared to continue his fight.[23]

The Tripolitan captain, nearly a foot taller than Decatur and much heavier, was able to turn over and get the advantage, pinning Decatur to the deck with his body while with a free hand he pulled his knife from its sheath.

Decatur struggled with one free hand to hold the Tripolitan's knife away from his throat. With the hand buried beneath the captain, Decatur was able to reach his pocket, where he found his pistol. Turning the barrel away from himself, Decatur cocked his pistol and pulled the trigger. The ball tore into the Tripolitan's abdomen, killing the man. Decatur disentangled himself from the captain's body, snatched an Arabic prayerbook from the man's pocket, and took command of the gunboat.[24]

By now the wind was shifting, blowing toward shore, and Preble signaled the gunboats and ketches to disengage. He brought the *Constitution* closer to shore so he could cover their retreat, then pulled away. Preble offered to tow the badly wounded Trippe, who declined, preferring to sail off under his own power. When all the smaller boats were safely out of range, Preble ordered the larger ships to tow them, and he began to receive after-action reports from each boat commander. How many men had been lost? He had watched Somers take on five Tripolitan boats, and seen Trippe and the Decatur brothers close in and board, as the *Constitution* and the other ships and all the Tripolitan batteries had kept up a barrage for more than two hours, and yet there were no reported deaths. His men had not lost a single boat, nor had they lost a single man.

But this would change. Preble learned that James Decatur was not likely to live. He dispatched Stephen Decatur, in Preble's own barge, to bring his brother back to the *Constitution*. Stephen found Midshipman Charles Morris cradling James's head in his lap. Carefully they lifted him into Preble's barge and steered for the *Constitution*. Morris continued to hold his lieutenant's head, and Stephen sat by his side. The setting sun cast a final glow on James Decatur's face; as they reached their flagship, he died. "I would rather see him thus," Stephen said, "than living with any cloud upon his conduct."[25]

James Decatur was the only American to die that day. Estimates of Tripolitan dead range above one hundred. The Americans had captured three of Tripoli's gunboats and sunk three others while losing none of their own. The American bombardment had damaged the masts of a Tripolitan schooner and brig beyond repair. The *Constitution* had lost a bit of the mainmast, and Preble nearly missed being killed by a shot that destroyed a gun on the quarterdeck, but none of the larger American vessels was seriously damaged. Preble, Decatur, Trippe, and Somers had shown that even against great odds, the Americans would fight and could win.

But the day was not a tactical success. Although Tripoli had lost six gunboats, its navy still had more gunboats than the Americans. Tripoli's larger vessels still controlled the harbor, and Preble noted that as quickly as his larger guns could clear away the Tripolitans manning the shore guns, more came to take their places. Preble's two bomb ketches had been particularly ineffective: between them they had managed to fire only fourteen shells, and only one had reached Tripoli, where it did little damage.[26]

The next morning Preble presided over James Decatur's funeral, committing his body to the Mediterranean. In his general orders for the day Preble lamented "the death of the brave Lieutenant . . . who nobly fell at the moment he had obliged an enemy of superior force to strike to him," and he praised the "very distinguished judgment and intrepidity of Captain Decatur," who had captured two gunboats of superior force.[27]

Preble decided to try again. He had learned that just west of Tripoli was a small, undefended bay. It seemed to offer a weak point in Tripoli's fortifications. If he placed his bomb vessels and some gunboats there, they would be out of range of Tripoli's main batteries but close enough to batter down Tripoli's western defenses and even lob shells into the city itself. Preble and his larger ships would engage the rest of Tripoli's fleet while this bombardment from the west distracted and weakened the land batteries. Preble ordered the three captured gunboats re-rigged from lateen sails to sloops and made preparations for a second attack on Tuesday, August 7.

Despite a message received through the French consul that Yusuf was now ready to negotiate, Preble ordered his fleet to advance on Tuesday morning. Friday's battle had been a moral victory for the Americans but a tactical one for Tripoli. Tuesday's attack would prove demoralizing for the Americans but not a clear victory for Tripoli.

Preble's information was wrong. Tripoli had managed to build a battery in the previously undefended bay. This "Vixen battery," as the American sailors named it poured shot onto their gunboats as the east wind kept the Americans from penetrating far enough into Tripoli's harbor to engage the enemy. Tripoli destroyed one of the American gunboats and damaged several others while keeping its own vessels hidden along the rocky coast, away from the damaging broadsides of the larger American ships.

Lieutenant James Caldwell commanded Gunboat Number 9, captured from Tripoli just four days earlier. Caldwell had begun his naval career with Decatur and Somers as a midshipman on the *United States*. At 3:30 on the afternoon of August 7, a smoldering bit of wadding from one of his guns dropped into the powder magazine on the gunboat. A terrific blast sent bits of wood, metal, and men smashing through the air and water. For an awful moment Tripolitans and Americans and their guns were silent. In the next boat, Decatur saw as the smoke cleared the bow of Gunboat Number 9 still floating, and on it the gun crew, led by Midshipman Robert Spence and gunner's mate Edmund P. Kennedy, loaded their gun to fire one more round. The rising water overtook them before they could fire, but Spence, Kennedy, and the rest of the gun crew gave three cheers as the deck fell beneath the tide. The survivors swam to nearby boats. Spence, whose father was a prisoner in Tripoli, could not swim, but floated on an oar. Once rescued, the men took positions at the guns of other boats. Caldwell and eleven other men were dead.

Preble had noticed a sail to the northwest and sent the *Argus* to investigate. The *Argus* came back with good news—which turned out to be bad news. The strange sail belonged to the *John Adams*, which Preble had been expecting since April. What a difference it might have made then, or even four days earlier during the attack on Tripoli. Now he was doubly disappointed to find that the frigate had come primarily as a supply ship, with only a few serviceable cannon. It had arrived as the advance guard of a new fleet of four frigates—the *President*, the *Congress*, the *Essex*, and the *Constellation*—sent to increase pressure on Tripoli. Preble welcomed the additional force. But there was also a blow: Secretary of the Navy Smith assured Preble that the administration had complete confidence in him, but the navy did not have enough junior captains to command all the vessels sailing to Tripoli. Command of the squadron would have to be turned over to Samuel Barron, senior to Preble. Preble would return home. "How much my feelings are lacerated by this supercedure at the moment of Victory," Preble wrote, "cannot be described, and can be felt only by an officer placed in my mortifying situation."[28]

CHAPTER 7

"The character of a great and rising nation"

PREBLE AND the men under him were now determined to win the war before his replacement arrived. "The officers here are all very anxious that a peace shoud be made before the arrival of Commodore Barron," *John Adams* purser John Darby wrote in his journal, "that Commodore Preble may have the credit of it." The officers and men of the *John Adams* were "opposed to it and we are praying for his [Barron's] arrival before a peace." They were particularly shocked at how the men of Preble's fleet, battle-hardened after a week of bloody fighting, "seem to talk of butchering and cuting up a Turk with as much indifference as one is accustomed to carve a Turkey or chicken."[1]

Secretary Smith tried to assuage Preble's wounded pride. Enclosed with the dispatches was a commission for the navy's newest captain, Stephen Decatur, retroactive to February 16, when Decatur had destroyed the *Philadelphia*. Preble had been referring to Decatur as "Captain" ever since. Now, just a week after Preble had officiated at the brief funeral for James Decatur, committing his body to the sea, Preble assembled his officers on the *Constitution*'s deck for the promotion of Stephen Decatur to captain. Decatur became, at the age of twenty-five years and a few weeks, the youngest man yet to hold the rank.

For all, the moment might have been tinged with irony. Preble was about to be displaced because of the navy's tight commitment to seniority. Decatur's commission as captain, postdated by President Jefferson, jumped him above seven of his comrades, including Stewart and Somers, Isaac Hull, and John Smith, who were now promoted to master commandant. They were all senior to Decatur in the service: Stewart had been a lieutenant on the day Decatur entered the navy as a midshipman. Now he outranked them. Preble hoped that rewarding deeds of valor would encourage more such deeds, and in fact this one did. But it also bred dissension. Lieutenant Andrew Sterrett, the first American hero of the Tripolitan war, resigned from the navy rather than be ranked below Captain Decatur. The secretary of the navy did not soothe Sterrett's feelings much by suggesting that Decatur's promotion should be a spur to his own ambition, as "the same principle" of a reward for valor "might ultimately raise you to the highest and most honorable command in the navy in preference to gentlemen senior to you in original appointment."[2]

Deeply disappointed, but eager to push on to victory, Preble ordered Decatur and Isaac Chauncey to reconnoiter Tripoli's harbor at dusk on August 18 in preparation for a nighttime bombardment. A week later, after midnight on August 24, Preble's gunboats pounded Tripoli, though "with what effect" Preble was uncertain. He did not know that one shot blasted through the wall of William Bainbridge's apartment, knocking down a cartload of stones which buried Bainbridge, and then bounced off the walls of his room. Bainbridge's junior officers had to dig out their bruised and cut commander (his ankle did not recover for months).[3]

Still waiting for Barron's fleet, Preble ordered another nighttime attack on August 28. This time he sank one enemy gunboat and a Tunisian ship and damaged others. But Preble's fleet was almost out of ammunition, and Yusuf was no closer to meeting his peace terms. To bring the Pacha to the table, Preble needed another bold, dramatic stroke, like Decatur's destruction of the *Philadelphia.*

This time, Richard Somers, now a master commandant, volunteered. He would pack the *Intrepid,* the little ship on which Decatur had made his name, with explosives—150 barrels of gunpowder and 300 shells—bring it into Tripoli harbor below Yusuf's palace late at night, light a fuse, and row away before it exploded. The mission promised glory to those who would undertake it, and "every man man on board the *Nautilus*" volunteered, just as every man had stepped forward when Decatur had asked for volunteers to destroy the *Philadelphia.*[4] Midshipman Robert Spence applied to both Decatur and Stewart to use their influence with the commodore, but Spence complained that Preble chosen his own favorite, Henry Wadsworth, for the honor.[5] Wadsworth would have been on the *Philadelphia* expedition had he not been suffering from syphilis. Now he was well enough to be Somers's second in command. With four sailors from the *Nautilus* (James Simms, Thomas Tompline, James Harris, and William Keith) and six from the *Constitution* (William Harrison, Robert Clark, Hugh MacCormick, Jacob Williams, Peter Penner, and Isaac Downs), the *Intrepid,* followed by the *Nautilus,* made for Tripoli harbor. The men had already good-naturedly divided their possessions among their shipmates ("I say, Sam Jones, I leave you my blue jacket and duck trowsers, stowed away in my bag"; "Bill Curtis, you may have the tarpaulin hat . . . I got in Malta—and mind, boys, when you get home, give a good account of us"). When Somers, realizing that its 150 barrels of gunpowder made the *Intrepid* a valuable prize, announced that "no man need accompany him, who had not come to the resolution to blow himself up rather than be captured," the crew rose as one man to give three hearty cheers.[6]

Before the *Intrepid* reached Tripoli on its second heroic mission, Preble sent Midshipman Joseph Israel with additional instructions for Somers. Israel had not been chosen for the mission but now seized his chance to be part of it. He refused to leave the *Intrepid*, but would join Somers and Wadsworth in pursuing glory.

The *Intrepid* set off on September 2, but the winds prevented the ship from entering the harbor.[7] On the next two nights Somers tried again, but not until September 4 could he get his ship through the narrow openings into Tripoli. The *Nautilus* stayed behind, just beyond the harbor, as Stewart and the *Siren* had in February. The deck officers on the *Nautilus* kept watch on the *Intrepid* through a spyglass. At ten a sudden blinding flash "illumined the whole heavens around" and the noise "shook everything far and near"; then there was silence. The *Intrepid* was gone.

After a moment, shrieking could be heard on shore. *Nautilus* showed a light—the signal for the *Intrepid*'s crew—and the guns of Tripoli opened fire. *Nautilus* waited all night under fire from Tripoli's shore batteries and ships, but no one returned. Preble speculated that Somers had made good on his promise to die rather than submit to capture. (Later, after his release from Tripoli and his return to America, William Bainbridge read Preble's speculations in the newspaper and felt that Preble was commenting on his own surrender of the *Philadelphia*.)

With this dramatic but unsuccessful attack, Preble determined that it was time to pull out of Tripoli. As the men prepared to set sail for Syracuse, Barron's squadron, the largest American fleet ever assembled, appeared on the horizon. Barron, with the *President* and the *Constellation*, "took command," Preble noted in his journal. The transition was smooth and immediate. Preble recalled the awkward moment in Gibraltar, a year earlier, when three American commodores—Bainbridge, Morris, and himself—had flown their pennants simultaneously. There would be no such awkwardness now, because for Preble, his pride already lacerated, the main goal still was victory. He and Barron met in the *Constitution*'s cabin to discuss strategy.

On board the *President* was William Eaton, formerly a colonel in the U.S. Army, and since 1798 U.S. consul in Tunis, where he had devised a bold plan. In Tunis he had met Ahmet Qaramanli, the older brother of Yusuf Pacha, who had been deposed by his ambitious younger brother. Eaton proposed to use Ahmet to advance American interests. If an army under Ahmet appeared in Tripoli, the people might rise to his support and overthrow Yusuf. Ahmet, restored to power with American aid, would naturally release the prisoners and maintain peace with the United States. Eaton had not completely convinced the administration that the plan was feasible, but Secretary of State Madison gave him qualified permission to pursue it. The United States would not pledge to restore Ahmet to power but would cooperate with him as long as doing so advanced American interests. Eaton was sent to the Mediterranean on Barron's ship with the title of naval agent, but Barron was not quite sure what to make of him.

Preble, however, knew Eaton and admired the ambitious soldier from New England. In their conversation in Preble's cabin, Barron was persuaded to support Eaton fully, sending him on board the *Argus*, commanded by Isaac Hull, to find Ahmet Qaramanli, who was somewhere in Egypt, and bring him to either Derna, Benghazi, or Tripoli. As a cover story, Hull would go to Alexandria to convoy any American ships that happened to be there.[8]

Eaton was relieved to find Preble. He was also astonished at the change Preble's force had wrought in the region. In the Mediterranean, "an American is no longer ashamed of an American Uniform," Eaton wrote home, and a "Barbary cruiser views an American flag in this sea with as much caution as a sculking debtor does a deputy sheriff in our country."[9]

Preble and Barron briefly put in at Malta for a few days of further discussion of strategy. There, Governor Ball, who had not been favorably impressed with the dueling and reckless Americans when they first arrived in the Mediterranean, now had nothing but praise for Preble and his fleet. He congratulated Preble on the "hair breadth escapes you have had in setting so distinguished an example to your countrymen whose bravery & enterprize cannot fail to mark the character of a great & rising nation," and especially for "not purchasing a peace with money—A few brave men have been sacrificed; but they could not have fallen in a better cause."[10]

For Preble's part, he was bitterly disappointed to be deprived of the ability to see the war through to victory. Having done well with a small force, he believed—with justification—that had the additional frigates arrived sooner, he could have reached a favorable settlement with Yusuf. Now the peace would be Barron's to win. Preble did take great pride in having restored order and discipline to the American forces. "It affords me much satisfaction," he wrote to the secretary of the navy, "to observe that we have neither had a duel nor a court martial in the squadron since we left the United States."[11]

Preble sailed from Malta on the *Argus*, the ship Decatur had sailed out of Boston just a year earlier. Decatur then had turned the ship over to his senior officer, Isaac Hull, in exchange for the *Enterprise*. Now Preble sent Decatur and the *Enterprise* to Syracuse, where he would hand the schooner over to a junior officer, Lieutenant John Robinson. Decatur's "present rank entitles you to a superior command," Preble informed him. Preble had already decided that command would be the *Constitution*.[12]

Not a sentimental man, Preble knew the importance of this gesture. A year earlier, in Boston, he had watched the ambitious Decatur take on the responsibility of building the *Argus*, while he himself had seen to the *Constitution*'s restoration. The younger officer, like Preble, was always pushing to get the job done, to get the ship to sea quickly and in good order. In their first weeks in the Mediterranean, Preble had had to chastise Decatur for his crew's lax discipline. But quickly Decatur had taken control of his men, not in the way Preble would have, but perhaps more effectively. His instinct always was the right one. He had taken the most difficult assignment Preble could have given—to bring the *Intrepid* into Tripoli harbor and destroy the *Philadelphia*, which a senior officer had lost—and succeeded brilliantly, without losing a man. In his negotiations in Tunis, Decatur had again succeeded where Commodore Morris had failed. In the attacks on Tripoli, Decatur had led not just his own crew but all the gunboats. Now Preble would leave Decatur in command of his own flagship, one of the largest in the American navy; and while Preble was bitter at having to leave the Mediterranean, he felt a "pleasure in leaving the *Constitution* under the command of an Officer whose enterprising and Manly conduct in battle, I have so often witnessed."[13]

At the moment, the *Constitution* was being repaired in Malta. The ship had weathered the battles of Tripoli but now needed caulking and painting, and its masts had to be repaired or replaced. There was no rush for Decatur to get to Malta to oversee the maintenance. First, he joined Preble and Eaton on a week-long journey through the Sicilian countryside, guided by the "attentive and intelligent" Lorenzo Abbate. Preble and Decatur had sailed often between Syracuse and Messina; now they took the land route. Unfortunately, Preble's and Decatur's impressions do not survive, though Eaton undoubtedly shared his views with them, that "every thing is stamped with wretchedness," and the author of his guidebook was "a graceless liar." Eaton was impressed with the "melancholy proofs" he saw in Sicilian villages of "how fatal to human happiness is the hypocrisy of religious bigotry in the hands of a privileged priesthood."[14]

Preble and Decatur had come to Messina to determine the value of the three gunboats captured on August 3. Decatur had more than a casual interest since he had seized two of them, worth $4,731, which would be distributed among his crew.[15] After ten days in Messina, Preble and Decatur sailed for Syracuse and then Malta.

Decatur's command of the *Constitution* would be brief. John Rodgers, who was his senior officer, had been encouraged to switch the *Congress* for the *Constitution*. Tobias Lear, the American consul in Algiers, had arrived in Malta. He wrote Rodgers that the *Constitution*, which would be ready for sea in a week or so, "is as fine a ship as swims on the Sea. You will be tempted to take command of her, not withstanding your partiality for your excellent

Ship, the Congress." Lear predicted that the *Constitution* "will be a most fortunate Ship; and I am sometimes good in my predictions."[16]

Decatur and Preble boarded the *Constitution* on October 24. The ship was loading, and sixty of the crew were on the sick list. Four days later Preble went ashore at Malta "and left Capt. Decatur in command of the *Constitution*."[17] The squadron cruised to Syracuse, and there on November 9 Decatur and Rodgers exchanged command, Decatur taking the *Congress*.

The new squadron was as much a disappointment for Decatur as it was for Preble. Decatur had been Preble's most trusted junior officer. He and the other officers in the squadron had come to form a fighting unit. Now the new officers—Samuel and James Barron and Rodgers—were their seniors, and Decatur was not in the inner circle. Peripheral now to the central naval action, he was put back on convoy duty, relegated to protecting merchant ships assigned to bring Maltese sheep to the American squadron. Decatur would not see Tripoli again until 1815.[18]

Decatur could have accepted the situation had Samuel Barron taken up where Preble left off. But Barron arrived in the Mediterranean a very sick man. His liver ailment grew so severe that he spent most of the winter completely incapacitated. With the commodore unable to perform his duties, and with no clear line of succession, there would be no action against Tripoli. Instead, the other captains—John Rodgers on the *Constitution*, and James Barron, Samuel's brother—disputed which would lead the squadron. Rodgers and Preble had never liked each other, but they were able to work together. Rodgers, like Preble, wanted to fight Tripoli (though Preble's purser, Noadiah Morris, believed that Rodgers's "reputation as a fighting man has originated . . . in his black looks, his insufferable arrogance, and the frequent and unmerited assaults he has made on poor and inoffensive citizens").[19] Preble's working relationship with Rodgers had been good as long as they were far apart. Rodgers naturally felt that he, not Barron, should have succeeded Preble as squadron commander.

The Barrons and Rodgers, however, seem to have not just a personality clash but a policy clash as well, and their private disagreements took on political overtones.[20] While Rodgers wanted to wage war against Tripoli, Samuel Barron had been instructed to consult with Lear, the consul in Algiers, and try to negotiate a peace. Lear had been advising both Rodgers and Preble to negotiate, but both felt secure enough in their own strategy to ignore him. Now, Barron brought Lear to Malta and moved the American base there, keeping his fleet secure while pursuing a diplomatic solution.

The only significant military activity came from the irrepressible William Eaton, who had found Ahmet Qaramanli in Egypt. With a dozen marines and an army of several hundred Arab horsemen and Albanian mercenaries, Eaton and Ahmet crossed six hundred miles of the Libyan desert to besiege Derna. Isaac Hull brought the cannon and other supplies to Eaton's army at Bomba, and on April 27 Hull and the *Nautilus* appeared off Derna, while Eaton and Ahmet Qaramanli's forces came from behind the city to capture the fort. Marine Lieutenant Presley O'Bannon, Midshipman George Mann, and others from the fleet entered the citadel at Derna, took down Tripoli's flag, and raised the American flag which flew for the first time over a captured foreign city. Marine John Wilton died in the attack, while two other marines and several of Eaton's Greek soldiers were wounded. Eaton, Ahmet, and the marines held Derna, but outside the city Yusuf's forces mobilized, preventing any further advance.

In early June the standoff finally ended. In Tripoli harbor John Rodgers on the *Constitution* oversaw negotiations between Tobias Lear and Tripoli's prime minister, Mohammed D'Ghies. The two sides agreed to terms: the United States would pay Yusuf Qaramanli $60,000, and he would release Bainbridge and the other prisoners but renounce any future tribute. Instead of marching to Tripoli, Ahmet and Eaton were evacuated to an American ship.

Rodgers now dispatched Decatur to Tunis, whose ruler was threatening war. The *Constitution* had taken a Tunisian corsair and two of its prizes, which were attempting to deliver contraband to Tripoli. Hamouda Bey believed that this seizure violated Tunisian sovereignty. Rodgers promised to send Lear, and come himself, to avert war, but when American chargé George Davis delivered this message, the Bey refused to receive any American negotiators until his ships were returned. Decatur arrived in Tunis on July 11, delivering Rodgers's letter to Davis, who brought it to Hamouda. All weekend Hamouda and his advisers met, as Davis was called in for long sessions only to be told that the American position was unacceptable. On Sunday night, after three days of negotiation, Davis reported that war was almost certain. "Nothing but the famine restrains him," the Bey had told him.[21] Davis was prepared to leave Tunis, though he told Decatur that his departure should not be considered a formal declaration of war.

When a Tunisian gunboat opened fire on the brig *Vixen* as it entered the harbor on Thursday, the *Vixen* simply kept going. The gunboat pursued. The wind died, allowing the gunboat to row closer to the brig, which swung around to fire broadside at the pursuing boat. But before this could happen, a fresh breeze came up, which carried the brig closer to Decatur on the *Congress*. The two American warships waited in the harbor for the Bey to declare war. Eaton predicted that their presence in Tunis would prevent hostilities, as Hamouda Pacha "finds a better Account in stealing Sheep, than in hunting Tigers."[22]

The Bey refused to allow Decatur to step on shore, so the young captain took the opportunity to study the wildlife in the Bay of Tunis. Captain Decatur, armed with his gun, spent long hours being rowed about the harbor in his gig. Reuben James, who would later claim to have saved Decatur's life in Tripoli, now served as his cockswain, steering the barge through the calm waters off Tunis. Seeing a devilfish eight or ten feet down under the crystal-clear water, Decatur shot it and asked James to dive in and retrieve the specimen.

"I don't like to trouble that chap," James told the captain. "He looks as if he would make an ugly customer." A different captain might have charged the sailor with insubordination. But Decatur laughed, and without another word was over the side, diving to the bottom to bring back his devilfish.[23]

Decatur sailed for Syracuse, visiting with Eaton during his one night in town. Preble's fleet had brought an "air of life" to Syracuse, according to Washington Irving, and stirred "a faint return of commerce." Two new inns had opened to accommodate the American officers and men, and a new opera company entertained Americans and Italians alike. The singer Cecilia Fontana Bertozzi was warmly admired by the Americans and, rumor had it, supported by one captain, whose pennant she proudly displayed.[24] From Syracuse Decatur sailed for Malta, seeking out Rodgers, but by this time Rodgers was in Tunis with four frigates, three brigs, two schooners, one sloop, and eight gunboats and Tobias Lear.

If the presence of the *Congress* and the *Vixen* had stalled war, Rodgers anticipated that the larger fleet would prevent it entirely. Rodgers had come prepared to negotiate "the subject, by the Language of our Cannon," but found the Bey now willing to negotiate at the bargaining table.[25] But when Rodgers sent Davis and Decatur ashore, the Bey refused to receive Decatur as a negotiator. Decatur, "in a Spirited manner, refused visiting him on any other terms," and returned to the *Congress*. Rodgers had promised that war would commence if the Bey did not negotiate. Davis, already packed, left Tunis for the safety of the American fleet. But after sending away Decatur and Davis, the Bey sent a message to Lear on the *Constitution*, urging negotiations and awaiting Lear's visit with pleasure. "[I] repeat I wish to speak with you," wrote the Bey.[26]

The Bey insisted throughout that he had made his treaty with the president of the United States and so was reluctant to negotiate with Decatur or Rodgers, or even with Lear. But now Lear assured him that he could deal with him as readily as with the president, and thus opened negotiations. The fact that

Lear stepped in when the Bey had all but driven the American chargé, Davis, from the city infuriated Davis, who left Tunis angrily. The Bey for his part agreed to send an ambassador, Soliman Melli Melli, to the United States.

Decatur was assigned to bring Melli Melli to Washington, along with a "present of Lions, Tigers, Ostriches, &c.," to preserve peace. Rodgers suggested that Melli Melli be escorted by an officer "to prevent those impositions which are often practiced in every Country on Strangers, particularly on people of his discription, and in his situation." Lear asked that a cultural ambassador join Melli Melli, and that he and his retinue be accommodated "as much in the Style of their Country, as the difference of climate & circumstances will permit," as he knew that the Tunisians would be "very backward in expressing their wants or wishes" for fear they might "not accord with our ideas of the propriety of things."[27] As it turned out, Melli Melli was not at all backward in expressing his wants.

The *Congress* sailed from Tunis on the afternoon of September 5. After watering at Gibraltar, Decatur steered the ship across the straits to Tangier as the Spanish and French prepared to attack Britain's fortress. From the tranquillity of Tangier, the Americans heard cannons blasting away across the straits.[28] The "Dogs of War, are now, of a sudden let loose," Rodgers wrote, and though "it is impossible to say what will be the result," the changing affairs of Europe presented "a favorable opening for the Extention of our Commerce, into Russia and Turkey," provided the United States could connect the "security of the Merchant with the pride of the Government, and honor and General Interest of the Nation."[29]

At ten o'clock on the morning of November 4, 1805, Decatur had the *Congress* drop anchor at Hampton Roads, Virginia. Just two years earlier he had sailed from the United States a lieutenant, with his first command on one of the smallest ships in the American fleet. He returned a captain commanding one of the navy's largest vessels. He soon discovered that his deeds in the Mediterranean had made him a hero in the United States.

CHAPTER 8

"I neglected the opportunities of improvement"

A LHOUGH TWO honorary swords presented by Congress awaited him in Philadelphia, and newspapers sang the praises of the "gallant Decatur," the young captain was not sure he had earned the adulation. He had seen his brother die, had watched Somers and his men sail off to glory, never to return. He had risen to the top, but he could not be certain that the Jefferson administration—long opposed to naval expansion—would maintain the fleet now that the war was over. Would there continue to be a U.S. Navy in which men like Decatur could rise? He had achieved all he could; what more was there?

Decatur's few days in Norfolk changed his life. As he was escorting the Tunisian ambassador into town, a party of sightseers came aboard the *Congress* to see the exotic animals brought back from Africa. One of the guests, the twenty-nine-year-old daughter of a Norfolk businessmen, caught sight of the miniature painting of the handsome young captain. Decatur may have had the miniature done for his mother, or perhaps for the mysterious girl in Philadelphia to whom he had been engaged. The portrait stirred Susan Wheeler much more than the lions or leopards, and she told her friends that she had seen the man she would marry. They knew her well enough to know she was not making an idle boast.

Susan Wheeler was born at Elk Ridge Landing, Maryland, where her father, Luke Wheeler, had an iron foundry. Her mother's name is not recorded; Susan's parents never married. When Luke Wheeler moved to Petersburg and then Norfolk in the 1790s, he brought his daughter with him. He sent Susan to one of the country's finest schools for young ladies, a Baltimore academy where she excelled academically and socially. Beautiful and intelligent, Susan made lasting friends at school, among them the equally lovely and bright Catherine Carroll, whose father, Charles, had signed the Declaration of Independence. Kitty Carroll and Susan would remain close throughout their lives.

While Susan was away at school, her father was becoming one of Norfolk's leading citizens. Norfolk was a boomtown, its population more than doubling in the 1790s from three to seven thousand. The U.S. government's decision to build ships at nearby Gosport was part of the reason for this economic boom, and Wheeler's iron business thrived. He invested his profits in local real estate, became a founder of Norfolk's Chamber of Commerce, was elected to the city council in 1800, subscribed to the fund to build the Presbyterian church (though he did not buy a pew), and the year after Decatur came to town he was elected mayor.[1] Wheeler was an example of how quickly an ambitious man could advance in American society. His own origins were obscure, and his daughter was illegitimate, but that did not prevent him from becoming mayor and his daughter an intimate friend of the republic's leaders. This rapid advance from obscurity echoed the stories of other Americans, including the gallant captain of the *Congress*, whose grandfather had arrived in the New World half a century earlier not speaking the language, friendless, and barely alive. Now, as one of Norfolk's leading citizens, Wheeler prepared a welcome for Decatur.

Susan had become a center of social life in both Norfolk and Baltimore. Her friend Kitty Carroll had married the South Carolina lawyer and former congressman Robert Goodloe Harper; a staunch Federalist, he had chaired the House Ways and Means Committee, but lost his seat in Congress in the Republican sweep of 1800. He decided to stay in Baltimore, where he married Kitty, practiced law, and raised their family. In 1816 Maryland's legislature briefly sent him to the U.S. Senate. When Susan was courted by Jérôme Bonaparte, the French emperor's younger brother, Harper had advised her to steer clear of this foreign entanglement. He knew that Napoleon was "ambitious of allying his family with the royal families of Europe" and would repudiate any American wife foolish enough to marry Jérôme.[2]

Another Maryland belle, Elizabeth Patterson, did not have as clear-headed an adviser. She married Jérôme Bonaparte. As Harper had predicted, Napoleon repudiated the marriage and refused to allow Elizabeth and the couple's child to land in France. Jérôme was married off to a German princess; Elizabeth, calling herself Madame Bonaparte, came home to America nursing her infant and her international humiliation. She circulated a rumor that her erstwhile royal husband had been interested in Susan Wheeler only as a lover, not a wife. Harper detested Madame Bonaparte and respected Susan enough to demand an explanation through diplomatic channels. From Europe, Jérôme Bonaparte sent word that his relationship with Miss Wheeler had been strictly honorable. (A descendant of Madame Bonaparte and the hapless Jérôme later served as secretary of the navy in Theodore Roosevelt's administration; his tenure ended shortly after he suggested using the venerable U.S.S. *Constitution* for target practice.)

By November 1805 the brilliant, beautiful Susan Wheeler was at home in the refined (though sometimes vicious) society of Baltimore and the boomtown of Norfolk. At the ball her father hosted for the Tunisian ambassador, she met the man whose face she had glimpsed in the Italian miniature. Nei-

ther she nor Captain Decatur ever looked back. They made an elegant couple—the dashing war hero, solidly built, standing about five feet eight or nine
inches, with an "aquiline nose, large mouth, black eye, dark visage," appear-
ing, according to one contemporary, "more like a Frenchman than an American," but without the unfortunate baggage carried by the real Frenchman in
Susan's past.[3] Decatur stayed just a few days in Norfolk, but long enough for
Susan to persuade him to return.

Decatur tore himself away from Norfolk, sailing the *Congress* up the Chesapeake and into the Potomac. After firing the traditional salute as his ship
passed Mount Vernon, he delivered Melli Melli and his menagerie to Washington. Then Decatur took a brief leave to visit Philadelphia. Rather than
staying with the family in Frankford, Stephen spent his leave with friends at
the house on Front Street. When Preble passed through on his way to Washington to lobby for more naval spending, Decatur joined Bainbridge and
Stewart at dinner with the former commodore. All agreed that their triumph
in Tripoli had been only a limited success. Along with Stewart and William
Eaton, Decatur was a guest at the Philadelphia Conversation Society, where
Eaton criticized the treaty for paying $60,000 "when the Tripolitans were
seized with terror by the news of the capture of Derne & the formidable
appearance of our fleets come to renew their attack on Tripoli itself."[4] Eaton's
vociferous public comments on the way "Aunt Lear and her Lieutenants,
Barron and Rodgers," had bought peace had already provoked James Barron
to challenge Eaton to a duel.[5] Less flippant than Eaton, Decatur was also
critical of the treaty. He told the business and civic leaders at the Conversation Society that he "had offered to land the men from the fleet, about two
thousand & bring away the Bashaw in open day."[6]

Decatur spoke boldly, but his encounter with the elegant and polished
Susan Wheeler, and with the business and civic leaders he was now meeting
in Norfolk, Washington, and Philadelphia, made him aware that he was lack-
ing something. The Quaker merchant Thomas Cope noted that Decatur "was
unreserved & appeared much at his ease" at the Conversation Club, but that
Decatur's mind did not seem "to have been so highly cultivated" as Eaton's.[7]
How could it be otherwise? His father was barely literate, and he had misspent
his own schooldays. Now, as an adult, Stephen was so self-conscious about his
own writing that he wrote very little. "I have always thought," he confessed in
one of his few surviving personal letters, "that they who write badly should
write little or by the way of practice a great deal." Thinking that no amount
of practice could make him "become an adept," Decatur seldom wrote
anything.[8]

The lure of the brilliant Susan Wheeler, the knowledge that he now would have to communicate with better-educated people—including secretaries of the navy and the president of the United States—increased Decatur's anxiety about his lack of intellectual polish. Fortunately for Decatur, he knew that if he applied himself, he could learn; as a young midshipman he had written down the names of lines and sheets, had studied navigation, and while based in Syracuse had learned Italian. What he needed was a guide as to what to learn. Just as fortunately, during his visit with his family at Frankford, the right mentor appeared. Benjamin Rush was the family physician, and one of the republic's most accomplished men. He had been a friend of Franklin's and now was an intimate correspondent of both John Adams and Thomas Jefferson (a few years later Rush would persuade both men, for the sake of the country, to put aside their political differences and renew their friendship).

Rush had come to Frankford not on a social call but to treat Decatur's ailing father. Before he could leave the Decatur home, the young captain stopped him. Stephen Decatur and Rush's son Richard had been at school together, but while young Richard had been a good student, and was now making himself a respectable success, Stephen had been more interested in sport and fun. Now Stephen realized his error. "Doctor," Stephen said, "I am going to speak to you as a friend. By good fortune, I have risen fast in my profession, but my rank is ahead of my acquirements. I went young into the navy; my education was cut short, and I neglected the opportunities of improvement I had when a boy. For professional knowledge, I hope to get along, expecting to increase it as I grow older; but for the other kinds of knowledge, I feel my deficiencies and want your friendly aid towards getting the better of them. Will you favor me with a list of such books, historical, and others of a standard nature, as you think will best answer my purpose, that I may devote myself at all intervals to the perusal of them?"[9]

Decatur could not have found a better mentor. Rush supplied a list of works of classical and modern history and political theory to help make the successful captain a better, more educated person. Decatur took this new opportunity to complete his education with more appreciation and zeal than in his reckless and high-spirited youth. Rush would repeat this story many times, impressed that Decatur recognized his own shortcomings. Richard Rush came to know Stephen quite well ten years later, when both men were in their thirties and living in Washington. "Whatever he may have been in earlier days," he wrote of the mature Stephen Decatur, the formerly troublesome youth now was "a man of ten thousand; great resources of native intelligence and propriety upon all subjects."[10]

Decatur's former employer Francis Gurney organized another testimonial dinner for Decatur and Eaton. ("I am arrested here and put under keepers for trial next Thursday," Eaton jokingly wrote Preble.)[11] The guests of honor at these dinners were expected to listen graciously as they were toasted, and then to offer their own reciprocal toasts to their hosts. Accordingly, Decatur toasted his hometown as "enterprising, generous, honorable," and continued, "May her approbation ever be considered by her sons a fair incentive to, and an ample reward of, exertion."[12] The self-conscious speaker had worked out his toast ahead of time, as he always did when speaking in public. He had to prepare; he found it difficult to speak otherwise. When the Hibernia Greens paraded to the house on Front Street to serenade and cheer him, Decatur's friends inside urged him to go out and bask in the crowd's applause. He protested, "I cannot; it is impossible; if it were anywhere but about here in Front Street, where everybody knows who Steph. Decatur was, I might do it."[13] This reticence, this reluctance to become a popular hero, this constant mindfulness of how far he still had to go impressed his listeners. Benjamin Rush wrote to former president Adams, "Captain Decater charms his fellow citizens as much by his modesty as he once delighted and astonished them by his exploits in the Mediterranean."[14]

On the Tuesday after the banquet, Decatur was guest of honor again, this time at the Shakespeare Tavern. This gathering, the *Aurora* noted, "banished party passions" by the "animating sentiment of love of our *common country*," as Federalists and Republicans joined together to honor young Stephen Decatur. His father, a hero of John Adams's war against France, sat beside the son, the hero of Thomas Jefferson's war against Tripoli. On his other side was another son in uniform, John P. Decatur. The theater artist Edwin Holland provided a transparency of the burning of the *Philadelphia* to decorate the room. All would have noted the symbolism here: *Philadelphia*'s merchants had built the ship for the senior Decatur, and his son had earned their undying gratitude by destroying it.

Before the serious toasting and drinking began, James Milner, the presiding officer, read a brief speech welcoming Decatur back to Philadelphia from "the shores of a distant land" where he had "recorded the first testimonials of [his] country's honor." Philadelphia joined the nation in hailing Decatur "as one of her favorite sons," but was not satisfied with merely joining "the general voice of admiration." The "friends and companions of your recent youth," Milner assured the guest of honor, felt the "warmest personal attachment and esteem," and would open their "admiring hearts" to him each time he returned to his native city.[15]

Decatur had prepared his own brief speech. "To be thought worthy of the applause of my countrymen impresses me with the liveliest sense of gratitude," he said. "But on the present occasion, when I look round and see myself surrounded by the companions of my earliest youth, my feelings are such as cannot be expressed. I have only to offer you, whose good opinion is particularly dear to me, my warmest thanks, with my assurances that, if an opportunity should again be afforded me, I will endeavor to merit, in some degree, the high opinion you have been pleased to express."[16] That there might be further opportunities for valor was in doubt. The Jefferson administration had been trying to cut the navy's budget since 1801, but the Tripolitan war had prevented it. Now, with the war over, Jefferson could restore the economy, as he had hoped to do five years earlier.

The company celebrated Decatur but also remembered those who did not come home. "The memories of Caldwell, [James] Decatur, Somers, and [John] Dorsey, four sons of Philadelphia," were toasted: "The ocean their grave, the hearts of their countrymen their monument, fame their epitaph."[17]

Decatur's toast seems more spontaneous than his formal remarks. "Our native city," he began, "the scene of our earliest happiness," then a pause; "may her sons ever emulate the virtues of their ancestors." Decatur, the son of immigrants, now could claim Philadelphia's founders as his own ancestors, and his family would become the ancestors of future generations. At this invocation of Philadelphia's founders, Milner rose and proposed a toast to the senior Decatur: "The gallant father of a gallant son."[18]

The old man—he was only fifty-five, but they had been fifty-five hard years, and his health now was failing—rose to propose his own toast. He was seated between two of his children but had heard the toast to his son James, dead in Tripoli, and to his son-in-law James McKnight, also dead in the Mediterranean. This country, where he had been left without a father, now honored his sons, who would devote their lives to it. Simply but forcefully, the old man spoke the only words anyone would later remember from the long night of speeches and toasts: "Our children are the property of our country."[19]

By the end of January, Stephen was back in Norfolk, and on March 8 he and Susan were married in Luke Wheeler's house. Presbyterian minister Benjamin Grigsby performed the ceremony. The young couple stayed with Wheeler, except for a visit to the Decatur family in Frankford, while Stephen awaited his country's orders. He hoped to be sent north, possibly to Maine, because "a Southern climate does not accord with Mrs. Decatur's constitution." A posting to Maine would also reunite him with Edward Preble.[20]

While Decatur awaited orders, President Jefferson was changing the size and mission of the navy. Preble's voyage to Naples to borrow gunboats had inspired the administration to see these smaller vessels as indispensable, and better suited to defending American harbors and rivers than the larger frigates. Jefferson's annual message in 1805 called for more of them, since for the cost of one frigate (about $220,000), the navy could build twenty-five gunboats. Congress authorized fifty gunboats, and also called for limiting the navy to 928 men. Once again the Decaturs had returned in triumph from a war to wonder if they would still be employed.[21] Once again, though, Stephen Decatur was kept on active duty. He was sent not to Portland, where Preble was handling gunboat construction, but to Newport, Rhode Island, where his ailing grandfather had landed half a century earlier.

Decatur and his bride arrived in Newport on July 20, 1806. Stephen immediately set about building the gunboats at Newport, Westerly, and "Grunage a town about twenty miles up the river." By the time the boats were ready to launch, Decatur would know the town's name was actually spelled "Greenwich."[22]

Like most of the navy's officers, Decatur believed that the gunboats would be completely ineffective. While less expensive than larger ships, gunboats were next to useless beyond sight of land. And though twenty-five gunboats cost as much to build as one frigate, they would require more than twice as many officers and crew to man them and would be more expensive to maintain. A single frigate with fifty cannon had more than twice the firepower of twenty-five gunboats. When one of the gunboats capsized in the Chesapeake, sinking in six fathoms of water, Decatur asked Bainbridge, "What would be the real national loss if all the Gun Boats were sunk in 100 fathoms water[?]"[23]

Despite recognizing their strategic futility, Decatur tried to build the gunboats to be as effective as possible. His and his men's lives would depend on it. The Navy Department' specifications called for him to use yellow pine, which was cheap and plentiful in the southern states. But he found no yellow pine in Newport. Instead he asked for and received permission to substitute white oak, a harder wood available in Rhode Island at nearly the same price as southern yellow pine. Decatur also noted that the gun carriages, which had been designed for a warmer climate, "can not be used in a cold climate during the winter." The moisture collecting between the bed and the deck "being frozen will prevent the carriage being moved at all," and in warm weather would "in a very short time rot the deck."[24]

Decatur had proved himself capable of leading men into battle; now he showed his abilities to organize work crews and to think through the practical details of building warships. At the moment, the Jefferson administration had a special need for men like Decatur. Jefferson had learned that former vice president Aaron Burr, dropped from the Republican ticket in 1804 (his failure to distance himself from the arch-Federalists who tried to elect him over Jefferson in the disputed election of 1800 had not endeared him to the president), was scheming to create an independent empire in the American interior and to invade Mexico. In the summer of 1804, Burr and Alexander Hamilton were both involved in the New York gubernatorial election. When their political disagreement turned personal, Burr challenged Hamilton to a duel and killed the former treasury secretary. Having alienated most Republicans and killed the leader of the Federalists, Burr found his political opportunities limited. He knew how disaffected some navy officers were from the Jefferson administration, which unceasingly argued against naval spending and had bought peace from Tripoli while the navy was trying to win the war. Burr reportedly told the still bitter Thomas Truxtun that he hoped to see him an admiral, and also plotted in New Orleans with the utterly corrupt General James Wilkinson, military governor of Louisiana. Jefferson decided to send Decatur and Preble to New Orleans to take charge of American forces there and make sure that no more American sailors went over to Burr's side.[25]

At the end of October, though, when Wilkinson suddenly turned against Burr and arrested citizens who knew of his own involvement in the conspiracy, Jefferson realized that the situation was back under control and he would not need to send Decatur and Preble. Burr was arrested and charged with treason, partly on Wilkinson's evidence. Decatur was instead sent to Norfolk to take charge of the Gosport Navy Yard. He temporarily turned the Newport operations over to Lieutenant Oliver Hazard Perry, who would keep things moving until Isaac Hull arrived to take charge. Three years earlier Decatur had turned the newly built *Argus* over to Hull, his superior officer; now he once again turned operations over to Hull, though this time it was Decatur who was moving on to a bigger assignment.

On their way to Norfolk, Stephen and Susan Decatur stayed a month in Philadelphia. They left his parents' Frankford home a few days before Christmas and arrived in Norfolk on the first day of 1807. The operations in Norfolk were not as far along as at Newport. While Lieutenant Arthur Sinclair had "shewn great indefatiegable judgment" in getting the gunboats and bombards ready for service, Decatur found that the "Muskets & pistols" were "unfit for service, & cannot be repaired at this place"; the gunpowder, too, was "in bad order," and once the weather was dry it would have to be "aired, the lumps broken, & sifted" to make it fit to use. Decatur took inventory and was astounded at how much was missing. It was "extraordinary . . . that so many articles should be wanting," but "the fact is, the stores have been broken open three times, & three fourths of the articles delivered from the boats, have been stolen, & the greater part of the things have been rendered useless in consequence of having had no care taken of them."[26]

Sinclair happened to be away when Decatur arrived. But Decatur realized that Sinclair was not the problem. The real power at the Gosport yard, and the real problem, was naval agent Daniel Bedinger. Bedinger and his clerk refused to cooperate with Sinclair or anyone else. When in Sinclair's absence Lieutenant Arthur Hunt, commander of the bomb ketch *Spitfire*, had received orders from the secretary of the navy to outfit the ships, he had gone to Bedinger's clerk for rigging and supplies, but the clerk had refused to act without Bedinger's order.

When Hunt told him this story, Decatur called the clerk in. Showing him Secretary Smith's order, Decatur told him that he had already "retarded the public business three days, unnecessarily," and that the secretary of the navy would not be pleased. Decatur "requested he would suffer the men attached to each boat, to examine their rigging & go to work upon it." The clerk refused. Naval officers commanded ships; their power did not extend to the stores on land. Bedinger, not Decatur, had the power to direct work in the navy yard. Decatur was furious. He informed him, he wrote Smith, "that unless he gave me permission, I should execute your orders by force." Still, the clerk refused. Decatur, who had stolen into Tripoli's harbor to burn the *Philadelphia*, had fought the enemy hand to hand aboard their gunboats, defied the Bey of Tunis, been the toast of Philadelphia and been given two swords by Congress, now found himself stymied by a clerk. Decatur "ordered the men belonging to the boats to take their rigging & to commence working upon it immediately." He knew that the clerk and Bedinger would claim "that I have assumed a power I had no right to," but he told Secretary Smith that he had a "duty to carry into effect your orders, with, or without particular instructions." Decatur assured the secretary that he would "continue to superintend, & hasten the equipment of the boats, until the arrival of Lieut. Sinclare."[27]

CHAPTER 9

"Give us a man *to lead us to glory"*

THE GUNBOATS were impractical for defense, but the irregular chain of command could be an advantage. When Sinclair returned to Norfolk, he opened a "recruiting Service at this Place" to enlist men for the frigate *Chesapeake*, being fitted out in Washington as part of James Barron's Mediterranean squadron. The British consul in Norfolk informed Decatur in March 1807 that Sinclair had enlisted four deserters from the Royal Navy, and requested that Decatur return the men. Decatur referred the consul to Lieutenant Sinclair, who was acting not under Decatur's orders but "under the immediate Orders of the Navy Department."[1]

These four deserters would lead to a crisis in American-British relations. They had deserted from British ships that were in the Chesapeake watching French warships that had taken refuge there during the hurricane season. The French had sailed up as far as Baltimore, and could not leave while the British were waiting in Norfolk. The British would not leave while the French were still in the Chesapeake. So the British warships had anchored close by the Gosport base, where Sinclair was recruiting for the *Chesapeake.* It surprised no one that with the slightest opportunity, British sailors would flee their navy's poor pay and harsh treatment to sign aboard an American ship. Lord Nelson estimated that forty thousand British sailors deserted from 1793 to 1801, and it was an article of faith among Royal Navy captains that the American fleet was manned by British deserters.[2]

The four men—William Ware, Daniel Martin, John Strachan, and John Little—had undoubtedly deserted. In fact, they had escaped under fire from the frigate *Melampus* in the captain's gig But were they British? Three of them had been born in America, and one, William Ware, was actually part Native American. He and Strachan were both from Maryland, and Martin was an African American from Westport, Massachusetts. The three Americans had been impressed into the British service, though they had subsequently chosen to remain.[3] Had the men not escaped from *Melampus* under fire, the British consul might not have taken such an interest in their case. But in March, when five more sailors deserted, the consul in Norfolk contacted Decatur. Four of these five additional deserters were British-born; the fifth was a Philadelphian who had enlisted voluntarily.[4]

Early in March the *Chesapeake* arrived in Norfolk under the command of Charles Gordon, the navy's youngest master commandant (the rank between lieutenant and captain). Gordon's merits are still disputed. Captain Alexander Murray had praised Gordon as an "excellent and inspiring officer," though Barron, who would command the entire squadron while Gordon had command of *Chesapeake*, thought Gordon "addicted to pleasure"; one historian called Gordon a "foppish young man."[5] All would agree that no officer had better political connections: one uncle was a congressman from Maryland, and an aunt was married to Treasury Secretary Albert Gallatin. The fact that Gallatin had long been a critic of naval expansion may have been an asset to Gordon; even when the ranks were being thinned, his position was secure.

Barron expressed dissatisfaction with Gordon as ship's commander but was too conscious of Gordon's political connections, and too relieved at being given command of the squadron, to force the issue. The Barron brothers were still under a cloud as a result of the Tripoli treaty, a cloud that had darkened in the summer of 1806 when John Rodgers returned home. Rodgers, like Decatur, Eaton, and Preble, believed that the treaty of June 1805 had ended the war too soon, and that a full victory could have been won if the navy had fought on through the summer. Rodgers also resented the way Samuel Barron had held on to command of the squadron when he was too ill to function. Rodgers did not believe James Barron's insistent story that he had urged his brother to step aside; instead, Rodgers thought that James was privately encouraging Samuel to stay on as commodore. When Rodgers returned home, he and the Barrons alternately tried to provoke each other into a duel and then backed off from fighting. "R. wrote J.B. a note at Hampton roads, another from Washington," William Eaton wrote, telling Preble that Rodgers and the Barrons "have been reconnoitring each other but cannot fix on a battle ground." Finally, James Barron "declined any further interference in his brother's behalf" since the ailing Samuel by this time had "so far recovered as to be able *to fight his own battles!*" Rodgers waited for either Barron to appear in Washington, then proposed an "interview" in Delaware. Thomas Tingey, commandant of the Washington Navy Yard, served Rodgers as second; Marine Commandant Franklin Wharton served Barron. The seconds made the arrangements, but then the Barron brothers quickly "returned to Hampton." Eaton commented that by threatening each other and then evading any action, Rodgers and the Barrons "seem to be fighting the battles of the Mediterranean over again."[6]

Navy Secretary Smith put a stop to these challenges and evasions. He ordered Barron and Rodgers to remain at their stations. The men printed a private circular to announce their reconciliation. They had averted a duel, but their mutual dislike did not abate. James Barron spent the winter and early spring of 1807 in Washington preparing to sail for the Mediterranean, then went to Hampton to await Gordon's arrival with his flagship, the *Chesapeake.*

Gordon's voyage from Washington to Norfolk was disastrous. Twice the *Chesapeake* ran aground. When the ship paused at Mount Vernon to fire the traditional sixteen-gun salute, the gunners discovered that only twelve cannon worked, and neither cartridges nor sponges would fit. This unforgivable embarrassment should have been a warning. Some sailors sensed disaster and deserted; others simply gave up.

Before sailing from Norfolk, Gordon had found time to muster the crew to quarters only three times, and perhaps because of the Mount Vernon fiasco he never had them practice at their guns. Barron visited the ship only twice while in Norfolk, and he had to cut the second visit short because Gordon was hosting a party on board that evening. Both men thought that they would have enough time to drill and muster during the Atlantic crossing. On June 22, as he put to sea, Gordon reported back to Secretary Smith that "every thing on board is now in order. The Officers and Crew perform to my satisfaction" on what they expected to be a routine voyage across the Atlantic.[7]

While Barron and Gordon focused on their mission to the Mediterranean, British officers in Norfolk grew increasingly frustrated with desertions of their sailors and the noncooperation of American authorities. Decatur sent the British consul to Lieutenant Sinclair, who told the consul to see the mayor; the mayor referred the matter to lawyer Littleton Tazewell, Decatur's close friend and personal attorney. Tazewell wrote a learned treatise saying that he found nothing in either treaties or state law about desertions, so there was nothing the mayor could do. While the British were being given this bureaucratic runaround in Norfolk, the consul learned that local authorities in Baltimore were being more than helpful in recovering sailors deserting from the French fleet.[8]

The British minister in Washington appealed directly to Secretary of State James Madison for help. Madison passed the matter along to Navy Secretary Robert Smith, though he reminded the British minister that, as Tazewell had found, the United States and Britain did not have a treaty covering deserters. Smith wrote to Barron, and Barron reported back to Smith, that four of the men the British wanted back—Ware, Martin, Strachan, and Little—actually were American citizens who had been impressed into the British navy.[9]

While the British officers in Norfolk were pressing for recovery of deserters, the government in London was tightening its policies toward neutral nations. Britain and France were embroiled in war, Britain controlling the seas and the French controlling the European continent. Americans traded

with both. When Britain announced in 1806 that it would blockade the continent, France retaliated by declaring that no ship could enter a British port
and then sail to a port under French control. Napoleon pledged to seize any
merchant vessel bound for a British port; then Britain announced that it
would seize any merchant vessel bound for a European port. The British ships
hovering off the American coast now were looking for American merchant
ships as well as French warships and British deserters.[10]

As France and England tightened commercial restrictions, relations between the United States and Britain reached a crisis point. Britain's naval
commander in North America, Vice Admiral Sir George Canfield Berkeley,
angered at reports that British deserters "openly parade the streets of Norfolk
bearing the American flag" while preparing to ship out on the *Chesapeake,*
ordered his commanders to stop and search American ships. He dispatched
his flagship, the fifty-two-gun HMS *Leopard,* to Chesapeake Bay.[11]

On the way south, the *Leopard* stopped and searched a number of merchant ships. When Captain Salusbury Pryce Humphreys reached Lynnhaven
on June 21, he learned that the *Chesapeake,* which he had expected to sail in
May, was still in Norfolk. The next day the *Chesapeake* put out to sea, and at 3:
37 in the afternoon Captain Humphreys hailed the American vessel. The
Chesapeake, about nine miles off Cape Henry, was waiting for the pilot boat
from shore so it could send its harbor pilot back to Norfolk. Some of the
Chesapeake's officers noted that the *Leopard*'s gun ports were open and the
tompions out of the cannon. Neither Barron nor Gordon suspected any hostile intent, and although navy regulations required American crews to be at
quarters when any foreign ship approached, Barron later said that the idea
of an attack from the *Leopard* "was so extravagant that he might as well have
expected one when at anchor at Hampton Roads."[12]

After hailing the *Chesapeake,* the *Leopard* sent a boat over. Barron thought
that the *Leopard* might be sending dispatches for him to bring to Europe, a
common practice. He was stunned when Lieutenant John Meade gave him a
note from Captain Humphreys and Vice Admiral Berkeley's order to search
the *Chesapeake* for deserters from seven British vessels—not including the four
from *Melampus.* Humphreys's note expressed the hope that the two captains
could resolve the problem "in such a manner that the harmony between the
two countries, may remain undisturbed."[13] Barron responded, in writing, that
he knew of no such men as the order listed (he was aware of the deserters
aboard from the *Melampus,* but that ship was not mentioned) and that his
recruiting agents were under orders not to enlist British deserters; furthermore, though he too hoped to "preserve harmony," he would never permit
"the crew of any ship that I command to be mustered by any other but her

own officers."[14] After Meade left with this response, Barron told Gordon to clear the gun deck quietly while he went above to survey the *Leopard.* Immediately he saw that the *Leopard* was prepared for action, though he still thought its appearance "more menace than any thing serious." He nevertheless called below to hurry the work and get the men to quarters silently, without beating the signal drum.[15]

While Barron and Gordon conferred with the British lieutenant, some of the American lieutenants had been belatedly preparing their guns. They had them loaded, but discovered they did not have rammers, wads, gun locks, powder horns, priming powder, or matches. The gun deck itself was still cluttered with baggage. The sick were slung in hammocks over some guns. Three pork barrels and a grog tub blocked Lieutenant William Henry Allen's gun, and Lieutenant John Creighton's was buried under trunks and furniture belonging to the captain's servants.[16]

It took five minutes for Meade's boat to return to the *Leopard,* but Midshipman Jesse Elliot speculated that it would have taken at least twenty just to clear the Third Division's guns, let alone prepare them for action. Captain Humphreys read Barron's note, then called through the trumpet, "You must be aware of the necessity I am under of complying with the orders of my commander-in-chief." Barron replied through his trumpet, "I do not understand what you say." Humphreys fired a warning shot across the *Chesapeake*'s bow, then fired a broadside directly at the ship.[17]

The *Chesapeake*'s crew, trained poorly in their ordinary duties and not at all in how to return enemy fire, performed as would be expected in the circumstances. The *Leopard* had sent three broadsides into the *Chesapeake* before a single American gun was ready to fire. Three sailors were killed, and sixteen, including Commodore Barron, were injured, and masts and hull were damaged. Barron, wounded in the leg, implored someone to fire at least one round before he had to surrender. Lieutenant Allen's crew had cleared away luggage and found powder and shot. But Allen had no matches. Running to the ship's stove, he reached in and with his bare hands picked out a burning coal, then raced back to his cannon juggling the scorching ember. He touched it to the fuse as the flag was being lowered on the deck above. Just as the American flag touched the *Chesapeake*'s rail, Allen's gun fired—the only shot *Chesapeake* would take at the *Leopard.* It missed.

Barron, wounded in the leg, retired to his cabin. The *Chesapeake* sent a boat to the *Leopard* to informing Captain Humphreys that the American frigate was his prize. Humphreys sent back Meade and other officers, who mustered the *Chesapeake*'s crew. The British took four men: Martin, Ware, and Strachan, the American-born deserters from the *Melampus,* as well as Jenkin

Ratford, a deserter from the *Halifax*, whom they had found hiding in the coal hole. Barron sent a formal note of surrender to the *Leopard*, but Humphreys replied that he had "nothing more to desire" with the *Chesapeake*. Having done his duty, Humphreys sailed off to join the British squadron in Lynnhaven Bay.[18]

Barron called his officers into the cabin. He knew what a disaster loomed for the nation; he may have been less concerned about the personal ignominy that would fall to him. Preparing to defend the nation was the first order of business. He would send Captain Gordon to Washington with news of the attack.

A year earlier, when Barron had presided at the court of inquiry into Bainbridge's surrender of the *Philadelphia*, every officer and crewman had spoken up for Bainbridge, who had given up his vessel without firing a shot. Barron may have expected his junior officers to show the same loyalty to him. But they did not. The officers were "mortified, humbled—cut to the soul," knowing that the "finger of scorn" would be pointing each one "out as one of the Chesapeak." Lieutenant Allen would have cursed Barron, "but I leave him to his own conscience, while he possesses the power of recollection *no curses* can add to its tortures." The immediate threat, all knew, was that a British fleet off the American coast could stop and disable American warships. This was a problem for the Jefferson administration and for each man in the navy. Allen protested, "Give us a Commander give us *a man* to lead us to glory and there is not an officer in this ship that will not immolate himself to serve his country."[19]

Secretary Smith recognized these problems and immediately ordered Stephen Decatur to take command of the *Chesapeake*, then making its way slowly back to Norfolk, and all U.S. naval forces in the Southeast. Was the attack on the *Chesapeake* a prelude to a full-scale invasion? Decatur did not know, but he needed to prepare. A delegation of Norfolk citizens called on him vowing to help resist a British attack. An assault seemed to be more imminent when Norfolk's authorities pledged to refuse British vessels the privilege of resupplying in their city. Captain John Douglas of the British ship the *Bellona*, anchored at Hampton Roads, demanded that the town's impudent "infringement" of Britain's rights be "immediately annulled" or he would "prohibit every vessel bound either in or out of Norfolk," as "the British flag never has, nor will be insulted with impunity."[20]

Decatur had "no doubt, from the threats the British have made, we shall have to fight." He had few weapons: four gunboats, the wounded *Chesapeake*, then making its way back into Norfolk, and the French frigate *Cybelle*. He anticipated that the British would attack at night, and knew that the enemy could bring five hundred men to shore, while his land forces would "be composed of volunteers, who notwithstanding their great zeal, will not possess all the skill we could wish." But, he wrote Secretary Smith, he would expect as much from this force "as ought to be expected from any four gun boats, more, I hope, will not be expected." Decatur closed by declaring that he would be ready to serve the country in any way he could, but "if the Frigates are to be fitted out," he hoped that he would not "be continued in Gun Boats."[21]

Decatur boarded the crippled *Chesapeake* on July 1, hoisting the American flag and his own broad commodore's pennant. He and Barron spent hours surveying the ship. The main and mizzen were beyond repair. The foremast and sails were damaged, but could be mended; the mizzen rigging was "very old, much cut and incapable of repair." Decatur estimated that the hull could "be repaired in four days by six Carpenters," and the entire vessel could be repaired in three weeks. Nine years earlier, in 1798, Lieutenant James Barron had first introduced Midshipman Decatur to his first naval frigate; now, at four in the afternoon on July 1, 1807, Barron relinquished his last command in the United States Navy to Captain Decatur.[22]

After relieving Barron, Decatur called the crew to quarters. His ship could be repaired, but the British fleet still threatened Norfolk. The Chesapeake channel was deep enough for three British men-of-war to attack Norfolk, the *Chesapeake* would take three weeks to repair, and its gunpowder was spoiled. But Decatur noticed something else about his own damaged ship. The *Leopard* had fired three broadsides, more than seventy shots, at the *Chesapeake*, but only fourteen had hit the hull. Some had raked the deck, but still less than half the shots had hit the target. The British had overwhelming firepower, but with a crew properly drilled and trained Decatur believed he could hold his own against the mighty British Navy.[23]

As Decatur surveyed the damage to the ship, his friend and attorney Littleton Tazewell met with Norfolk's mayor to draft the town's reply to Captain Douglas, telling him that "the American people are not to be intimidated by your menace." Tazewell delivered the message personally to Captain Douglas, aboard the *Bellona* at Hampton Roads. Tazewell, like Decatur, recognized weakness of the American position. It was one thing for citizens to pass proclamations and declare themselves prepared for the worst, but Decatur recognized what the worst might be. To his relief, Tazewell and Douglas managed to avert a war. Douglas assured Tazewell that his proclamation was not meant to be menacing, and he had "no hostile intention against Norfolk."[24]

Decatur still prepared for the worst. A pilot from the Eastern Shore came aboard the *Chesapeake* to report that the *Bellona* was lightening, preparing to ascend the Chesapeake. Decatur assured Secretary Smith that if the British did not leave the bay, he would use his four gunboats "to render their situation extremely uncomfortable." Decatur would also use his frigate: "I beg you sir to rely most confidently on the *Chesapeakes* retrieving her reputation if any thing shoul'd be attempted."[25]

Invasion was fresh in the minds of Virginians. Less than thirty years earlier Benedict Arnold's forces had swept into the Chesapeake, and a British force ascended the James River far enough to chase Governor Thomas Jefferson from his breakfast table at Monticello. Now President Jefferson (who had been accused of failing to prepare Virginia's defenses as governor) called for 100,000 militia, and asked Governor William Cabell of Virginia to send his militia to defend Norfolk and the unfinished gunboats Samuel Barron was building at Hampton.[26]

Decatur knew that these volunteers would be useful in an emergency, but not for long. He told Secretary Smith that while he could find "volunteers to man" his four gunboats, and he admired them for the "Patriotic spirit they have displayed," the "small trial" of their abilities showed them "entirely ignorant of the duty that must be performed, and extremely averse to control." He asked to be sent "men, who will be subject to the articles of War. Men who if not disposed to do their duty, I can force to do it—give me those, and If I fail to do everything you expect from me, I beg you will not spare me."[27]

By July 14 Decatur had the *Chesapeake* nearly completed. He learned that Samuel Barron had his gunboats nearly finished at Hampton. The moment seemed safe to send the boats to Norfolk. Captain Douglas planned to move the *Bellona* at the first fair wind. Did that mean that he "intended to go out at first fair wind?" Decatur asked. "Douglass said his answer should be given, 'that he would go where he pleased the first fair wind.' "[28] Douglas sailed for Halifax in mid-July.

The new British commander in the Chesapeake was Sir Thomas Masterman Hardy, Lord Nelson's flag captain on the *Victory* (Nelson had died in Hardy's arms at Trafalgar). Hardy knew that there was a time for war and a time for conciliation. He pulled the British fleet from the Chesapeake, and no longer had them stop every vessel going in or out.[29] The British government agreed. When it learned in late July that the *Leopard* had attacked the *Chesapeake*, it denounced the attack and recalled Berkeley.

With the immediate threat of war passing, Decatur could attend to other problems of administration. The arrival of Isaac Hull to supervise the gunboats at Norfolk would be a great help. Under the threat of war, neither man reflected that Hull was the senior captain, now under the direction of the twenty-eight-year old commodore. Both men had other problems. First and foremost, now that the British threat was past, was to find sailors.

Decatur would need nearly five hundred crewmen to man the forts and gunboats. But finding men for the *Chesapeake*—by enlisting British deserters— had led to the crisis in the first place. In early August, with the *Chesapeake* repaired, Decatur moved the ship to Craney Island, "to prevent desertion & keep the crew healthy, neither of which could have been effected lying in the harbour of Norfolk."[30] Patriotism would not be enough to keep his men both healthy and on board.

CHAPTER *10*

"I cannot suffer men to be taken from me by force"

ECATUR SET to work restoring discipline and order on the ship. He had two men court-martialed, "one for desertion, the other for mutinous & seditious expressions, & insolence to his officers," in order, he told Secretary Smith, "that proper punishment will check those evils, which otherwise may become serious."[1] When he had first stepped aboard the *Chesapeake*, he found Midshipman William Sim under arrest for "ungentlemanly conduct." Decatur freed Sim, thinking that with war imminent "I should have immediate use for all the officers." But Sim "unfortunately drinks hard," and fearing that "his example will be injurious to the younger Midshipmen," Decatur gave him "permission to leave the ship."[2]

Among the officers Decatur found similar problems. Lieutenant John Davis, he reported, "for a long time past" had been "in the habit of drinking to excess," which left his mind "in a deranged state for some weeks" before he shot himself through the head. Davis left behind many debts. The *Argus*'s purser, John Lyon, was "in the habit of frequenting gambling houses," and was a regular at the Eagle Tavern's gambling table. Decatur at first tried to convince Lyon of the "impropriety of any person entrusted with public money visiting such places." Lyon gave his word of "honour if [Decatur] would not report him" to the navy secretary, then "he would not visit such places for the future." Lyon nevertheless continued "to gamble," and just a few nights later was "betting as high as Thirty Dollars on a card" at the Eagle Tavern. Decatur did not have another purser for the *Argus*; he warned the brig's captain of Lyon's gambling, and when Lyon came to collect his ship's cash before sailing, Decatur withheld it, knowing that Lyon would use it to cover his gambling debts before sailing out of Norfolk.[3]

Gambling was not the only problem on board. Decatur's former secretary, a Mr. Petty, was too often drunk, and he and Richard Crump had "disgrace[d] themselves by boxing while on shore at Norfolk." Both had been drinking and were "equally to blame." Neither man's behavior, Decatur reported, "since they have been under my command has been correct." He kept both boxers in the brig.[4]

Court-martialing, dismissing, and incarcerating troublemakers would, Decatur hoped, be a lesson for other sailors. The marine detachment, however, was another story. "The Marines on board the Chesapeake are the worst detachment I have ever seen," he complained. "More than four fifths of them are foreigners, they are bad soldiers, turbulent men, & few of them able bodied." When the *Leopard* attacked, these marines had refused to fire unless given a direct order to do so. This was unacceptable to Decatur. "Our marines," he told Smith, "we have ever considered as our sheet anchors, men whom we can rely upon in the worst of times." But these men were worthless. He knew there were better marines in Washington but was "told they have selected their worst for us."[5] He asked Smith to send him better marines.

Drunken and disorderly sailors, incompetent marines: these were not Decatur's only problems. Britain threatened the nation at sea, and Aaron Burr threatened from the west. As Decatur was preparing the fleet against a British attack, he was summoned away to Richmond to testify before the grand jury investigating Burr's conspiracy. In September he returned to Richmond for the trial, though he was not called to testify. The government's star witness against Burr was his former co-conspirator, General James Wilkinson, who challenged Congressman John Randolph to a duel after Randolph publicly charged Wilkinson with corruption. Decatur's friend Littleton Tazewell thought that the idea of meeting the disgraced Wilkinson "on the field of honor" was absurd, and predicted that Jefferson would dismiss Wilkinson from the army just as he had dismissed Richard Morris from the navy. But Army Captain John Saunders, commander of Fort Nelson in Norfolk, knew the army and Jefferson better than Tazewell did; he bet that Wilkinson would not be dismissed. Tazewell and Saunders wagered a coat on the outcome. Decatur thought this a safe bet. Wilkinson had even arrested innocent civilians who threatened to betray his duplicity. Surely Jefferson would not keep such a tarnished officer in the ranks. Saunders won two coats, as Decatur and Tazewell lost their bets, as well as some faith in Jefferson's integrity.[6]

Decatur and Tazewell returned to Norfolk and the *Chesapeake* for the court of inquiry on the loss of the ship. Tazewell would prosecute James Barron, who was to be defended by his cousin Robert Taylor. Secretary Smith had wanted Edward Preble to preside over the court, as it would help restore public confidence in the navy. But Preble's ill health kept him in Maine, where he died in August. Instead, Alexander Murray, Isaac Chauncey, and Isaac Hull conducted the inquiry. The news of Preble's death reminded the assembled captains of the differences among commanders; the tough, irascible Preble had fought, while Barron and his brother had bought peace in Tripoli. Preble was gone, but the assembled captains would learn from his example. William Ray, the poetic marine from the *Philadelphia*, wrote an elegy mourning Preble's death. Although Preble was dead, Ray wrote, "a Second Preble!—A DECATUR lives!"[7]

Barron thought he would be exonerated. After all, the men of the *Philadelphia* had rallied to Bainbridge's defense, and he knew that Charles Gordon was at least as responsible for the *Chesapeake*'s failure as he was. But by sending Gordon to Washington with the official word of surrender, Barron had committed a tactical error. He may have thought the loss such a calamity that no single scapegoat would be sought, or that by bringing the word to Washington, Gordon himself would be blamed. Either way, Barron was wrong. Gordon made sure to direct responsibility toward Barron, the overall commander, reminding all that the commodore had visited the *Chesapeake* only twice while the ship was being prepared to go to sea.

As the captains conducted their official inquiry, midshipmen and civilians were fighting duels—a total of seven by the late summer of 1808—in their own attempts to sort out the blame for the *Chesapeake*'s surrender. Midshipman James Broom had been on the quarterdeck with Barron during the attack and believed that the captain had acted correctly. Midshipman Richard Crump, the boxer, disagreed, and in their ensuing duel Broom "received a flesh wound in his thigh." Decatur's investigation found "both gentlemen have been to blame in this affair."[8] He arrested them both.

Two of Barron's Norfolk relatives took exception to the way Gordon had shifted the blame to their kinsman. Dr. Bolling Stark challenged Gordon to duel, with the other relative, A. J. McConnico, acting as second. "I regret much Sir the disagreement which has arisen between Capt. Gordon & two of the younger citizens of this place," Decatur wrote to Secretary Smith. The two younger citizens, Stark and McConnico, "it is said are the connections of Comr. Barron & have cast some reflections on the conduct of Capt. Gordon, in the affair between the Chesapeake & Leopard.—from their standing in society they are not entitled to notice from Capt. Gordon—one of them is a clerk in some merchants counting house—I shall do all in my power to prevent anything further from taking place."[9] Secretary Smith ordered Decatur to put a stop to this dueling; three weeks later Decatur was "happy to inform" the secretary that "all differences between the officers & gentlemen at this place I am informed are adjusted."[10]

At the same time that Decatur was trying to prevent these disputes over the *Chesapeake*, his brother John, a lieutenant stationed in New York, joined four other lieutenants (including Oliver Hazard Perry and James Lawrence) in proposing a "Court of Honor" to resolve differences that might otherwise lead to duels. Stephen Decatur thought this a good idea. He even took it a step further. Recognizing that midshipmen were more sensitive to challenges of honor than senior officers, and were thus more prone to dueling, Decatur required all his midshipmen to pledge that they would bring their disagreements to him rather than to the dueling field.[11]

Back in Norfolk, the court of inquiry charged Barron, Gordon, gunner William Hook, and marine captain John Hall with negligence. The court found that Barron had neglected to clear his ship for action, had failed to encourage his men to fight courageously, and had not done his utmost to take or destroy the *Leopard*. Secretary Smith asked John Rodgers—who had attempted to provoke Barron into a duel just a year earlier—to preside over Barron's court-martial. Like the court of inquiry, the court-martial would be held aboard the *Chesapeake*. Smith appointed William Bainbridge and Stephen Decatur to serve as well.

Decatur protested his appointment. Even before the *Chesapeake* had sailed, Decatur told Secretary Smith, his opinion of Barron "as a Soldier, was not favourable." Barron's conduct of the Tripolitan war had not impressed Decatur, who had been relegated to convoy duty. He had attended the court of inquiry, and had read its report, which he thought too lenient. "It is probable that I am prejudiced against Commo. Barron," he wrote to Secretary Smith, "& view his conduct in this case, with more severity than it deserves." He asked to be excused from the court-martial, though if the secretary insisted he serve, he would try to "conscientiously decide" Barron's case.[12]

When Smith did not excuse him, Decatur sent copies of the correspondence to Barron's lawyer, Robert Taylor, hoping that Taylor would request his removal. But Taylor did not challenge Decatur, perhaps still hoping that the panel would completely exonerate Barron. Barron, after all, had presided over Bainbridge's court-martial and had cleared him for the loss of the *Philadelphia*. Some of Barron's friends even planned a testimonial dinner to celebrate after the verdict. When they asked Lieutenant William Allen of the *Chesapeake* to buy a ticket to the dinner, he had a better sense of what the verdict would be. He told them "they need not worry themselves about it!"[13] The public would not be celebrating James Barron.

The court-martial cleared Barron of negligence and of not encouraging his men to fight courageously. But he was found guilty of failing to prepare the *Chesapeake* for action when he was warned that the *Leopard* would take the British deserters by force. He was suspended for five years without pay. Captains Gordon and Hall were found guilty of minor charges and sentenced to be privately reprimanded by the secretary of the navy. Hook, the gunner, was dismissed.

The court of inquiry and the court-martial had an unintended result. For the first time since the American squadron cruised off Tripoli, the navy's senior captains were brought together in one place. The gunboat system had decentralized the navy's operations, putting lieutenants and sometimes midshipmen in command of their own vessels—often the only naval installation in a small port. Though given command earlier, these junior officers did not have the opportunity that Decatur, Barron, Lawrence, Stewart, and Somers had had to form a cohort of young officers under the direction of a senior captain such as John Barry or Edward Preble. Barron's trial brought the navy's senior officers together for several months, meeting daily, either on Decatur's ship or in a tavern on shore. Barron's court-martial panel—Captains Rodgers, Bainbridge, Hugh Campbell, Decatur, and John Shaw, along with Commandants John Smith and David Porter, and Lieutenants Joseph Tarbell, Jacob Jones, James Lawrence, and Charles Ludlow—may have been the most distinguished panel of American naval officers ever assembled. Some of these men had already met: Decatur and Jones had been midshipmen under Barron on the *United States* ten years earlier; Porter had served as a lieutenant under Rodgers in the French war, and had been a prisoner with Bainbridge in Tripoli; Campbell had commanded the *Constellation* when Rodgers commanded the Mediterranean fleet. Now, as these officers spent a month together, whether consciously or not they were establishing the standards that would guide their profession. They were considering not only the specific cases of Barron and Gordon but also the more fundamental question of how an officer should prepare his ship, and how an officer should respond to a crisis. While deciding the future of Barron and Gordon, the court was also deciding the future of the U.S. Navy.

In hearing witnesses, they were evaluating junior officers as well. Jesse Elliott, the junior officer most supportive of Barron, never gained the confidence of the other officers. By contrast, William Henry Allen, the junior officer most critical of Barron (he had carried a burning coal to fire the *Chesapeake*'s only shot), told his father that one member of the court of inquiry (either Murray, Hull, or Chauncey) had offered him a lieutenant's position on his ship, and Commodore Rodgers, president of the court-martial, had invited him to take a position in his squadron in New York. Allen declined both offers. Decatur had kept him on the *Chesapeake*, where he had moved up from fourth to second lieutenant. "Should I now leave him," Allen wrote, "I might change a freind to a foe."[14] Allen remained with Decatur for the next five years.

In addition to considering Barron's actions, the captains were also considering ways to respond to the British. As the court sat in the *Chesapeake*'s cabin on January 6, a visitor was announced on deck. Decatur went up to find

R. H. Bromley, captain of H.M.S. *Statira*, a fifty-gun Royal Navy frigate. Decatur apologized. "I informed him we were on Public Duty & I could not invite him below." But Bromley "informed me he had waited on me for the purpose of paying his respects to me &c.," and he stayed on board only briefly, "during which time he was treated with politeness." In addition, Decatur was proud to report, "the Chesapeake could not have been in better order."[15]

Bromley's was a courtesy call, but it covered up a serious problem. The *Statira* had brought envoy George Rose to resolve the question of reparations due the United States for the attack on the *Chesapeake*. Although the British agreed to apologize and make good the damages to the ship, the British government still believed that the American service was taking in far too many British deserters. Rose estimated that two-thirds of the *Chesapeake*'s crew were British subjects. The British government wanted these men back. How many were deserters? Deserters would have been reluctant to be repatriated once they learned that John Strachan, the man from the *Chesapeake*, had been hanged. But in October the king had offered to pardon any British subject who quit the service of a foreign power. The day after Bromley visited the *Chesapeake*, Norfolk's customs collector, Larkin Smith, demanded that the British consul release George Fox, an American impressed aboard the *Statira*. Bromley again was polite. He was certain that Smith had made his application for Fox's return in good faith. But the *Statira*'s records showed Fox's story to be nothing but "impudent falsehoods."[16] Bromley demanded that the Americans release 3 British subjects known to be aboard the *Chesapeake*: Thomas Kelly, Elias Brown, and Thomas Addison.

Decatur responded through the British consul that he would gladly release British deserters, asking "no further proof" of their status "than such as [Bromley] demands on our part, for the release of those who may be claimed by us."[17] Decatur summoned the alleged British subjects to his cabin. There Decatur, Rodgers, and four other American captains faced the three sailors. After reading aloud Bromley's letter, which promised to release the Americans if Decatur would release the British sailors, Captain Rodgers opened the discussion. He thought Bromley's letter "very fair," Rodgers said, "but I will not deliver up a Man, I will fight him first."[18]

Brown and Kelly denied that they had asked to be discharged. Addison, though, said he had contacted the British consul on November 23 to apply for a discharge from the U.S. Navy. How long had he been in the United States? "On and off since 1775," he replied.

"Here is a pretty fellow to call himself a British subject," Decatur said, "after having been so long in the Country." It was longer than Decatur had been alive. Decatur asked Addison how old he was, whether he had taken the oath of allegiance to the United States, and if he had been married in America. Addison was forty-seven, nearly twenty years older than Decatur—in fact, older than every captain in the room. He had never sworn allegiance to the United States, and had not been married in America. Decatur sent for his first lieutenant, William Crane, telling him not to let Addison go ashore, instructing him to keep "a sharp Eye upon him, and to *touch* him up," or thrash him, if he got out of line.[19]

Decatur then took steps to discover how many foreigners were serving aboard the *Chesapeake*. "I think we shall find many," he predicted, though the estimate he gave the secretary of the navy—thirty French and sixty British—was short of the British estimate. Addison related the story of Decatur's muster on board the *Chesapeake*. With the men lined up before him, Decatur asked all the French to step forward. Twelve men did so. Decatur asked if they wished to be discharged. They did. Then he asked the British subjects to step forward. He may have recalled his *Enterprise* crew stepping forward as one to storm the *Philadelphia*, but this time a crowd of American sailors came forward clamoring to be released from service. He raised his hand and demanded that British sailors come forward only if they wished to "enter on board the Statira." The men all jumped back "as if fired on by Musketry." Decatur asked again for the British to step forward. When the men understood that discharge from the *Chesapeake* meant enlistment on the *Statira*, only four came forward.[20]

Captain Bromley told Decatur that he expected "to get the most of" the men discharged from the *Chesapeake*, and according to Decatur, the British were actively trying "to seduce the men of the boats of the Chesapeake to enter onboard the Statira." Decatur understood that he might lose men, but he was determined not to lose them to Bromley. When six more men on the *Chesapeake* claimed to be British subjects, Decatur put them in a gunboat and had them taken to Baltimore.[21] His ship and the gunboats were short by over 100 men by January 1808, and by April he had discharged 150 foreigners from his squadron.

Decatur knew that he and Bromley, despite the nationalistic tones of their exchanges, were both desperate to sign sailors. Bromley was not limiting himself to the suspected deserters on Decatur's ship; he was also wooing the unemployed sailors of Norfolk. Decatur wanted to sign these men on to the *Chesapeake*, and he believed that he could do it if the Navy Department would allow it.[22]

The sailors of Norfolk had been thrown suddenly out of work by the Embargo Act of 1807. Both Britain and France were harassing American shipping. President Jefferson's response was to cut off all American trade. The

economic rationale was that both warring nations relied on American grain
to feed their armies, navies, and civilians. Deprive them of grain, and they
would cease to fight, their people would rise up in rebellion, and all would
recognize that real power came not from military force but from agricultural
labor. It was a noble idea, for Jefferson reasoned that although the embargo
would hurt American commerce, a war with England, France, or both might
destroy the nation.

In the meantime, unemployed American sailors still had an option other
than the U.S. Navy. Pay in the British service was low, but Bromley could
promise any man who enlisted a chance to earn prize money if the *Statira*
captured a French ship. Decatur could not make the same promise because
the United States was not at war, and Jefferson was pledging to avoid war.
While sailors in the British navy would have opportunities to fight the French,
American sailors would be patrolling the coast inspecting American ships to
ensure that none was violating the embargo.

Decatur sailed for New England in July 1808. He patrolled off Sandy Hook
in July, then in August spent two weeks off the coast of Rhode Island. The
Chesapeake stopped twenty-six Rhode Island vessels and found that every ship
out of Providence and half the ships out of Bristol were violating the law.
Lieutenant Allen, a Rhode Islander, knew that merchants in his state were
going to evade the embargo in any way they could. To spare Allen having to
detain a merchant he knew "for a single keg of butter" or else be accused of
partiality, Decatur gave the lieutenant permission not to board any of these
ships.[23] The Rhode Island captains, meanwhile, tried to explain away their
smuggling. On one ship out of Providence "there was a considerable quantity
of Provisions found beneath her Ballast," but the captain assured Decatur
that he did not intend to sell any of these goods; he was using them as ballast,
"merely to serve as Pebbles or Rocks." Decatur sent the ship to New York.
Worse than deceitful captains was the fact that Decatur knew these vessels
had been "accompanied by an Officer of the Customs down to the Sea. It is
therefore a little surprising how the Shippers should be able to smuggle so
many articles on board in despight of so much precaution."[24]

Customs officers were either failing to inspect ships thoroughly or blatantly
aiding the smuggling merchants. In the years before the American Revolution, Rhode Island merchants had colluded with revenue officers to defy
British law. Now the merchants were joining with American revenue agents
to defy the embargo. From Rhode Island the *Chesapeake* cruised off Nantucket
and Martha's Vineyard, then sailed for the coast of Maine. There as well
Decatur found that "the people are much averse to the Embargo." His duty
was to enforce the law, however unpopular.[25]

Off the coast of Maine one morning, Decatur "had the mortification to be beaten . . . in sailing by two vessels." This was his first lengthy cruise since he had brought the *Congress* back from the Mediterranean in 1805. He found that the "Chesapeake as a vessel of war sails uncommonly dull." He also had time, as he coordinated his ship's movements with the *Argus*, the *Wasp*, and the gunboats, to study the signals that American ships were using. These signals, based on the British navy's system, used colored flags to signify letters and words. Decatur and other captains found them "defective, in as much as they are not sufficiently extensive." During this cruise Decatur expanded the signal system, selecting "such words from a common Dictionary as I supposed might be useful, to which I have added the names of Rivers, Capes, Shoals, Cities, &c." With these additions "there are no orders of intelligence that may not be conveyed." Decatur conferred with Rodgers and Chauncey in New York, who agreed that the new system would be an improvement.[26]

This mundane duty of enforcing the embargo gave Decatur ample opportunity to think of other ways in which the navy could improve. He had seen the disaster of the *Chesapeake*'s encounter with the *Leopard* as a lesson in preparation: the gun crews had never trained, their guns were not ready. But even in assessing the damage to the ship, Decatur had noted how poor the British aim had been. While the *Chesapeake* sat in wait for blockade runners, Decatur had the crew trained and drilled. Lieutenant Allen had been disgusted with the old *Chesapeake*'s lack of training; he now threw himself into the new commander's regimen. Drilling and artillery practice were aimed at making the crew an efficient fighting force. But the preparation also had the result of making the men a team. Knowing that his crewmen could easily find berths on other vessels—especially British ones—meant that Decatur had to give these men an incentive to stay and few incentives to leave. He accomplished this by treating them fairly and keeping them all involved.

Unlike Bainbridge and other captains known to be free with the lash, Decatur preferred milder forms of punishment, such as witholding the grog ration, and there may have been a correlation between sobriety and improved discipline. Order was best maintained, however, by teamwork. When a sailor or midshipman stepped out of line, Decatur acted quickly. William Barton, who had been the surgeon on the *United States*, could never get along with the other officers. Barton was an educated man (he later became a professor of botany at the University of Pennsylvania), and he found his companions in the wardroom as disagreeable as they must have found him. In March 1810 Decatur had to arrest Barton for hitting one of them. Barton had argued with sailing master John Gallagher, in the presence of the crew, "using provoking & reproachful words." Barton was a young man with great professional talents, but "his situation with his messmates has been for some time back, very disagreeable," noted Decatur, as a result of his temper. Decatur wanted to get Barton off of his ship but to do it while causing "the least injury to the Dr." Barton was honorable but imprudent; he and the navy would both benefit if he were permitted to make a fresh start on another ship.[27]

Decatur would not always be so lenient in punishing infractions against the good order of the ship. When Midshipman William Cutter committed a "crime of too detestible a nature to name" (Cutter had attempted to sodomize a boy on the ship), Decatur had "this monster," who was "in all respects dishonorable," dismissed from the navy.[28]

Along with proposing new signals for the navy, Decatur thought up the navy's overall strategy for the embargo. Rather than keeping the frigates off the port cities, he proposed keeping the squadron off Bermuda. Since most of the embargo violators were taking cargoes to the West Indies, it made sense to put the enforcing vessels on the main route southward. "One or two of our Vessels stationed about two degrees to the Eastward" of Bermuda, he wrote Secretary Smith, and another one or two west of the island "would stand a better chance of falling in with Vessels bound to the West Indies than if they were stationed before our ports, where with long stormy nights they would be able to evade us. On the contrary few vessels pass the Lattitude of Bermuda in the night."[29]

In this same letter Decatur informed the secretary that he had made a brief visit to Philadelphia to attend his father's funeral. He had left Lieutenant Allen in charge of the *Chesapeake* at New York and spent five days at home. The man who had declared that his children were the property of his country would have understood that his son could stay for no longer than was required to escort his father's body from Frankford to St. Peter's churchyard just a short distance from the Front Street home. Then Stephen left his mother and widowed sister and his nieces and nephew to return to New York. He signed his letter to the secretary of the navy simply "Stephen Decatur," for the first time dropping "Junior" from his name.

Susan also waited in New York, where she had taken a room in a boardinghouse. While the ship was in port, she and Stephen lived together on shore. His cruises on the *Chesapeake* were so far the longest separations in their brief marriage. While Stephen was away, Susan could not sleep; even when he was conducting the relatively routine enforcement of the embargo, she was overcome with worry. After another cruise off the New England coast, on October 25 the *Chesapeake* was back in New York harbor, where Stephen took Susan aboard and sailed for Virginia, dropping anchor in Hampton on November

9. From there he sailed to Washington, where he was given command of the largest ship in the American fleet, the *United States.*

Decatur had begun his career eleven years earlier as a midshipman on the *United States.* Perhaps the pencil marks he had drawn behind the lines to help him remember their names were no longer visible; or perhaps subsequent generations of midshipmen had emulated him. Future generations of sailors would emulate Decatur in other ways. For the moment, however, he could not think of past or future glory. His most pressing need was to find a crew. Most of the men on the *Chesapeake* had enlisted in 1807; their two-year terms were about to expire. These men were free to go—unlike their comrades who had claimed British protection and left to join the British fleet. Decatur no doubt recalled that embarrassing day when the crew had rushed forward to claim their freedom from the U.S. Navy. When he mustered the *Chesapeake*'s crew for a final time to tell them that he was leaving the ship, these men whose naval service now was over "came forward, & offered to reenter for the Frigate United States."[30] After a year of drilling and training, the team was prepared to follow its captain.

CHAPTER II

"No ship has better men than she now has"

T HE EMBARGO expired when Jefferson left office. President Madison did not renew it. Treasury Secretary Albert Gallatin and Navy Secretary Smith (who now became secretary of state) had opposed the embargo but had been required to enforce it. The embargo had failed to end the troubles with either England or France. Although the United States was at peace in 1809, the rest of the world continued to be at war.

Decatur took advantage of his long peacetime cruises to continue his exploration of the natural world. He sent back to Philadelphia samples of marine life collected off the Atlantic coast, impressing Judge Richard Peters with the "highly useful additions to our stock of esculents." Peters thought that Decatur's collections were "the most important of any attempt I have known to penetrate [the ocean's] secret recesses."[1]

Other captains did not share Decatur's enthusiasm for scientific exploration and experimentation. While in Washington to transfer to the *United States*, Decatur very likely heard of Robert Fulton's demonstrations at Kalorama, Joel Barlow's estate. Fulton had invited Jefferson, President elect Madison, and several members of Congress to observe his "harpoon torpedo" in operation. This torpedo—an underwater mine attached to the end of a harpoon—would revolutionize naval warfare. A torpedo costing $1,000 could destroy a frigate costing $200,000.

Fulton had long been developing underwater mines, submarines, and torpedoes. He had been in France helping to devise Napoleon's defenses against the British navy when Robert Livingston came to negotiate the Louisiana treaty. The temperamental Fulton had become disenchanted with the equally temperamental emperor, who rejected Fulton's idea of building steam vessels to prepare for an invasion of England. Fulton and Livingston entered into an agreement, and the inventor returned to America, where he launched the first successful steamboat in 1807. His real passion, however, continued to be mines, submarines, and torpedoes. After the Kalorama demonstrations, Fulton published his book, *Torpedo War and Submarine Explosions*. President Jefferson, mindful of both economy and ingenuity, supported Fulton, but the navy establishment resisted.[2]

With the publication of *Torpedo War* in February 1810, Fulton asked Congress for money to develop his experimental methods of warfare. Congress appropriated $5,000 and the navy secretary assigned Captain John Rodgers to report on Fulton's invention. Rodgers thought Fulton a madman, and set out to prove it. Fearing that Rodgers would thwart fair trials of his experiments, Fulton asked for and received a committee of civilian observers: Livingston, Governor Morgan Lewis of New York, former treasury secretary Oliver Wolcott, and Cadwallader Colden. Fulton hoped to stage a torpedo demonstration on the Potomac if all went well in New York.

Rodgers assigned Isaac Chauncey to prepare defenses against Fulton's explosives. Chauncey and James Lawrence prepared the *Argus*, the brig Decatur had built, to withstand attack. They strung nets beneath the ship to catch the torpedoes before they could reach the hull. The defenses worked, and Fulton's demonstration was a complete failure. Rodgers wrote in triumph to the navy secretary: "Having attended all the experiments, if experiments they may be called, . . . as far as we have yet seen, that not a single sentence of that ever memorable book, which he has published to the world under the title of 'Torpedo War' is in any degree the production of sound reasoning or even of a sane mind." Torpedoes, Rodgers insisted, were completely impractical and "of no importance at all" to the nation's defense.[3]

Rodgers had demonstrated that the old technology could defeat the new technology—for the moment. In the long run the demonstration was unfortunate, as the navy lost an opportunity to develop torpedoes. It was also unfortunate that Decatur was not yet involved; by 1814 he and Fulton would be collaborators in building the world's first steam-powered warship. Decatur became Fulton's only real ally in the navy. Unlike Rodgers, who sought to prove Fulton a madman, Decatur actually found ways to make Fulton's steam warship more effective. At present, though, Decatur was occupied with less exciting tasks.

When Robert Smith became secretary of state, Madison appointed South Carolina lawyer and planter Paul Hamilton secretary of the navy. Smith had been on top of all things—lobbying Congress for more money, pushing to build more ships, overseeing personnel problems. Hamilton's qualifications for the position remain a mystery, though he handled his duties for four years with some competence. Decatur immediately tried to make a friend of the new secretary, passing along to Hamilton information about the schooner *Ploughboy*, which sailed regularly between Baltimore and Charleston, South Carolina. On Decatur's suggestion, the ship's owner reserved a choice stateroom for the navy secretary, should he ever choose to return home by sea.[4]

Most of the captains would have been glad to have Hamilton return home. Smith, while thoroughly engaged in naval affairs, had left the officers to run their ships, squadrons, and bases. By the time he stepped down, after running the navy for eight of the twelve years of its existence, he and all the captains shared a common vision of their mission. Hamilton came in not knowing any of the navy's ways, and though these ways were still relatively new, the men who had created them, as Rodgers's successful discrediting of Fulton shows, were not eager to change.

The new secretary had to resolve the persistent problems of command. Would he, a civilian, be in charge of the navy? Or would its operations be in the hands of its officers? Who would be in charge in a navy yard—the commandant of the navy yard or the senior officer on a ship? Seemingly insignificant events provoked these questions. For instance, before sailing the *Nautilus* from Norfolk to New York, Captain Arthur Sinclair discovered that he needed a small iron stove. He turned to Decatur, commander of the squadron based at Norfolk. Decatur told Sinclair to take one from the *Enterprise*. But when Sinclair went aboard the *Enterprise* to get the stove, Lieutenant Edmund Kennedy refused to let him take it. Kennedy told Sinclair that Decatur was not commander of the navy yard, and that he would have to buy a stove when he got to New York. Decatur, probably remembering how he had had to use force to get anything done in Norfolk when he arrived in 1806, sent Sinclair to seize the stove and had Kennedy arrested for refusing to follow an order.

Kennedy protested to Secretary Hamilton, and Hamilton sided with Kennedy, not Decatur. He ordered Decatur to release Kennedy, who had been following navy regulations: captains could not transfer materiel out of ships in a navy yard; only the yard's commandant could do so. Decatur released Kennedy and apologized to Secretary Hamilton. He explained that William Bainbridge had given orders in the navy yard when he had been stationed there, but now he felt "much regret at having assumed a power which is considered as not belonging to me." He also offered "as an apology" to Hamilton "the general opinion which has obtained in the service, that the senior officer," in this case Sinclair, "had the power of ordering the junior."[5]

Decatur would comply with the secretary's orders consistently. He was preparing to leave Norfolk on the *United States*, but the ship did not have a doctor. He told Secretary Hamilton that he had ordered Dr. Schoolfield from the navy yard to join the ship, "but I do not now feel myself justified in keeping him." Rather than disobey the secretary's wishes, and reasoning that the rule for an iron stove would cover the case of a physician, Decatur would sail from Norfolk without a doctor. In the margin of Decatur's letter Hamilton noted that the issue "requires particular notice and attention." Irregular acts could be approved or disapproved, but he needed to maintain the principle that captains could not act arbitrarily or capriciously. "These sentiments are to be expressed explicitly but yet with tenderness of Language—Decatur may err but while he has his honorable feelings needs little admonitions."[6]

While Decatur and the secretary were working out their relationship, the United States, England, and France continued to work out theirs. England and France were at war, and each country believed that America's ostensible neutrality was unfairly helping the other. British ships cruised the American coast between Bermuda and Halifax, maintaining a presence but avoiding confrontations with American warships. They did, however, claim their right to take deserters from American merchant vessels.

Rumors of hostile actions swirled in the port cities, and when British and American warships did meet, their commanders tried to stop just short of war. When Lieutenant John Trippe of the *Vixen* met a British war brig in July 1810, the British ship shot away the *Vixen*'s main boom. As Trippe's men prepared to return fire, the British commander hastily raised a truce flag and sent an officer to apologize. Trippe, famed for his capture of a Tripolitan gunboat against overwhelming odds, this time recognized the virtue of diplomacy. He told the officer that he would accept only a written apology, which the British captain quickly supplied. Decatur was somewhat disappointed that Trippe had averted war. "Trippe has lost a glorious opportunity to cancel the blot under which our flag suffers" three years after the surrender of the *Chesapeake*, he wrote, "and to distinguish himself." But Decatur was "perfectly satisfied, that, although he may have shewn great moderation in this affair, he has not lost sight of what is due to the honour of his flag."[7]

When John Rodgers learned that an American sailor had been impressed off a merchant ship not far from Sandy Hook, he was equally mindful of restoring the flag's honor. Sailing off to investigate, he spied a vessel six miles south of New York. Shortly after eight in the evening Rodgers was close enough to hail the stranger: "What ship is that?" The answer came back: "What ship is that?" Rodgers repeated his question. Then the other ship fired a cannon. Rodgers, like Decatur, had learned from the *Chesapeake* fiasco to have his guns ready when approaching another ship. Even before he could give the order, one of the *President*'s cannon fired. The other ship answered with three cannon and then a broadside. A broadside from the *President* silenced the other ship. Rodgers called for a cease-fire, thinking that he had disabled the other. All was silent in the darkness, then the other ship fired again. Rodgers ordered another broadside. This time the enemy's guns stayed silent.

Now when Rodgers hailed, the other ship answered. It was the British warship *Little Belt*, a twenty-two-gun sloop built to look like a frigate. Rodgers had the *President*'s lanterns lit and spent the night watching the *Little Belt* drift in the current. In the morning he sent a boat over. The *Little Belt*'s captain, Arthur Batt Bingham, with his ship shot apart—masts, sails, hull damaged, thirty-one men dead or wounded—refused aid; he could make it back to Halifax.

In June, Decatur was ordered to sea to join Rodgers. He learned before leaving Norfolk that the British frigate *Guerriere* was off the Chesapeake. A pilot boat reported that the *Guerriere*'s captain "had heard of the mistake that the Little Belt had made," and had asked if the pilot knew when the *United States* would sail and if it was short of men. Decatur was in fact short of men (ten sailors and twenty marines) but would "feel proud to meet her tomorrow."[8]

Three days later, four miles off the coast, he met the British squadron. Seeing the *United States*, the thirty-eight-gun frigate *Eurydice* drew up under Decatur's leeward side. The *Eurydice*'s captain hoped to avoid the war the captains of the *Little Belt* and *Guerriere* were willing to provoke. He made a point as he approached of identifying himself, and by coming from Decatur's leeward side to signal peaceful intentions. But Decatur had learned the lesson of the *Chesapeake* and had all his gun crews ready to fire as the *Eurydice* approached.

The *Eurydice* had dispatches for the U.S. government and was anxious to avoid another violent confrontation. The captains exchanged questions and answers, the British commander having learned from the *Little Belt* incident to enunciate clearly. But just as they concluded their formal conversation, a gunner on the *United States* accidentally pulled the lanyard, setting off his cannon. The two frigates were at close range, but miraculously the shot did not injure any British sailors. Both captains remained calm. Decatur shouted that the shot was an accident, and no other gun was fired. The British captain acknowledged that "accidents would happen, and that he was willing to believe this to have been one." Mindful of the way his colleagues on the *Leopard* and the *Little Belt* had issued demands of the *Chesapeake* and the *President*, the captain pointedly asked "*permission* to send his boat on board," and Decatur agreed to his "*request*." When the British officer came aboard the *United States*, Decatur again told him that the shot had been an accident, and the officer assured him that no one had been hurt. In this way the *Eurydice* and the *United States* avoided hostilities. In his report Decatur noted the British captain's "pointedly polite and respectful" manner.[9]

The British officers were all beginning to learn better manners. At the same time, the discipline of Decatur's crew—being ready to fire, and then witholding fire after the gun accidentally went off—showed how effectively he and Allen had trained the men. The rest of the trip to New York was uneventful, though Decatur had a nagging thought: If he was serving under Rodgers, would he still have his "rank as Commo., or whether my rank as such is to cease"?[10] Decatur maintained his rank, but acted under Rodgers.

His first task in New York was to conduct the court of inquiry into the *President*'s encounter with the *Little Belt*. Decatur, Stewart, and Chauncey found that Rodgers had fired only after the *Little Belt* fired on him. Although the British government supported Captain Bingham's version of events (he claimed that the *President* had fired the first shot), the British did not want to risk war with the United States at the moment, and so let the matter drop. Rodgers and Decatur both regretted this. Now that Rodgers had the *United States* and the brig *Argus* with him, he was "willing to risk the consequences of an action with the two best Frigates and the best Brig of which England can boast; should such an event take place, I hope at least to prove to the world that British ships are not so perfectly invulnerable as British arrogance has described them." Rodgers knew that the British "never will voluntarily attempt a game of such hazard," because once an American frigate defeated a British frigate, as Rodgers was certain one would, "the character of the British Navy would be more injured than it was elevated by the victory of the Nile."[11]

Decatur agreed. The *Eurydice*'s captain had made much of his peaceful intentions, but Decatur and Rodgers both knew that the British still did not respect the U.S. Navy. The *Guerriere* was cruising off the Atlantic coast stopping American ships. Its captain had the name "GUERRIERE" emblazoned in enormous black letters on the foretop sail, a reminder to all American merchant ships that the British navy was patrolling the American coast. Hoping that one of his frigates would encounter the *Guerriere*, Rodgers had the name "PRESIDENT" emblazoned "on each of my topsails in letters that may be seen ten miles."[12]

After enlisting a full crew in New York, and plotting strategy with Rodgers, Decatur sailed back to Norfolk, where the *United States* needed its hull recoppered. Although he and Rodgers anticipated war against the world's most powerful navy, both men were confident. With pride and satisfaction, Decatur wrote of the crew enlisted on the *United States*, "No ship has better men than she now has."[13]

CHAPTER 12

"Aim at the yellow streak"

ECATUR AND his fine new crew sailed the *United States* to Norfolk, where they would spend the winter replacing the ship's copper. As commander of the navy's southern squadron, Decatur now had two frigates—the *United States* and *Congress*—under his command, along with the sloop *Wasp*, the brig *Nautilus*, and of course the gunboats. Gunboats aside, the U.S. Navy had fifteen ships in the water: five frigates, four schooners, three brigs, and three sloops. At this moment eighty of the Royal Navy's five hundred ships were cruising off the American coast and in the Caribbean. A war between the two nations would be a one-sided affair.[1]

The British had an overwhelming naval advantage, but their government was trying to avert a war. They were repatriating two of the surviving men taken from the *Chesapeake* five years earlier (one, John Strachan, had been hanged for desertion; William Ware, the Native American, had died). At sea, the British no longer seized American sailors. In fact, shortly after Decatur reached Norfolk, HMS *Macedonian* docked next to the *United States,* having escorted in an American merchant ship found damaged after a gale.[2]

Captain John S. Carden and his *Macedonian* crew would have much to do with Decatur and his men during the months their ships were in Norfolk. The officers and men had time to evaluate their potential enemy's strengths and weaknesses. Carden claimed that many of his men recognized sailors on the *United States*; the Americans maintained that these men had been impressed into the British service. Carden told Decatur he was reluctant to call the *United States* an "American Frigate," since so many of Decatur's men were actually "first rate *British Seamen*" absconded from the British fleet. As for the other seamen, the British navy had been at war for twenty years; while Decatur's "ships may be good enough, and you are a clever set of fellows, what practice have you had in war? There is the rub."[3] Carden also doubted that the *United States*'s cannon, which fired twenty-four-pound shells, were as effective as the *Macedonian*'s longer-range eighteen-pound guns.

Decatur disagreed. He believed that the future of naval warfare was in heavier guns, capable of disabling or destroying the enemy's ships from a distance. This had been one of the lessons of the Nile and Trafalgar, which Decatur knew well. A dinner guest years later recalled how Decatur had arranged nutshells on the table to represent the British and French fleets on the Nile, demonstrating that the key to Nelson's victory had not been superior seamanship, but artillery. Decatur was also keenly aware that the three broadsides from the *Leopard* had done only minimal damage to the *Chesapeake*'s hull, when such devastating fire should have sunk the ship.

To prepare his men to fight more effectively, Decatur and Lieutenant Allen had the *United States*'s crew drill constantly, synchronizing movements and perfecting their aim. Decatur also experimented with new types of shell. He had four small holes drilled into the outer casing of a hollowed-out cannonball, which then was filled with gunpowder. On impact with a target, the holes would crack, admitting enough air to react with the powder and explode. In tests of the new shells, Decatur found that they could shatter a timber wall when fired from a quarter mile away. This new weapon could destroy an enemy ship with a single broadside. But he would not use the weapon against the British. He told Treasury Secretary Gallatin that the French were developing similar weapons; he might use his experimental models against their navy but not against the British, who did not have this kind of shell. Decatur "meant to have fair play with" the British when the war began.[4]

Decatur also reported to Secretary Hamilton on the best way to defend Chesapeake Bay. The ships under his command could be anchored off Craney Island, about five miles south of Norfolk. If an enemy tried to approach through the narrow channel at this point, the American ships would deliver "a raking fire from our vessels, in the most intricate part of the navigation." This would probably force the enemy to "go on shore" rather than continue on. If the enemy did make it through, the same wind that allowed enemy ships to advance toward Norfolk would carry the Americans there first, and "they would again be exposed to our raking." The entire Chesapeake could be defended in this way.[5]

Decatur may not have shared his strategic thinking with Carden, but he and the British captain did engage in good-natured bantering. According to tradition, the two captains speculated about what would happen if their ships met in combat. "We now meet as friends," Carden is supposed to have said, "and God grant we may never meet as enemies; but we are subject to the orders of our governments, and must obey them. Suppose we should meet as enemies, what do you suppose will be the result?" Decatur also hoped "that you and I may never meet except as we do now. But if as enemies, and with equal forces, the conflict will undoubtedly be a severe one, for the flag of my country will never be struck whilst there is a hull for it to wave from."[6] The two men were said to have wagered a hat on the battle's outcome.[7] Carden, denied permission to load a cargo of gold in Norfolk, prepared to sail for Lisbon.

While the two captains dutifully said that they hoped war could be avoided, by this time it was clearly imminent. The secretary of the navy informed Decatur that the United States was instituting an embargo as a "precursor, in all probability, of a state of things which will call into action the whole energy of your character & afford you an opportunity of acquiring additional laurels. I need not therefore admonish you to be prepared. For in your love of fame you find a sufficient excitement."[8]

Before Decatur could be spurred by his love of fame, he had to make another trip to Philadelphia, owing to his mother's "extreme indisposition." He was there when she died on March 27. Ann Decatur had been living with her daughter Ann and her new son-in-law, Dr. William Hurst; she was buried in St. Peter's churchyard beside her husband, the two infants she had buried in the 1780s, and Dr. Hurst's first wife, Louisa Catherine Hurst, who had borne her struggle with tuberculosis with "resignation, fortitude, and even cheerfulness."[9] In the same year her mother died, Ann Decatur Hurst gave birth to a daughter, Catherine Louisa Hurst.

Returning to Norfolk, Stephen Decatur prepared for the war that was sure to come. He sent the *Argus* and the *Congress* to join Rodgers at sea, and readied the gunboats to defend the Chesapeake's entrance. The *United States* still needed work. Decatur and Rodgers, the commanders of the northern and southern departments, were in general agreement about overall strategy for deploying the navy's dozen or so seaworthy vessels against the five hundred ships of the British. Decatur wrote Hamilton that "the plan which appears to me to be the best calculated for our little Navy to annoy the Trade of Great Britain, in the greatest extent, & at the same time expose it the least, to the immense naval force of that Government, would be to send them out with as large a supply of provision as they can carry, distant from our coast, & singly, or not more than two frigates in company; without giving them any specific instructions as to place of cruising, but to rely on the enterprise of the officers."[10] The French had had great success with this method; Decatur believed that the American navy would as well.

The British could easily blockade the American coast. It was essential that the Americans get their forces to sea before the British fleet knew that war had been declared. By dispersing its few ships to Africa, South America, and even the coast of Europe, the United States would be able to attack British merchant ships in those places and force the Royal Navy to come out in search of American warships, rather than sitting off the American coast waiting to attack merchant ships. Decatur noted that the ports of northern New England—Boston, Portland, and Portsmouth—would be the most difficult for the British to blockade. Boston, Norfolk, and New London were the most easily defended. But with so few ships, the Americans should not risk all by keeping too many in a single port, where the British could destroy virtually the entire navy at a single stroke. Decatur recommended instead dispersing the American ships to force the British to come after them one by one.

Hamilton did not adopt this strategy. Whatever Decatur and Rodgers thought of their fighting prowess, Hamilton feared that having individual frigates cruise alone would expose them to attack. He ordered a joint cruise of the frigates *President, United States,* and *Congress* in pursuit of the British West Indian fleet, which protected the merchant ships carrying molasses and sugar to England.

Although the two nations were preparing for war, individual acts of civility still marked the exchanges between captains. Rodgers reported in early June that the British navy's schooner *Mackerel* had come into New York carrying official dispatches. Its commander had died on the trip, killed when a sailor fell from a mast and landed on him. The acting commander signaled Rodgers, off Staten Island, to ask for use of a boat to get his dispatches to shore since the *Mackerel*'s boat was too leaky to trust on such a mission. Rodgers complied, though he learned that the acting commander was not worried about a leaky boat but rather knew that his crewmen were ready to desert if given a chance.[11] The *Mackerel* quickly left port.

On June 18 Decatur passed the *Mackerel* and the ship *Tartarus* off Sandy Hook as he prepared to enter New York. He "was unfortunate," he said "in not knowing" that war had been declared, "else the harbour of New York would have been graced by their appearance as prizes."[12]

Decatur anchored the *United States* and the *Argus* off Sandy Hook to await Rodgers's squadron, while Rodgers waited in New York harbor for the official word, which came from Washington on June 20. Leaving Isaac Chauncey and his gunboats to defend New York and ordering David Porter to get the frigate *Essex* to sea as soon as possible, within "ten minutes after" learning that the United States had declared war on Britain, Rodgers had his frigate under weigh. "We are all in high spirits," he wrote of his squadron—the *President* along with the *United States, Congress, Hornet,* and *Argus*—"and hope to give our country a good account" of their cruise.[13]

Rodgers's account would not be as good as he had hoped. The weather was so foggy that the ships were never able to see more than four or five miles; for most of the cruise they could not even see one another. They chased every vessel they did see, and stopped all but four, but captured only seven British merchant ships and recaptured one American ship taken by the enemy. Three days out of New York the *President* spied the British frigate *Belvidera.* The squadron gave chase. *Congress* got close enough to fire a few shots, and the *President* fired two or three broadsides. But when Rodgers ordered the forward guns to fire, the cannon exploded. Three sailors were killed and sixteen wounded, including Rodgers, whose leg was fractured when he slammed into the *President*'s deck. The *Belvidera* escaped.[14]

In the fog Rodgers and his squadron tracked the British convoy by following its wake of coconut shells and orange peels. By mid-July the American squadron was off the English Channel. The ships turned south for Madeira, then west for the Azores, and then back toward Newfoundland. Rodgers was proud to have left New York within minutes of hearing that war had been declared. Now, after a month at sea, scurvy had ravaged his crew; he had been in too much of a hurry to leave New York to load more fresh fruits and vegetables. With a sick crew and one hundred British prisoners, Rodgers sailed back to the United States, reaching Boston on the last day of August.

He discovered the city in celebration. The day before, Isaac Hull had sailed in on the USS *Constitution* bringing great news. Hull had been cruising off Newfoundland on August 19 when he met the *Guerriere*, the British frigate that had long menaced the American coast. *Constitution* "in the space of thirty minutes" had shot away *Guerriere*'s masts, cutting the proud frigate apart until it was not worth saving. Hull reported that his crew had given "three cheers" as they went into battle, and "not a look of fear" was to be seen from the "smallest boy in the ship to the oldest seaman." *Guerriere*'s cannonballs had bounced harmlessly off *Constitution*'s hull, framed with tough Georgia live oak, earning it the nickname "Ironsides."[15]

The *Constitution*'s victory was exhilarating for Americans—particularly since Hull's uncle, General William Hull, had surrendered Detroit to a British and Indian force on August 16. Now Isaac Hull had redeemed the family and national honor, inflicting on the British navy an unexpected defeat.

Hull's victory in contrast with the squadron's lackluster results caused Secretary Hamilton to revise his policy. Instead of keeping the fleet together, the navy would send out three squadrons, one under Rodgers on the *President*, another under Decatur on the *United States*, and the third under Bainbridge on the *Constitution*. (Bainbridge had been appointed commander of the *Constitution* before Hull had sailed on his heroic cruise. Hull had rushed to sea before Bainbridge arrived to take command. When the crew returned victorious and learned that they would now be under the command of the "unlucky" Bainbridge, many tried to get off the ship.) While warning the captains not to engage in foolhardy actions motivated by patriotic zeal, the secretary authorized each to use his own best judgment in seeking out the enemy.[16]

Decatur and Rodgers sailed from Boston on October 8. Four days later, Decatur left the squadron to cruise with the *Argus* and the *United States*. He fell in with the American merchant ship *Mandarin*, which he found to be full of British goods. Perhaps its most valuable cargo was British certificates of protection for American merchant vessels—certificates that would protect American merchants doing business with the enemy. Decatur had the ship sent to Norfolk as a prize. For Decatur this was part of the war effort; the ship's American owners protested the seizure as a high-handed use of military power against civilians.

Decatur would eventually face the complicated issues raised by the seizure of the *Mandarin*. Now, however, he sailed for the coast of Africa, cruising after British merchant ships between the Azores and Cape Verde Islands.[17] The *United States* was at latitude 29° and longitude 29° at sunrise on October 25 when the lookout spied a ship twelve miles to the southeast. With the wind behind, the stranger was approaching the *United States*. On each ship the crew felt an air of expectation. Was the other vessel friend or foe? An enemy merchant ship to be taken as a prize, or an enemy warship to fight? Each captain set a course toward the other. Decatur steered the *United States* to the southwest, the stranger sailed toward him. When they had come within three miles, each ran up his flag. The *United States* was approaching a British warship.

Decatur tried to steer the *United States* across its bow so he would have the weather side. The enemy anticipated this and steered his own ship into the wind. Outmaneuvered, Decatur turned again. The two vessels now were a mile apart. Each tried to take the other's measure. Decatur ordered a broadside fired, but it fell short of its target. As the two ships sailed toward the southwest, on parallel courses, the stranger on the weather side, Decatur and his men recognized the ship. It was the *Macedonian*, the ship they had docked beside in Norfolk at the beginning of the year. He and its commander, Captain Carden, had discussed what would happen if they met as enemies. Now they would find out.

Some of the men on the *Macedonian* were sorry the enemy was not a French frigate. They had never fought an American frigate before and were not entirely sure what to expect. A delegation of American sailors asked Captain Carden to excuse them from fighting against their own countrymen. He told them if they failed to do their duty they would be shot, and he positioned midshipmen at the gun deck entryways to shoot any slackers. He then strode along the deck invoking Nelson's immortal cry, "England expects every man to do his duty!"

On the *United States*, nine-year-old Jack Creamer approached his captain. "And it please you, Captain," Jack said, "I wish my name might be put down on the roll."

"And what for, my lad?" Decatur asked.

"So that I can draw a share of the prize money, sir,"

Pleased at the boy's confidence, Decatur ordered it done.

It was just nine o'clock when the two ships drew close enough to open fire. Now the results of the constant drilling and training showed. The American gun crews worked so quickly and efficiently that they could fire off two broadsides for every one from the *Macedonian*. When Carden's crew saw flames blazing amidst the thick smoke on the *United States* they cheered, thinking that they had set fire to the enemy. Only when a barrage of shells hit them did they understand that what they had seen was the synchronized firing of the *United States*'s cannon.

When his mizzenmast fell, Carden thought the Americans had made a lucky shot. A gun captain on the *United States* called out, "Aye, Aye, we have made a brig of her." Decatur called back, "Well, my boys, take good sight at your object, and she will soon be a sloop." Seeing the *Macedonian*'s masts fall, Decatur shouted more instructions: "My good fellow, aim at the yellow streak; her spars and *rigging* are going fast enough; she must have a little more *hulling*."

Carden believed that his ship must have inflicted as much damage on the *United States* as his ship and his men were suffering. He ordered his foresail—the only sail still functioning—set to bring the *Macedonian* close enough to the enemy to board "& decide our cause Sword in hand."[18] This time Decatur anticipated his move, and the *United States* sailed ahead, still raking the *Macedonian* with devastating precision. With all its masts gone, the *Macedonian* rocked so violently that its guns touched the water as the ship rolled from side to side. As the *United States* crossed the *Macedonian*'s bow, the astonished British survivors waited for a final deadly barrage from the enemy; but the *United States* ceased fire and seemed to sail away.

The sudden silence "broken only by the stifled groans of the brave sufferers below" gave the men of the *Macedonian* a moment to review their situation.[19] Perhaps another British man-of-war or frigate had appeared to chase off the Americans. The survivors tried to clear the deck, throwing the dead overboard, as belowdecks the surgeons, "smeared with blood from head to foot," looking "more like butchers than doctors" worked on the living. Lieutenant David Hope urged Carden to keep fighting—let the ship sink rather than dishonor the British navy with surrender. He had advised Carden to close with the enemy sooner, not to wait for the enemy to bring the battle to the *Macedonian*. As Hope was urging further valor, the *United States* came astern of the "perfect wreck and unmanageable log" that had been the *Macedonian*. Decatur hailed, and Carden ordered the *Macedonian*'s flag lowered.[20]

Decatur sent Lieutenant John B. Nicholson to bring Captain Carden aboard the *United States.* Nicholson could not believe the damage his men had done to the British frigate. The gun deck looked like a slaughterhouse. The masts were shattered, and more than a hundred shots were lodged in the hull, allowing seven or eight feet of water to fill the hold. Thirty-six men were dead, another sixty-eight wounded. Only nine of the fifty-two officers and men on the quarterdeck had escaped death or serious injury. These were not strangers but men Nicholson remembered from Norfolk. When Nicholson asked the surgeon, "How do you do?" the doctor answered, "I have enough to do; you have made wretched work for us."[21]

If Nicholson could not believe the devastation on the *Macedonian*, Captain Carden could hardly believe that the *United States* had been in a battle. The ship was in perfect condition. Five men, out of a crew of four hundred, were dead, and seven wounded (two of whom subsequently died). Stepping onto the quarterdeck, Carden was greeted not by the sounds and smells of death but by the jovial Decatur wearing a straw hat and farmer's clothes.[22] When Carden offered his sword, Decatur refused it. "Sir, I cannot receive the sword of a man, who has so bravely defended his ship," said Decatur, "but I will receive your hand."[23] Another account has Decatur offering to accept the hat Carden had bet in Norfolk.

Decatur found that "half the satisfaction" he felt in his terrific victory was "destroyed in seeing the distress of poor Carden, who deserved success as much as we did."[24] He did his best to cheer Carden. He turned to the marines who had been stationed in the *United States*'s fighting tops, picking off British officers on the *Macedonian*'s quarterdeck. "You call yourselves Rifle Men," he chastised them, "& have allowed this very Tall & Erect Officer, on an open Quarter Deck to escape your Aim."[25] When Carden moaned that he was "an undone man," that he would never live down the shame of being "the first British naval officer that has struck his flag to an American," Decatur reassured him: "You are mistaken, sir; your Guerriere has been taken by us, and the flag of a frigate was struck before yours."[26] Carden had not heard of Hull's defeat of the *Guerriere*; it is likely that he took the news with mixed emotions.

Decatur sent Lieutenant Allen to take charge of the *Macedonian.* In the wake of its defeat and the death of so many officers, the surviving British sailors had raided the ship's rum supply. Drunkenness and despair did not make them well disposed toward the American conquerors. Allen quickly restored order, sending some men and surviving officers to the *United States* and leaving men from the *United States* in charge of the *Macedonian.* Within a few hours of trying to kill each other, the two crews were living and working in harmony on both ships. Decatur gave strict orders to respect the private property of the *Macedonian*'s officers and crew, and he helped the cash-strapped Carden by paying $800 for his wine collection and hiring from him the band of French musicians the British had captured from a French frigate. Decatur would bring these musicians to New York, where they would continue to perform for years to come.[27]

After restoring order, Allen surveyed the damage. The *Macedonian* had lost its mizzenmast, the main yard and topmast, and the foretop mast, and the hull was damaged. But Allen believed that the ship could be repaired. This news gave Decatur a daring idea. He remembered the jubilation in Boston after Hull had brought in the *Guerriere*'s flag, and he regretted that the last time he had captured a ship—the frigate *Philadelphia*—its flag had fallen into Tripoli harbor. He did not want to leave the *Macedonian* behind. Imagine the reaction if Decatur not only defeated a British ship but brought it home!

Allen put the crews to work, scrubbing down the blood-caked decks with hot water and vinegar, repairing the masts and jury-rigging them to carry sails, plugging the holes in the hull, and pumping water from the hold. Within a few days the *Macedonian* was seaworthy, and by some accounts sailed better than the *United States*. The *Macedonian* was a newer ship—just two years out of the shipyard. Its arrival would not just boost American morale; it could be refitted into a formidable fighting ship.

But it did not seem possible to sail both the *United States* and the jury-rigged *Macedonian* across two thousand miles of ocean and bring them into an American port without running into a British warship. Carden anticipated that he and his men would be liberated and Decatur taken prisoner before the two ships reached the Gulf Stream. After all, the British navy still controlled the Atlantic. Once again, though, Captain Carden was disappointed. "But NO!!" he wrote in his memoir. "We were nearly one Month on the American Coast, & never saw a British cruiser."[28]

As the ships made their way across the Atlantic, Decatur wrote to Secretary Hamilton. "I have the honour to inform you, that on the 25th inst., being in latitude 29 N. longitude 29 30' W. we fell in with, and after an action of an hour and a half, captured his Britannic Majesty's ship Macedonian, commanded by Captain John Carden, and mounting 49 carriage guns, (the odd gun shifting.)" He reported that the *Macedonian* was a two-year-old "frigate of the largest class," overhauled just four months earlier. Reputed to be "one of the best sailers in the British service," it had begun the battle with the weather advantage (being on the windward side of the *United States*). But the "enthusiasm of every officer, seaman, and marine on board this ship, . . . their steady conduct in battle, and precision of their fire, could not be surpassed." Decatur's "fullest expectations" had been met. "Our loss compared with that of the enemy, will appear small." Decatur would have continued on his cruise but "deemed it important that we should see our prize in," and so was returning to the United States.[29]

Although he did not want to discriminate among his officers and crew, he recommended that Lieutenant Allen be promoted to captain. Decatur recalled how Preble had sought his promotion back in 1804, and that Captain Hull had successfully won a promotion for Lieutenant Charles Morris after the victory over the *Guerriere*. (Morris and Decatur had jumped onto the *Philadelphia* together in 1804.) Now Decatur wanted this honor bestowed on Allen. William Allen had distinguished himself in battle, but he had also spent five years as Decatur's right hand. His "unremitting exertions in disciplining the crew" over those years had resulted in "the obvious superiority of our gunnery" which had won the battle. But despite Decatur's persistent lobbying, Secretary Hamilton did not want to create a precedent of promoting every victorious first lieutenant.[30]

Decatur was more successful with other rewards. He summoned Jack Creamer, the boy who had asked to be put on the muster roll just before the battle. "Well, Jack, we have taken her," Decatur told Creamer, "and your share of the prize, if we get her safe in, may be two hundred dollars." At the time an ordinary sailor earned ten dollars a month. Decatur asked Creamer what he would do with his share. Jack answered, "I will send half of it to my mother, Sir, and the other half shall pay for my schooling." Decatur was so impressed that he had the boy appointed a midshipman.[31]

By early December the two ships were off Montauk Point, and on the night of Thursday, December 3, when it was so dark they could not see each other, they parted ways. Allen brought the *Macedonian* into Newport, and Decatur the next morning sailed the *United States* into New London. He sent Lieutenant Archibald Hamilton (Secretary Hamilton's son) to Washington with his report and with the *Macedonian*'s flag, and wrote a short note to Susan in New York. In capturing "His Brittanic Majesty's Frigate *Macedonian*," Stephen told his wife, he had "gained a small sprig of laurel, which I hasten to lay at your feet." He did not mention the dead and wounded or the ship's size and armament, hoping to minimize in her mind the danger of battle. Instead, he recalled Tripoli. "I tried burning on a former occasion, which might do for a very young man," he wrote, "but now that I have a precious little wife, I wish to have something more substantial to offer in case she should become weary of love and glory."[32]

By this time Decatur had spent more than a month with Carden, and now

The burning of the *Philadelphia*, February 16, 1804, made Decatur a national hero.
(Courtesy: Beverly R. Robinson Collection, United States Naval Academy)

Susan Wheeler fell in love with Stephen Decatur when she saw this miniature by
Italian artist Olivio Sozzi.

(Courtesy: United States Naval Academy)

Commodore Preble commissioned artist Michael Corne to record on canvas the battle of Tripoli, August 3, 1804.

(Courtesy: Maine Historical Society)

Dennis Malone Carter's painting of Decatur boarding the Tripolitan gunboat to find the man who had killed his brother.

(Courtesy: Naval Historical Foundation)

This popular 1857 engraving shows Decatur wrestling with the Tripolitan captain who had killed his brother James and includes Daniel Frazier (with "R. James" tattooed on his left arm) preparing to save Decatur from a surprise attack.

(Author's Collection)

Susan Wheeler Decatur, by Gilbert Stuart.

Stephen Decatur, by Gilbert Stuart.
(Courtesy: Stephen Decatur House, National
Trust for Historic Preservation)

The *United States* defeats the *Macedonian* in Thomas Birch's 1813 depiction.
(Courtesy: Museum of Fine Arts, Boston)

Thomas Sully's portrait of the heroic Decatur has hung in New York City Hall since 1816. Sully shows Decatur as a bold leader striding through the columns of the Pantheon. He remembered that Decatur was a very impatient sitter.

(Courtesy: Art Commission of the City of New York)

Painted by T. Sully – Eng. by A.H.Durand from a Copy by James Rozzing.

STEPHEN DECATUR

Stephen Decatur

Nineteenth-century engraving after the Sully portrait. Note Decatur's signature in facsimile.

(Author's Collection)

Nineteenth-century engraving after the Stuart portrait.
(Author's Collection)

The home of Stephen and Susan Decatur in an 1822 watercolor.
(Courtesy: Stephen Decatur House, National Trust for Historic Preservation)

was even more moved by his distress. Stephen assured Susan that he was doing "all I can to console him." As for himself, "Do not be anxious about me, my beloved. I shall soon press you to my heart." And he added a couplet:

> Love turns aside the balls which round me fly
> Lest precious tears should drop from Susan's eye.[33]

CHAPTER *13*

"The trophies won by the Athenians"

W
HILE DECATUR was laying his laurels at Susan's feet, Lieutenant Archibald Hamilton continued on to Washington. Hamilton left New London on Friday, December 4, and reached the capital on Tuesday, December 8.

His timing could not have been better. That night at Tomlinson's Hotel on Capitol Hill, all of Washington society would gather to honor the nation's naval heroes.[1] Isaac Hull, Charles Stewart, and Charles Morris were all in town, as was Jacob Jones, captain of the *Wasp*, which had defeated the *Frolic*. Stewart had hosted a celebration on board the *Constellation*, moored in the Potomac. President and Mrs. Madison had been among the five hundred dignitaries rowed out to dance and dine on the *Constellation*'s deck.

As Washingtonians prepared for the ball at Tomlinson's Hotel, a handbill circulated through town with the stunning news that Decatur had captured the frigate *Macedonian*. Immediately, Washington's homes were illuminated in celebration, and as the architect Benjamin Latrobe and his wife Mary left for Tomlinson's, they saw "Pennsylvania Ave. and the scattered houses on the hills" lit with "a most singular and splendid dash of scattered fires."

The revelers arrived in high spirits, but they were soon brought to earth. None of the officials present—including the secretary of the navy—could confirm the rumor about Decatur and the *Macedonian*. "People were ashamed to have wasted their candles on a false report." But with the captured flags of the *Guerriere* and the *Wasp* hanging on the walls, and Hull, Morris, and Stewart with them, the revelers—who included Dolley Madison, Elizabeth Monroe, Hannah Gallatin, and Paul and Mary Hamilton and their daughters—celebrated anyway. They would consider their illuminations to be in honor of capturing the *Guerriere*. The dancing began with the usual "crowding . . . upon the toes and trains of those that did not dance," and went on for several happy hours. Shortly after nine a loud "huzza" brought the music to a sudden stop. All eyes turned to the door, where a tall, fatigued lieutenant stood, carrying in his arms a British flag.

Mary Hamilton nearly fainted. She had not seen her son Archibald in three years—and only a year before he had narrowly escaped death in a horrific fire in a Richmond theater. All day, as she had heard rumors of a battle between the *United States* and the *Macedonian*, she had been frantic with worry. Even in victory men died. Now suddenly here he was, alive. The false, almost forced gaiety gave way to "profound silence" as Hull, Stewart, and Morris marched to the door. The three captains raised the lieutenant onto their shoulders and carried him across the room to his mother. He "sprang into her arms," and his sisters threw their arms around him as the band struck up "Yankee Doodle," the song with which the British had once mocked the colonial Americans, and then "Hail, Columbia."

Leaving Mary Hamilton and her children, Hull, Morris, Stewart, and Secretary Hamilton unfurled the *Macedonian*'s flag and raised it over their heads like a canopy as they paraded around the crowded ballroom. The crowd cheered in delirium as the four men made their way to the front of the room, where they spread the flag at Dolley Madison's feet. Benjamin Latrobe thought that this last gesture "degraded the whole scene," but still could think of nothing more "affecting and at the same time dramatic" as this "unexpected and unprepared" celebration, which "went off as long rehearsed."

Mary Latrobe worried that this celebration, like those for the *Guerriere* victory, might be premature. The English navy still was much stronger than the American, and despite these victories, she thought, "there are ten chances to one that we are beaten." And how could she look with any pleasure at the captured flags, "the taking of which had made so many orphans and widows." As the crowd pressed to touch the *Macedonian*'s flag, she blurted out, "Good heavens! I would not touch that color for a thousand dollars." One man in earshot quickly walked away. Another asked, "Is it possible, Mrs. Latrobe?" She turned to see who had caught her uttering such unpatriotic sentiments. She recognized Senator William Hunter, a Rhode Island Federalist, and so knew she was safe in her apostasy.

Secretary Hamilton took up the flag from the floor for safekeeping, and Congressman Samuel Mitchill, a physician and man of letters from New York, carried it across the room to give the ladies there a closer look. Unlike Mrs. Latrobe, Dr. Mitchill found the show exhilarating. "After I got home," he wrote his wife, "I believe I was in the very condition of Themistocles after viewing the trophies won by the Athenians from the Persians at the battle of Marathon—*I could get no sleep.*"

Lieutenant Hamilton's dramatic arrival in Washington reminded all of the navy's accomplishments and made Decatur a hero once again. But just as Mrs. Latrobe cringed at some aspects of the spectacle, not all celebrated Decatur's valor. William Bainbridge was at sea on the *Constitution*, about to encounter the British frigate *Java*, as Decatur was becoming the toast of the nation. Bainbridge thought that bringing the *Macedonian* across the ocean was too risky an operation in proportion to the momentary glory it had won. "The applause of my countrymen has for me greater charms than all the gold that glitters," Bainbridge wrote. By putting some of his men aboard the prize, Decatur would weaken the conquering ship, making it susceptible to capture. A captain had an "indispensable duty" to destroy a captured ship "on account of the gauntlet he would have to run with both the prize and his own ship," and the likelihood of losing both. Although Decatur had succeeded brilliantly, Bainbridge calculated that the loss would have been insurmountable had he failed.[2]

But Decatur had not failed. Now with the two ships safely in American ports, he eyed a greater opportunity to display his trophy. He would bring both of his ships to New York City. What a spectacle it would be to dock a captured British frigate in New York. The city, home now to Susan and to many of his sailors, would appreciate the honor. New York's Park Theatre was already displaying transparencies of the victory over the *Macedonian*. A week later New York's Common Council commissioned a portrait of Decatur for City Hall and voted Decatur "Freedom of the City."[3]

The council also decreed that a "national salute" would be fired when the *United States* and the *Macedonian* reached New York: every vessel in the harbor would hoist its colors, and every church in New York would ring its bells for an hour. Others prepared their own celebrations. Some of New York's clergy objected when the Park Theatre announced special shows on Christmas night, "between the play and a farce, a patriotic sketch in one act, called, 'America, Commerce, and Freedom: or More Laurels for Gallant Tars.'" The clergy applauded the American victory but did not think that theatrical performances were appropriate on Christmas.[4]

While New York prepared to welcome him, Decatur prepared his ships to sail to the city. The *Macedonian* prisoners went ashore at New London to await their exchange (except for the boy Samuel Leech aboard the *Macedonian*; American sailors helped him hide on the ship). Decatur kept the French band aboard the *United States*. The Americans took full command of both vessels. His ships ready, Decatur sailed for the western end of Long Island Sound, all along the way being saluted by sloops and fishing vessels. "Most of them honored us with three cheers, as they passed," Leech recalled. "Of course, the prize crew could do no less than cheer again, so that we passed our time amidst continuous cheering."[5]

While the frigates waited just east of Throg's Neck for the right wind to bring them through the treacherous passages into the East River, visitors streamed out of Manhattan and Brooklyn to see the captured *Macedonian*. Leech "found a profitable business in conducting them about the ship, describing the action, and pointing out the places where particular individuals fell." But he also knew that if he stayed on the ship, he would be found out and sent back to England. The boy struck up a friendship with a black youth who had his own profitable enterprise rowing visitors to the ship, and made his escape from the *Macedonian*. He was not soon missed, as streams of visitors continued to come aboard.[6] The novelist Washington Irving reported that one "old gentleman" of threescore years was so "highly tickled" and "power-fully excited" by the victory that he ventured out to "where the frigates lay wind bound; and he brought a way a piece of the Macedonian, which he seemed to treasure up with as much devotion as a pious Catholic does a piece of the True Cross."[7]

Susan was already in the city, staying at Mrs. Bradish's boardinghouse on the corner of Rector and Greenwich streets. Decatur slipped into the city ahead of his ship, and on December 29 he and Isaac Hull were guests of honor at the City Assembly Room. Washington Irving, also staying at Mrs. Bradish's, reported that it was "the most splendid entertainment of the kind I have ever witnessed."[8] The room had been transformed into a maritime palace: the columns were the masts of ships, and the *Macedonian*'s colors hung from the walls. A thirty-square-foot area of greensward lay in the middle of the room; in the center was a pool of real water, and in it floated a minia-ture of the frigate *United States*.

Decatur sat at the right of Mayor De Witt Clinton; Isaac Hull sat at the mayor's left. They faced on the opposite wall a topsail, and behind them rose a mainsail thirty feet wide and sixteen high emblazoned with an American eagle. In its beak the eagle held a scroll proclaiming, "Our children are the Property of Our Country!"[9] Decatur's father had shouted those immortal words six years earlier when the young captain returned from Tripoli; they now hung over his head at a banquet in his honor in New York. As supper ended, the rounds of toasts and songs began. The first toast was to "Our Country! May it ever be distinguished by wisdom in council and energy in action!" Then the band struck up "Hail, Columbia." "The President's March" and "Governor Tompkins' March" followed the toasts to President Madison and the governor. After the toast to the navy—"With such an auspicious dawn, what may we not hope will be its meridian splendor!"—the assembled men gave three rousing cheers, and "as if by magic" the mainsail behind Clinton, Decatur, and Hull suddenly furled, revealing "a transparent painting of its whole extent" depicting the *Constitution*'s battle with the *Guerriere*, the *Wasp* capturing the *Frolic*, and the *United States* taking the *Macedonian*. "The company were electrified and instinctively arose and gave six cheers."[10]

At a toast to "American Gallantry," the topsail on the opposite wall furled to reveal another illuminated transparency—this one an American eagle with three medallions, of Hull and the *Constitution*, Jacob Jones and the *Wasp*, and

Decatur and the *United States*. The band struck up "Yankee Doodle" and the men gave nine cheers. Then the glee club sang "Decatur, Hull and Jones are here," a song specially written for the night (Jones had been invited but did not attend). After this the guests of honor offered their own toasts. Hull gave a toast to Isaac Chauncey, who had been sent to the Great Lakes to build ships. Then it was Decatur's turn. He raised his glass to "the Citizens of New York," and as all rose he exclaimed, "May their great liberality stimulate us to acts more proportioned to their approbation."[11]

So far only the men of New York had publicly celebrated the triumphant year. But on New Year's Eve the City Hotel decorated its supper room to look like the cabin of a battleship, and three hundred women, including Susan Decatur, sat down to supper at eleven. The men—including Decatur, Hull, and their lieutenants—waited outside while the ladies dined and then returned to dance into the small hours of the New Year.

Decatur's "New Year's gift" to New York City arrived later that day: the *Macedonian* with the "star-spangled banner proudly waving over the British cross," sailed down the East River to anchor between Governor's Island and the North Battery. Every church bell in New York answered the *Macedonian*'s New Year's salute to the city. Many New Yorkers had already made their pilgrimage to see the ship at Throg's Neck; thousands more now clamored to view the prize. One of the visitors was Samuel Leech, who slipped aboard to pick up the belongings he had left behind. He tried to avoid being noticed, but Lieutenant John Nicholson recognized him. Leech was terrified. But Nicholson smiled. The prisoner's cartel, Nicholson told him with mock sorrow, had already sailed for England. Leech now would be an American.[12]

The *Macedonian*'s conversion into an American ship was somewhat delayed. So many visitors continued to stream aboard that Decatur finally closed the ship to public tours and ordered it to the Brooklyn Navy Yard. But even with the ship under repair, the celebrations continued. A steam ferry brought Lieutenant Allen and the prize crew—many of them New Yorkers—from Brooklyn to the Battery, where "they received the welcome of thousands of spectators."[13] The *Macedonian*'s captured French band led them up Pearl Street to Wall Street, then along Broadway to City Hall. After Mayor Clinton welcomed the sailors home, the parade marched on to the City Hotel, where another military band—this one featuring George Washington's old trumpeter—played as the sailors and as many celebrants as could fit crowded in. The boatswain piped for silence, and Alderman Cornelius Vanderbilt rose in front of the mainsail emblazoned with the eagle and the legend "Our Children are the Property of Our Country!" He gave the official greeting: "Brave American Tars, the corporation of the city of New York have ordered you this entertainment. It is given as a tribute to your valor displayed in the capture of the British Frigate Macedonian." As he finished, the sail furled to reveal the illuminated transparency of the three naval triumphs—the *United States*, the *Constitution*, and the *Wasp*. The repeated "huzzas" and the whistle of the boatswain "made an impression never to be forgotten."[14] After the dinner the sailors enjoyed "more than a usual amount of drinking, laughing, and talking" until nearly every sailor was drunk.[15]

Suddenly the boatswain whistled for silence. The gunner stood and with the ship's speaking trumpet announced that when Decatur and Allen arrived, the company would give them nine cheers. The men gave more than that. As Decatur and Allen entered the room, their crew rose, "every man standing on tiptoe and flourishing his glazed hat over his head," cheering their heroic leaders. Allen and Decatur stood beneath the transparency, where Decatur offered a simple toast: "Free trade and no impressments!" He reminded the sailors that the war was being fought to protect them.[16] After Allen graciously toasted the other victorious captains, Hull and Jones, the men gave their nine rousing cheers for Decatur and Allen.

After this the sailors left the hotel in another procession, this one to a special six o'clock performance at the Park Row Theater. Again crowds lined the streets to cheer the heroes. The theater had reserved the entire orchestra section for the three hundred sailors who filed in as the band played "Yankee Doodle." The stage was already decorated with a transparency of their victory. The show featured dancers and an Irish comedian who sang a song specially written for the occasion:

> No more of your blathering nonsense
> 'Bout Nelsons of old Johnny Bull;
> I'll sing you a song, by my consience,
> 'Bout Jones, and Decatur, and Hull.

As the sailors watched the special performance, highlighted by "the engagement between the United States and the Macedonian, which had been dramatized, and re-enacted," their "demonstrations of pleasure were unbounded, and their huzzas almost endless." The boatswain stunned the house by playing his whistle "as skillfully as loud." In the third box from the stage sat Decatur and Allen, the captain "in full uniform, his pleasant face flushed with the excitement of the occasion."[17]

As the nation celebrated, Decatur reflected on his achievement. Less than a year earlier, he and Carden had speculated about what would happen if the two met in battle. The British captain had told Decatur, "I should be obliged to capture you." Decatur had predicted his own victory—he expected to win.

But what now struck him even more was a "remarkable fact": "that I brought this prize—the Macedonian—two thousand miles over sea, and never met a British vessel." The British supposedly controlled the seas, but Decatur with two ships had eluded them. What would he have done had he met a British frigate? a visitor later asked. "I'll tell you what I would have done," Decatur answered. "I would have taken my crew out of the United States, put them on board the Macedonian, and would have whipped and captured the enemy with one of their own frigates. That's what I would have done."[18]

After the performance, Decatur gave the men a night's liberty. Most of them took a whole week. Each returning sailor made sure to call at Mrs. Bradish's boardinghouse before returning to the *Macedonian*. There they would tell Susan Decatur "a piteous tale" and beg her to "intercede for them with their captain." Susan and Stephen were both inclined to be generous, and "with almost constant success" she would persuade her husband not to punish the tardy celebrants. The sailors would go away from the boarding-house praising Susan, "the sailor's friend." "Good luck to her," they would say, "she has a soul to be saved."[19]

Decatur's men had done something no American crew had ever done before: they had captured a British frigate and brought it safely to an American port. The capture had made the men heroes. It had also made some of them wealthy. The *Macedonian* was worth $300,000. Under the prize law passed during the French war, if the *United States* were weaker than the *Macedonian*, the *United States*'s crew was entitled to all the prize money. If the *Macedonian* were weaker, then the crew of the *United States* would receive half the *Macedonian*'s value, while the rest went into a sailors' pension fund. Decatur argued that the *United States* was the weaker vessel, though in fact it was the stronger. But the government felt generous to the captain and crew who had brought the *Macedonian* into port.

Under the law, the captain received 15 percent of the ship's value—or, if the government was taking half, 15 percent of half its value. The ship's lieu-tenants, its sailing master, and the captain of its marine squadron divided 10 percent of the prize money; another 10 percent was divided by the chaplain, the marine lieutenants, the surgeon, carpenter, boatswain, and gunner. The midshipmen, surgeon's mate, clerk, schoolmaster, boatswain's, surgeon's, carpenter's, and gunner's mates, sailmaker, and cooper all divided 17.5 per-cent. The noncommissioned officers among the marines divided up 12.5 percent, and the ship's crew—seamen, boys, and marines—divided 35 per-cent of the prize money.[20] No captain in the War of 1812 would earn more prize money than Stephen Decatur. His salary as a captain was $1,200 a year; he earned $30,000 in prize money.[21] Decatur had his lawyer, Littleton Tazewell, collect the money in Washington and bring it to New York, for he wanted "the crew to dispose of it to their liking before we leave port."[22]

The men apparently did. Samuel Leech noted that all New York welcomed the *United States*'s crew, not only because of their patriotic valor but because of the prize money all the tavern keepers, restaurateurs, and theater managers knew the men would be receiving. "That was the key that unlocked coffers; the warmth that melted the heart; the spirit that clothed the face with smiles. But for that—THE PRIZE MONEY—poor Jack's credit and favor would, as usual, have been below par."[23]

Receiving the money—and the gratitude of the republic—made these winter months a happy time for Stephen and Susan. In Mrs. Bradish's boardinghouse they came to know Washington Irving, who had been in the Mediterranean during the Tripolitan war but had not met Lieutenant Decatur. A lifelong Federalist, Irving had opposed the war. But he was also a longtime friend of John Nicholson, and he became a close friend of the Decaturs. Decatur and the other naval heroes were not at all what Irving had expected. "No vain-glorious boastings, no puerile gasconades, are ever heard from their lips; of their enemy they always speak with courtesy and respect; of their own exploits, with unaffected modesty and frankness." When Irving's friend James Kirke Paulding's *Analectic Magazine* began a series of biographical sketches of naval officers, Irving wrote about his friend Stephen Decatur. Irving's biography was published along with an engraving made from Gilbert Stuart's portrait of the young captain. The portrait and biography show Decatur "in the very prime of life, pleasing in his person," his face "intelligent and interesting," with "brilliant lustre, spirit, enterprise, and urbanity" all "happily blended." His "manly and unassuming" manners, so "gentle and engaging," combined "the polish of the gentleman with the frank simplicity of the sailor." Irving admired the way these heroes made so little of their accomplishments. In their hands, "without apprehension or reserve," the nation could entrust its "interests and honour." To this "handful of worthies" lay the task of establishing the U.S. Navy's reputation. These brave men did not dwell on the deeds of the past. "Their whole souls seem stretched towards the future."[24]

CHAPTER 14

"A caged eagle"

URING THESE happy weeks in New York, Decatur also came to know Robert Fulton. Fulton took advantage of the fact that John Rodgers was at sea, and Isaac Chauncey on the Great Lakes, to present his ideas again to the navy, this time in the person of Stephen Decatur.

Rodgers had regarded Fulton as a madman; Decatur thought he was a genius. Fulton explained why his invention had failed in the 1810 trials and what he had done to correct its defects. Chauncey and James Lawrence had hung underwater netting beneath the *Argus's* hull, which easily deflected Fulton's torpedoes. Fulton saw that without an efficient way to cut through underwater netting, his explosives would be useless. He had invented an underwater cable cutter, though it proved ineffective. Cutting the nets and cables required sharp blades propelled somehow through the water, and this had led Fulton to a new idea: an underwater cannon.

Fulton's original idea was to attach the torpedo to a mooring line or a harpoon and let the victim ram into it. But now he realized that if he could find a way to shoot the torpedo through the water, it could strike the enemy between two and ten feet below the waterline. Decatur was intrigued. Armed with a "submarine gun," a small vessel—even one of Jefferson's gunboats—could sink a battleship. If Fulton could make this weapon work, Decatur predicted that it would "anihilate the present System, by rendering Small vessels equal to large ones, for both must Sink if attacked in a like manner."[1] The submarine gun would change the nature of naval warfare. But their prediction "that if this invention proves as perfect as they have reason to believe, it will lead to the destruction of military navies, and give liberty to the seas" was too optimistic.[2]

Decatur and Fulton entered into an agreement to develop this submarine gun. Fulton would get a patent and work on developing a cannon that could send a shot "from ten to twenty feet through water" and break through three feet of oak timber.[3] While he worked out the technical problems, Decatur would work toward getting the weapon into use. He would secure its deployment by the U.S. Navy, or, if the United States happened to be at peace by the time Fulton perfected the weapon, Decatur would introduce the gun "into practical use among the maritime nations of Europe."[4] The two men would split the profits.

Decatur began by writing an enthusiastic report, which Fulton sent to former president Jefferson. Jefferson had seen the possibilities in Fulton's torpedoes; Fulton hoped that Jefferson could use his influence on President Madison and on Congress to get the navy to adopt his new submarine gun. Decatur told the former president that "he perfectly agree[d] with Mr. Fulton" about the potential of the new weapon. What a change this was for Fulton. Three years earlier Rodgers had dismissed him as a lunatic. Now he was optimistic that with Decatur's backing and Jefferson's support, Congress would appropriate $100,000 to develop his submarine gun, for the endorsement of "so experienced an officer must carry weight with those who are not familiar with nautical affairs."[5]

Developing this exciting new weapon would take time. Meanwhile, the British fleet had the entire American coast effectively blockaded. Decatur would not wait for the submarine gun, but proposed a conventional strategy to attack the enemy and liberate the coast. He proposed to the new secretary of the navy, William Jones, a cruise of the *United States* and the *Argus* "to the Eastward of Bermuda" to strike at the force blockading Charleston, South Carolina. Once this "subordinate enterprise" was accomplished, the two ships would turn on their primary target, Britain's merchant fleet. He and William Henry Allen, now in command of the *Argus*, would sail to the far eastern edge of the Grand Bank. From there they would cruise along the forty-second parallel toward the coast of Ireland, where "I shall be in the track of all the British Commerce returning from beyond the Cape of Good Hope from the Brazils & the West Indies."[6]

Decatur anticipated that he and Allen could evade the British fleet on their way out; but getting back would be a problem. They would sail with three or four months' provisions to avoid the necessity of returning too soon. But Decatur proposed a new system of provisioning vessels once initial supplies were exhausted. The United States, through an agreeable third party, should charter a neutral vessel that could sail through the British blockade to the Cape Verde Islands. There on St. Iago this neutral merchant would set up a shop where his goods would be "ostensibly for sale but at prices to prevent purchases" by any except Americans.[7] Decatur had learned during the Tripolitan war the value of having neutral bases from which to conduct his operations. From this base in the Cape Verde Islands, Decatur could not only be resupplied, but also attack British merchant ships bound to and from the Mediterranean, damaging Britain's supply lines to its forces in Spain.

As Decatur was preparing his squadron—the *United States*, the *Macedonian* commanded by Jacob Jones, and the sloop *Hornet* under Lieutenant James Biddle—to sail from New York, the British fleet appeared in full force. Allen aboard the *Argus* had already slipped out, carrying envoy William Crawford to Europe. But now Decatur and his squadron were trapped. Two British line-of-battle ships and two frigates blockaded New York.

Decatur sailed back into New York harbor. He knew that the British fleet would wait for him, aware that he had no other way out. Or did he? He had brought the *United States* and the *Macedonian* through Hell's Gate from Long Island Sound into the East River. Why not bring them back the same way and escape into the Atlantic off Montauk? No ship of this size had ever before navigated successfully through this narrow passage; but the mere fact that no one had done something before would not stop Decatur. On the night of May 24, the three ships made their way through Hell's Gate, anchoring off Riker's Island the next day. For the next four days they made a difficult passage down Long Island Sound, sailing always into the wind—lightning struck the *United States*'s mainmast, briefly grounding the ship—but by May 29 they reached Montauk Point.[8]

As his squadron prepared on the last evening in May to slip out to sea, Decatur spied the battleship *Ramillies* off Montauk Point. The next morning he prepared his two frigates and the *Hornet* to pursue. As the *United States* was nearly within range of the enemy three more British ships hove into view from around the point—the frigates *Orpheus* and *Acasta* and the line-of-battle ship *Valiant*. Sir Thomas Hardy deployed his ships to prevent Decatur from slipping back into Long Island Sound. Decatur had the squadron tack back into the sound as he and the *United States* covered the retreat, exchanging fire with the *Acasta*. His three ships made it safely. More than a year would pass before Decatur again reached the open sea.[9]

His squadron would spend the rest of the war in New London. The British anchored just off the entrance to the Thames River and stayed there for twenty months. Decatur had recommended New London before the war as an easily defended base for an American squadron. Unlike the rest of Connecticut, which was solidly Federalist and antiwar, New London was evenly divided between Federalists and Republicans. Now Decatur began to have second thoughts, and would continue to have throughout the next year. Not only could the British easily blockade the Thames, but also the people of New London treated the presence of Decatur's fleet as an enemy occupation.

When Decatur had brought his victorious *United States* and the British prisoners from the *Macedonian* to New London the previous December, the town had reacted with patriotic enthusiasm; but after Decatur left, the mood changed. Then the town's citizens had showered their attention on Captain Carden as he awaited his parole to England, giving the defeated British officer so many "Invitations to the Tables of the Inhabitants of the first order" that he and his officers found it a "great inconveniance" to "pay constant & equal attention" to all. The people of New London left Carden with "no vacant hour" during his months of captivity, with their sleigh rides by day and parties by night.[10]

No state had been more opposed to the Jefferson administration than Connecticut; first the embargo and now the war made many of the state's leading citizens, and many of their followers, bitterly opposed to the Republicans and all their works. Decatur sailed into New London not as a victorious American captain seeking to protect the town from the British, but as an intruding representative of the bungling Madison administration. During his stay in New London, he and the people of the town would grow "heartily tired of each other."[11] Decatur found the locals reluctant to support his fleet. While they remained hostile to him, there was "a constant communication kept up with the enemy," who wanted to recapture the *Macedonian*.[12]

Decatur had learned in Tripoli that a blockading force needs a neutral base to resupply. The British fleet blockading New London found plenty of fresh water on Long Island and even on the Connecticut shore. The British consular agent in New London, a man named Stewart, supervised the loading of cargoes onto neutral vessels bound for the West Indies or American ports— cargoes that went instead to the British fleet. Decatur had Stewart ordered out of New London. When the consul refused to leave, the marshal "was compelled to use force" to move him to Tolland. There the consul declined to accept parole, which would have forbidden him to return to New London. Instead he was put in jail; but by October he was back in New London. "How he has been discharged, I am as yet uninformed," Decatur wrote. But the marshal claimed to have no legal power to detain a British consular agent, so Stewart remained in town. While the citizens showed hostility to Decatur and the American sailors, their homes and shops were open to British men and officers, who were coming ashore dressed as civilians, buying supplies, exchanging gossip—and studying the positions of the American ships.[13]

Decatur had been in New London barely a week when he received an urgent message from across Long Island Sound. Four men had deserted from the British fleet; one, a black man from the *Valiant*, and reported that the British planned to retake the *Macedonian* and capture the *United States*. This intelligence was confirmed by a report from Easthampton, Long Island, where a lieutenant from the *Acasta* had told a Mr. Parsons in Montauk that the British would take the American frigates when the "Orpheus & Remilies arrived from New York which they were momentarily expecting."[14] Decatur knew that the British were planning to invade New London, if only to take the American ships. He remembered the desperate days after the *Chesapeake* disaster when the citizens of Norfolk had urged him to mount a defense against a British invasion that never came. Now the citizens of New London had a British fleet within sight of their town and threatening invasion, but their reaction was one of indifference. If the British took Decatur's fleet, it would spare the citizens of New London this unwelcome intrusion.

Decatur urged Brigadier General Jorah Isham of the Connecticut militia to fortify the relics of Revolutionary era forts above New London. Isham replied that he had been studying the militia laws, and "in examining the law he found, that there is no obligation on the part of his men, to obey" commands from a naval officer. Regarding Isham as "totally unfit for his command," Decatur finally persuaded him to restore Fort Griswold. But despite having won over the militia, Decatur could not find anyone in New London to supply lumber. Their town was threatened, but "there is no person here, who feels authorized to incur this expense, which could not exceed three or four hundred dollars," Decatur reported in disgust.[15] "I thank God, that our safety does not mainly depend upon them," he wrote of the militia. To protect his squadron, he moved the ships five miles up the river, and there had his own men build a fortification on Dragon Hill overlooking the ships. They called it "Fort Decatur."[16]

When Decatur moved upriver, he noted that almost immediately General Isham and the British fleet began exchanging flags of truce. He knew that the British would use these opportunities to observe New London's defenses, and he suspected that Isham would point out anything the British missed. When he asked Isham the meaning of all these visits from the British fleet, the militia commander rebuked Decatur, saying that he did not need to consult with Decatur before communicating with the British fleet. In the midst of this dispute General Henry Burbeck of the U.S. Army arrived, but Isham insisted that he, as head of the state militia, would remain in command. Burbeck wrote to Washington for clarification. When word came back that Burbeck was to be in charge, Isham for once acted "with an alacrity and promptitude quite unexampled in his military performances, and with a zeal never manifested when it might have been serviceable." He ordered his militia force to disband, "forbidding them to assemble or turn out in case of an alarm without orders from him," which in turn would come from the governor, "who resides near a hundred miles from this."[17] In other words, Isham would leave New London undefended.

Conventional forces could not have averted an invasion. But unconventional tactics kept the British from taking Decatur's ships. When the master's mate on the *Ramillies* spied a schooner heading for New London on June 25, he set out after it in a boat. The schooner's crew spotted him and turned toward shore, abandoning their vessel on the beach. Under fire from the Americans, the British mate and his men secured the abandoned schooner, the *Eagle*, out of New York, which was full of fresh vegetables and naval supplies. Normally a prize taken by men from the *Ramillies* would have been unloaded next to the frigate; but the wind and tide made that impossible, so the *Eagle* was tied up next to a British sloop to unload. As the men furled the *Eagle*'s sails, the schooner "blew up with a most tremendous explosion." The *Eagle* was an American booby trap, packed with explosives set to go off when the British tried to unload the cargo. Ten sailors and a British lieutenant died in the blast, "a sacrifice to this new mode of Warfare," wrote Captain Hardy, who thought it "most providential" that the *Eagle* had not been brought alongside the *Ramillies*, for it might have destroyed the frigate. [18]

Although Decatur disavowed any knowledge of the *Eagle*, Admiral Sir John Warren of the Royal Navy knew that Decatur had been cooperating with Fulton on his explosives experiments, and he may also have recalled the Americans' use of exploding vessels in Tripoli. After the *Eagle* incident Warren forbade any prizes or boats to be brought alongside one of His Majesty's ships or vessels, as the "Enemy are disposed to make use of every unfair and Cowardly mode of Warfare, such as Torpedoes." [19]

Even though he may not have sanctioned the trap, Decatur did use other new methods of warfare. Just five days after the *Eagle* explosion, a Captain Holsey or Halsey set out from New London in a submarine boat, built by a Norwich boatbuilder. The one-man underwater craft had torpedoes attached on harpoons; Halsey hoped to get close enough to a British ship to attach one of the explosives to its hull. But within minutes of his departure, gunfire from the Connecticut shore signaled the British fleet, which returned the signals, and Halsey was never seen again. When Fulton heard of the experimental craft, he expressed doubt that the vessel could have withstood the water pressure at the depth Halsey had hoped to reach. Decatur, however, believed that Halsey had been betrayed by Connecticut traitors. [20]

Captain Hardy had his own worries about Decatur's network of spies. In September he apprehended a Long Island man named Penney who had come aboard the *Ramillies* under the pretext of "selling clams, &c." It turned out that Penney had piloted American boats to Gardiner's Island, where Decatur had sent a small force either to capture British provisioning parties or to kidnap Sir Thomas Hardy himself. Hardy claimed that Penney was a spy; Decatur denied that the man had been employed as anything other than a pilot. [21]

Although the mines and submarines had limited success in destroying British ships, they did succeed in getting the British to stay clear of the coast.

Hardy took the precaution of having cables sweep his hulls every two hours to check for mines, and he kept his ships away from the shore. If Hardy believed (with some accuracy, Decatur thought) that many in Connecticut would welcome a British landing, the threats from torpedoes and submarines nevertheless prevented him from attempting it. One of Decatur's officers entertained a visitor from Pennsylvania by describing "in a ludicrous manner" the enemy's perpetual state of alarm. The British were under constant "apprehension of the torpedoes floating around their vessels, which they feared, every night, would attach to their ships' bottoms and blow them up." The British had to keep a lookout around the dock, "and had boats sailing round their ships after it was dark." With their threat completely imaginary, the visitor from Philadelphia, Alderman John Binns wrote, "the torpedoes proved to be a very innocent and harmless warlike instrument."[22]

Once the likelihood of invasion abated, Decatur brought his squadron down closer to New London to prepare for an escape. On the night of December 12 the wind and tide were right. The three ships slipped down to the mouth of the Thames. As they began to enter Long Island Sound, Decatur saw blue lights shine from either side of the river—signals to the British fleet. He returned angrily to New London. Secretary of the Navy Jones was "truly astonished" to hear of this betrayal "in the bosom of our own happy country," for he had believed that "every American heart vibrated in unison with the gallant Squadron."[23]

The people of New London just as indignantly denied Decatur's charge. The blue lights were from fishing boats, or were reflections of the setting sun, or were the product of Decatur's own "warped and excited imagination." Years later, New Londoner Samuel Griswold Goodrich speculated that the lights might have been signals from British sailors on shore, since men and officers from the British fleet were constant visitors, welcomed in the homes and shops of people openly hostile to Decatur's fleet. The editor of the *New London Gazette* agreed with Decatur; but when he denounced the New London traitors who had alerted the British, his neighbors denounced him in return as a traitor to the town.[24] For years afterward, Connecticut Republicans would use the epithet "blue light Federalist," with its hint of treason, against their political opponents.

Relations between Decatur and the people of New London were strained. Goodrich, who attributed the blue lights to Decatur's imagination and blamed his "ill humor" on a "mind diseased by disappointment," described in his memoirs the three American captains, contrasting the "quiet, thoughtful Jones" and the "dark, handsome, complacent Biddle" with Decatur, who seemed in New London "like a caged eagle, ready to rend in atoms the bars which restrained him." Goodrich is one of the few among Decatur's detractors to leave a detailed description. He remembered Decatur as "rather below the middle size, but of a remarkably compact and symmetrical form. He was broad-shouldered, full-chested, thin in the flank: his eye was black, and lit with a spark of fire. His nose was thin, and slightly hooked; his lips were firm, his chin small, but smartly developed. His whole face was long and bony; his complexion swarthy; his hair jet black, and twisted in ropy curls down his forehead and over his ears. Altogether he was a remarkable looking man, and riveted the attention of everyone who saw him."[25]

The charismatic American captain and his British counterpart now were taking the other's measure. Decatur and Hardy realized that they had each other trapped. Decatur could not leave New London as long as Hardy lay off the coast; Hardy could not retake the *Macedonian*, nor could he send his fleet against other American ships or against the French, without allowing Decatur to escape. Understanding their situation, the two captains began an indirect communication. Alderman Binns was startled during dinner aboard the *United States* when Decatur called to the steward to "have that double Cheshire cheese set on the table which Commodore Hardy sent me yesterday." For his part, "Commodore Decatur frequently sent vegetables, and other acceptable presents, to the British commodore, which he, in the politest manner, reciprocated."[26]

But beneath these polite exchanges lay the reality of war. One day in January the British captured an American trading sloop. Captain David Hope of the *Endymion*—he had been first lieutenant on the *Macedonian*, and still regretted that Captain Carden had not taken his advice to go down fighting—told the American captain that he would like nothing better than to retake the *Macedonian*, or at least to meet the *United States* again in combat. Captain Hassard Stackpoole of the *Statira*, the *Macedonian*'s sister ship, offered another idea. Imagine a contest between the *Macedonian* and *Statira*—identical ships, but one manned by American crew, the other by British. Which would win? Captain Hardy was intrigued. He told the two captains that he would not prevent the fight, but the challenge had to come from the Americans.

When Decatur learned of this, he immediately issued a challenge. Biddle paid a call on Hardy, bringing Decatur's proposal: the *United States* and the *Macedonian* would take on *Endymion* and *Statira*. As Biddle met with Hardy, Decatur mustered the *United States*'s crew, who had been languishing for half a year in New London. He promised that "you will shortly be called upon again to try your skill and valor. . . . You are accustomed to victory, and you will not tarnish the glory you have already won. I have no fear for the result."

Jacob Jones told his crew on the *Macedonian*, "My lads, our cruise will be short, and I trust a very profitable one."²⁷

"There is a fight making up between this ship and the Macedonian, against the Endymion and the Statira," Decatur wrote to naval agent John Bullus in New York. Although he had no dread of battle, he was "fearful" that advance news of the duel might "find its way into the public prints." Decatur therefore asked Bullus "to wait on all the editors with whom you may have influence, and request them to withhold publishing until the affair is settled." This would "perhaps prevent several bright eyes," including Susan's, "from being dimmed."²⁸

But the contest never happened. Hardy, as interested in laurels as the other captains, wanted only a single-ship duel between the *Statira* and the *Macedonian.* Hardy knew that *Endymion* was lighter and carried fewer guns than the *United States.* He appreciated the "gallant spirit" behind the suggestion, he told Decatur; he knew there was "no personal feeling towards each other" but only "a laudable ambition to add to the Naval renown of our respective countries."²⁹ Decatur could not accept these terms, knowing that Hardy could pull the best sailors from each of his ships to man the *Statira.* So Decatur notified Hardy that although Jones and the men of the *Macedonian* were ready to take on Stackpole and the *Statira* in single combat, Decatur could not allow it. The battle was off, though not without one last verbal salvo. Stackpole wrote that he welcomed a chance to add to the "glory of the British flag" and the "honor of my King," as well as the "defense of my country engaged in a just and unprovoked war."³⁰ Decatur replied that "whether the war we are engaged in be just or unprovoked on the part of Great Britain" was "a question exclusively with the Civilians, & I am perfectly ready to admit both my incompetence & unwillingness to confront Capt. Stackpole in this discussion."³¹

Even though the sea duel did not materialize, Decatur wanted to publish the correspondence among the captains as a spur to American patriotic sentiment, since the letters showed the fighting spirit of the American sailors. Decatur sent the letters to Secretary Jones, who showed them to President Madison. Madison, however, saw where this kind of correspondence would lead: the entire British fleet might appear off the coast and offer individual challenges to American ships. He not only forbade publication of the letters but also ordered Jones to forbid any of his commanders to accept or receive challenges from their British counterparts.³²

CHAPTER 15

"To die well"

S USAN STAYED at Mrs. Bradish's New York boardinghouse while Stephen was bottled up in New London. She had had no reason to leave the city with him when he first sailed, expecting that he would be at sea for months. When it became apparent that he would not get his ships out of the Thames, he insisted that she remain in New York, much as he wanted her with him. Since there were "more persons in the world disposed to find fault than to approve, it might be said, if he had his family with him, that he did not make every effort to get to sea."[1]

Stephen paid a visit to New York at Christmas. Although seeing Susan was his primary motive, he also paid several calls on Robert Fulton. He and the inventor had been corresponding since Decatur left New York in May, and in October Fulton had visited New London. Fulton now had built a prototype of his underwater cannon, which had a firing range of ten to twenty yards. Decatur knew that this was not enough. A sailing ship that close to an enemy risked tangling lines and crossing masts, allowing the enemy to board. Fulton saw a solution: have his attacking vessel powered by steam, not sail. But he and Decatur knew that steam vessels were especially vulnerable, with the wheel and the engine both exposed on the deck. So Fulton designed a new type of vessel, with the wheel and engine concealed inside the hull. There would still be sails to power the ship at sea, but "when within one mile" of the enemy, the crew would retract the masts and use steam power to ram the vessel into the enemy. Four of these battering steamships could destroy a seventy-four-gun battleship by attacking simultaneously from four quarters.

Their collaboration created a new kind of fighting ship, and ultimately the world's first steam-powered warship. Fulton sent the plans to his former sponsor, Thomas Jefferson, who was "highly pleased." Steam power would allow Fulton's vessel to get within six to twelve feet of the enemy and pull away safely. Adding steam power to the torpedo boat and submarine gun, Fulton now saw, gave "perfection to the whole system." He wrote to Decatur, "It is one of my best combinations."[2]

But even with steam power Decatur still foresaw the problem of enemy boarders. Four small steamboats could attack an enemy battleship, but that ship would have four hundred men aboard. Once the steamboats were as close to the battleship as they needed to be, one hundred men from the battleship could board each of the smaller vessels and overpower their crew.

Decatur therefore proposed making the steamboats impossible to board. Fulton had been planning conventional flat upper decks. Decatur proposed sloping the upper deck sharply toward the water and covering it with sharp spikes to make boarding difficult, with a gun mounted on the spiked deck, fired from inside the vessel, to destroy any approaching boats or boarders.

On Christmas Eve, Fulton hosted a gathering in his home to form the Coast and Harbor Defense Company. Decatur was present, along with the men who had been sponsoring Fulton's experiments since 1810. These were influential Republicans and Federalists from throughout the Northeast. Henry Dearborn of Massachusetts, Republican and secretary of war in the Jefferson administration, was chosen president; also present were Oliver Wolcott of Connecticut, secretary of the treasury in the Washington and Adams administrations; Congressman Samuel Mitchill of New York; former New York governor Morgan Lewis; and Adam Brown, Thomas Morris, Cadwallader Colden, and Henry Rutgers. They named Fulton the "engineer." Their stated goal was to build a steam warship to defend New York harbor.[3] When Decatur returned to New London, he enlisted Biddle and Jones in the plan. Both signed a testimonial approving Fulton and Decatur's design for the ship and urging the navy to begin construction.[4]

While Decatur was trapped in New London, working toward the navy's future, the war went on without him. He had not succeeded in getting Lieutenant Allen promoted to captain; but Allen had been given command of the *Argus*, Decatur's first ship, and had sailed it to the English Channel, where he spent the summer of 1813 capturing and destroying British merchant ships. His life and career were both cut short by a cannon shot from the British ship *Pelican*, though he had stayed on deck giving commands even after the shot blew off his leg. The enemy gave Allen a hero's funeral. Eight Royal Navy captains carried his casket, draped in an American flag, into St. Andrew's Church, Plymouth, England, accompanied by a Royal Marine honor guard, followed by the *Argus*'s American crew.

Closer to home, in May 1813 Captain James Lawrence had learned that the British frigate *Shannon* was off the Massachusetts coast eager to engage with an American frigate. Lawrence took the *Chesapeake* to sea on the first day of June. It was Lawrence's first time commanding this ship and the first cruise aboard for all but one other officer and many of the men. They met the *Shannon* just off Boston Light, and though Lawrence rallied his crew enough to inflict damage on the *Shannon*, his men were so confused and desperate that their resistance was ineffective. After fifteen minutes at close range Lawrence was mortally wounded, and he was carried below just as British boarding parties began to climb over the rail. He gave his final command to the men on deck: "Don't give up the ship!" Fifteen minutes later, the *Shannon*'s crew captured the *Chesapeake*. They wrapped Lawrence's body in his ship's flag and brought him ashore in Halifax with full military honors. His body and that of Lieutenant Charles Ludlow were brought to Salem in August; Supreme Court Justice Joseph Story delivered a eulogy at their second funeral. In September, Lawrence and Ludlow would receive a third funeral at Trinity Church in New York.

Asked if Lawrence's qualities as an officer merited this veneration and the extravagant mourning, Decatur answered, "Yes sir, it did; and the fellow died as well as he lived: but it is part of a soldier's life to die well." Decatur had known Lawrence as a midshipman; Lawrence had been with him when he took the *Philadelphia* in Tripoli, and had commanded a gunboat during the battle there. "He had no talk," Decatur said, "but he inspired all about him with ardour; he always saw the best thing to be done; he knew the best way to execute it; and had no more dodge in him than the mainmast."[5]

As Lawrence's and Ludlow's bodies were making their way from Halifax to New York, another of Decatur's former junior officers, Oliver Hazard Perry, was preparing to face the British fleet on Lake Erie. Perry named his new flagship the *Lawrence*, and Purser Samuel Hambleton prepared a blue battle flag with Lawrence's last words in white letters: "Don't Give Up The Ship." Although the *Lawrence* was shot out from beneath him, Perry perservered; in the midst of enemy fire, he and his flag were rowed from the sinking *Lawrence* to the curiously unscathed *Niagara*, commanded by Jesse Elliott. Perry was too exuberant at his triumph to heed other officers' queries about why Elliott—the only officer who had defended James Barron after the first *Chesapeake* disaster—had held the *Niagara* back from the action. Why was the *Niagara* undamaged when the British had battered the rest of the fleet? Perry thought it better to shield a coward than to let the enemy know you had one. To the secretary of the navy Perry wrote simply: "We have met the enemy and they are ours. Two ships, two brigs, one schooner & one sloop."[6]

Decatur's task was less heroic. From mid-April to early May 1814 he presided over the navy's court-martial arising from the loss of the *Chesapeake*. The frigate's only surviving officer, Lieutenant William S. Cox, was charged with cowardice and desertion. He had gone below with his wounded commander; then when he returned to the main deck, he found such a horrific scene that he had gone below again. In addition, four men were charged with cowardice: James Forrest (also charged with drunkenness); Henry Fleishman (also known as Henry Brown); William Brown the bugler (he had spent most of the battle hiding under a boat); and Edmund Russell, the midshipman in charge of the second gun (he had deserted his post, returned to it, and then deserted again).

It disturbed Decatur that one person had leveled most of the charges, and most of the evidence came from one witness. He demanded more evidence, more witnesses; and as a fuller picture emerged, he was convinced that the accused were not to blame for the disaster. The *Chesapeake* was a strong ship evenly matched with the *Shannon* (fifty guns to the *Shannon*'s fifty-two; 379 men to the *Shannon*'s 330), and its commander Decatur personally knew to be fearless. The crew were likely not cowards but only poorly trained. Decatur had come to understand the importance of training and drilling. He could not now fault Lawrence for not having prepared sufficiently; Decatur and Allen had spent five years training the crew of the *United States*. He would not make scapegoats of Cox and the others. All but William Brown were acquitted of cowardice. Cox was found to be neither a coward nor deserter; he had simply obeyed his human instinct to accompany his wounded captain below. Since he should have stayed on the quarterdeck to rally his forces, however, he was dismissed from the navy. Forrest was also dismissed; acquitted of cowardice, he pleaded guilty to drunkenness. The court took Fleishman's youth and good conduct into account, and sentenced him merely to a public reprimand. Midshipman Russell, who had deserted, returned, and deserted again, had his wages stopped, but stayed in the navy, becoming a lieutenant. The only man convicted of cowardice was the bugler Brown, who had hidden under a boat. The absence of the bugler had contributed to the crew's confusion. Brown, an African American, was sentenced to three hundred lashes and had his wages withheld during the remainder of his service. President Madison reduced the sentence to one hundred lashes.[7]

For Decatur the lessons here confirmed what he already knew. Victory was a matter not of gallantry but of discipline and training. Lawrence simply had not had time to turn his crew into a disciplined fighting unit. None of them wanted to "give up the ship," but the sheer terror of war had left them no alternative. Decatur had come to understand that to win the war, a fighting force must be one unit, trained and drilled. In New London he was constantly confronted with evidence of deception, division, and borderline treason. He could not instill military discipline in the people of Connecticut, but the disciplined fighting force under his command, and the machinery of war he and Fulton were creating, could protect their freedom to act like cowards and fools.

New London was an anomaly to Decatur. In New York, men such as Dearborn and Wolcott, political adversaries, had united for the common good.

Among his own officers there were differences, but Decatur had forged a spirit of unity. James Biddle was from Philadelphia, but from a different social world; his father, like Stephen's, had been a merchant captain, but he had turned to land-based enterprise and by the 1780s was vice president of Pennsylvania's Supreme Executive Council. Two of Biddle's brothers would later serve in Congress; another would become president of the Bank of the United States. Biddle's relationship with Decatur would later cool, but when William Biddle visited the squadron in August, he reported home that James "likes Decatur very much & that of course they agree very well."[8]

When Alderman Binns visited in March 1814 to present the Philadelphians Decatur and Biddle with ceremonial swords, Decatur may have been reminded of the social gulf between himself and Biddle as well as the political differences in his home city. Binns, editor of Philadelphia's *Democratic Press*, had arrived in Philadelphia in the 1790s after being imprisoned for his role in the Irish rebellion. Stephen Decatur, grandson of a French immigrant, had enlisted to serve in the war against France, and was fighting his way through pro-French mobs in the streets of Philadelphia. The city's Republicans like Binns had opposed the French war. Now Decatur was fighting the British from New London, most of whose Federalist citizens opposed the war.

Experienced in military matters, Decatur was just beginning to understand politics. He was still not a confident speaker, and knew that a formal occasion like this required a formal statement. Biddle was a better-educated man, and Decatur instinctively sought Biddle's judgment on the remarks he had painstakingly prepared, thanking the people of Pennsylvania, his officers, and crew, and pledging to take up the sword in their defense again. Decatur showed his successive drafts to Biddle and Jones, seeking their comments until they were satisfied or simply worn out.

All men were mustered aboard the *United States* for the presentation of the swords from the Commonwealth of Pennsylvania. Binns delivered Biddle's sword, reading the legislature's proclamation and the governor's letter, which predicted that when "future opportunities present themselves I doubt not your distinguished skill and gallantry will call for fresh honors and rewards which will cheerfully be paid by a grateful country." Biddle took the sword and delivered his speech of thanks—modest, yet expressing pride in the accomplishments he and his men had achieved on behalf of their native state and country. The other officers, including Decatur, could hardly contain their laughter: Biddle had memorized and delivered Decatur's speech, word for word. Binns would later recall his visit to Decatur's squadron as one of the proudest moments of his career; the officers would recall his visit for the joke Biddle had played on Decatur.[9]

By this time, Secretary Jones and Decatur had concluded that the *United States* and the *Macedonian* might never leave New London. Three more British line-of-battle ships now were stationed off the Thames, threatening to move in and take the two American frigates. Since Decatur could not get his ships out of port, he and the navy secretary decided his best course would be to take them so far up the river that the British could not reach them. Then he and his men would go to New York, where he would take command of either the *Guerriere* — a new ship being built there, named for the British warship destroyed under Bainbridge's command—or Rodgers's ship, the *President*. As long as the British still thought that Decatur was in New London, they would continue to blockade it, and this would allow Decatur to slip out of New York. Alternatively, when they saw the frigates move up the river, the British might relax their blockade, allowing Biddle in the *Hornet* to pass out to sea. In either case, Decatur and the navy would have to abandon the two frigates. Within days of concluding the *Chesapeake* court-martial, Decatur had moved the *United States* and the *Macedonian* fourteen miles up the river, placing cannon in their sterns and leaving gunboats to guard them from downstream.

Decatur attended to a few political matters before leaving New London. He reported to Secretary Jones on the case of Nathaniel Senter, whom Decatur had arrested as a spy. The Connecticut civil authorities had released Senter, arguing that Decatur did not have the authority to arrest civilians. Senter had since been seen going aboard the British fleet, and after coming ashore again in Connecticut had gone on to Rhode Island—proof enough for Decatur that Senter was in fact a spy.[10]

John Thayer, a Massachusetts farmer, had come to Decatur seeking the release of his son Hiram, impressed ten years earlier by the British. Decatur was so struck by the length of Hiram's service in the British fleet that in a letter to Jones he put it in bold: Hiram had been impressed into the British service "in August **1803**." Hiram was now a boatswain's mate on the *Statira*. Captain Stackpole denied that Hiram was an American citizen, and had told him that if they met an American ship and he refused to "do his duty, he should be tied to the mast and shot at like a Dog."[11]

Decatur arranged for father and son to meet—for the first time in ten years. The British officers agreed to allow the meeting but insisted they needed more proof that Hiram Thayer was an American citizen. As the father's boat approached the *Statira*, Hiram told the officers that he could see his father, and when John Thayer climbed aboard, Decatur reported, "the feelings manifested by the old man on receiving the hand of his son, proved beyond all other evidence the property he had in him" There "was not a doubt left on the mind of a single British officer of Hiram Thayer's being an

American Citizen—and yet he is detained not as a Prisoner of war, but compelled to under the most cruel threats, to serve the enemy of his Country." The British admiral released Thayer.[12]

Decatur dealt not only with British spies and impressed Americans but also with local political issues. When the New London customs inspector, Nathaniel Richards, learned that the Madison administration was going to replace him, he turned to Decatur for help. Decatur was aware that the navy and the Madison administration had few friends in New London, and Nathaniel Richards was one of them. Decatur knew how to plead Richard's case. He wrote to Secretary Jones, attesting that Richards had performed many services to "the squadron under my command," and from the "lively & personal exertion he displayed in placing the town in a state of defense on probability of an attack, & his efforts in preventing supplies going to the enemy—I do not hesitate to declare that I believe Mr. Richards, Patriotic & deserving." As to the important question of political affiliation, "Mr. Richards is reputed by all to be a republican, & has been unequal in his support of the present administration." He asked Jones to present the letter to Secretary of State James Monroe.[13]

CHAPTER 16

"Every sword should be prepared"

W ITH THE squadron out of immediate danger, Jones and his men left for Sackett's Harbor on Lake Ontario, Biddle waited for a chance to get the *Hornet* to sea, and Decatur went to New York. Stephen WAS relieved to be back with Susan, in a city where he and the navy had friends, and to have a chance to sail again. He would take command of the *President*, re-copper the bottom, replace the masts, and enlist a crew.

The term of the fine crew signed aboard in 1811 expired in 1813. After bringing the *Macedonian* safely across the ocean, they had spent the rest of their service idle in New London. This dull service with no chance for prize money gave them few incentives to reenlist. Many of Decatur's men found opportunities elsewhere in the fleet: on the Great Lakes or on the ships sailing out of Boston. Decatur had difficulty signing new recruits in New York. He was able to sign men from the gunboats, eager for a chance to serve on a frigate at sea rather than on a boat patrolling New York harbor, and he also sent a lieutenant to recruit in Philadelphia.

Decatur divided his time between the Brooklyn yard where the *President* was being refit and Brown's Shipyard on the East River, where Robert Fulton was supervising construction of his steam frigate. It was becoming apparent to Fulton that the vessel would be best suited to defending a harbor or small inlet, and only on a calm day. While the *Demologos*, as Fulton and Decatur had named the ship, was under construction, Fulton began building models of similar vessels. In time they would revolutionize naval warfare, just as the commercial steamboat he had designed was now speeding communication between New York City and the Great Lakes. But in 1814 work on Fulton and Decatur's warship proceeded slowly.

The *President* was out of the navy yard by July, and final preparations were being made for going to sea. Anticipating another separation, Stephen and Susan enjoyed the social life of New York. They spent evenings of "tea & gin" with Washington Irving's circle of friends. Irving had been an opponent of the war, but he developed a warm friendship with the Decaturs, and Stephen found the moderate Federalism of Irving and the New Yorkers a welcome contrast to the "blue light Federalism" of New London.

Decatur also had time to attend to other naval responsibilities. He and Oliver Hazard Perry were ordered to conduct a court of inquiry on David Porter, who had sailed the *Essex* into the Pacific, attacking British whalers and merchant vessels between Chile and Hawaii before a British warship captured him. (This was the same *Essex* that Captain Preble had taken to the Indian Ocean during the French war, the first U.S. Navy ship to go to the Indian Ocean and the first in the Pacific.) Decatur and Perry absolved Porter of any blame in the loss of the *Essex.*

On a more delicate matter, Secretary Jones had Decatur conduct an inquiry into the case of purser Robert Ormsby. Ormsby had left Baltimore with a large sum of money; he was arrested at Sag Harbor under suspicion of trying to desert to the enemy. Decatur began the inquiry but dropped it under instructions from the navy Secretary after Congressman Stephen Ormsby, a relative of the purser, protested and vouched for his kinsman's integrity.[1]

But while Decatur was handling these matters, he received a new set of orders from Secretary Jones. Late in July the secretary had heard from the northern frontier that Isaac Chauncey was too ill to command the fleet he had heroically built on Lake Ontario. Newspapers and other sources reported that the British were increasing their forces—on land and on the lake—and it was imperative that the Americans stop the British from crossing Lake Ontario into New York. Jones ordered Decatur to take charge of Chauncey's fleet at Sackett's Harbor. Decatur responded with a long and barely legible letter pledging to follow the secretary's orders but asking for a few more days. Decatur's own recent information from Lake Ontario was that Chauncey had recovered, and his "personal friendship & respect" for Chauncey made Decatur reluctant to replace him. He delayed his departure long enough; on August 9 he was about to leave when the Albany steamboat arrived with the news that Chauncey's fleet had sailed and was out of sight of land. Chauncey himself wrote Jones, expressing regret "that so much sensation has been excited in the Public mind because this Squadron did not sail so soon as the wise heads that conduct our newspapers have presumed to think I ought."[2]

Chauncey's fleet would take on the British on Lake Ontario. But this was only a preliminary objective for the British. Once they had destroyed Chauncey's fleet, they would move into upstate New York, reaffirming their alliance with the Iroquois. They already were sending a fleet to Lake Champlain and preparing an army of ten thousand men to march down the Hudson River valley to take New York City from the interior. This would force Decatur to divide his troops to protect the city, and his squadron would be caught between the land and naval forces of the British Empire. New England would be cut off from the rest of the Union. The British knew well that New Londoners had treated Decatur's squadron like an occupying force, and that a movement was growing in Connecticut and Massachusetts to break those states away from the United States. The British also were sending a fleet and an army to the mouth of the Mississippi River. Once they had taken New Orleans, they would unite with the Creeks and other Native people in the Southeast. The British and their Indian allies had begun the war by taking Detroit; they planned to end the war by taking New York and the western country, setting up an independent Indian territory stretching from the Great Lakes down the Ohio River to the Mississippi and the Gulf of Mexico. New England would be an independent country. The Virginians might be permitted to maintain their own sovereignty in an enclave along the Chesapeake. The fate of the United States, though, was of little concern to the strategists in London.

Decatur had been preparing to go to Sackett's Harbor when he learned that the British planned to strike at "decidedly the most important" target, New York City. The British fleet was gathering off New Jersey and Long Island, preparing to attack while the fleet on Lake Ontario struck at Chauncey's defenses at Sackett's Harbor. New Yorkers, unlike the citizens of New London, mobilized quickly and did not hesitate or wait for Washington to clarify who would be in charge. They turned to Decatur to lead them. The common council formally asked Decatur to take over of the city's defenses. Nicholas Fish, chair of the council's committee of defense (he had also chaired the committee that organized the dinner in Decatur's honor in December 1813) expressed the councillors' confidence in Decatur's "skill and judgment," which they also knew to be "cherished by the public." The city pledged to provide him "with the means of executing such additional plans of defense as he may conceive essential to public security." Quickly Decatur ordered a new fortification, Fort Green, built in Brooklyn. The council was especially interested in torpedoes or mines, which could be strung across the Throg's Neck channel and across the Narrows to prevent invasions from Long Island Sound or the sea.[3]

Decatur tried to push ahead the work on Fulton's steam frigate. Secretary Jones ordered Decatur to suspend the *Essex* court of inquiry so that David Porter could take command of the *Demologos*, which was not yet ready for service. The weight of its steam engine, guns, and thick protective skin made it slow and cumbersome, more a moveable island fortress than a fighting ship. One of the heaviest vessels afloat, it could block narrow channels or the harbor entrance, but it was too slow to lead an attack on the enemy.

Decatur also needed land forces. He had five thousand sailors under his command. They would not be required on their ships, so he had his marine captain, Robert Wainwright, drill them in land tactics. Armed with pike poles, pistols, and cutlasses, the men were trained to run in straight lines screaming at an imaginary enemy in preparation for warding off a British invasion.

Marines typically had only a small detachment on board a navy ship; now Wainwright found himself commanding what Decatur called a "small brigade" and acting as a brigade major. Decatur suggested to Secretary Jones that Wainwright be paid more for this service.[4]

In the midst of these preparations came a reminder of the petty problems that had stymied Decatur in New London. One of his gunboat captains hailed a strange boat along the New Jersey shore. The stranger did not respond even after the captain called three or four times; finally he had to have it "brought to" by firing muskets. The stranger stopped. Its commander identified his vessel and crew as New Jersey "sea fencibles," a maritime militia. The boat was allowed to proceed. When the gunboat approached a nearby fort commanded by New Jersey militia, the fort fired on the gunboat and ordered the captain ashore. When the gunboat captain stepped inside the fort, the militia officer knocked him to the ground. The officer was angry that the captain had stopped a company of sea fencibles. On hearing the story, Decatur complained to New Jersey's militia authorities, who chastised the officers involved. But a few weeks later Decatur learned that the offenders had been restored to their rank. This time he complained to Secretary Jones. He did not wish to prolong a feud "at a time like this, when every sword should be prepared to act against the enemy of the Republic," and he wanted "no private considerations" to "destroy that unanimity of exertion which alone can lead us to an honorable result."[5] Jones referred the matter to the president.

Decatur, Jones, and President Madison had before them more pressing issues than tensions between the navy and the New Jersey militia. Jones realized that he had misread the intent of the British. Eventually they would strike New York, but the fleet that had mobilized off Long Island was now sailing into the Chesapeake. Twenty-one British ships, carrying thousands of soldiers, entered the bay and quickly overwhelmed the gunboat defenses along its shores. Secretary Jones and Secretary of War John Armstrong disputed whether the real target was Baltimore, the shipping center, or the capital itself. It was a moot point, as the British were able to take both. By August 22 the British had forced American sailors to run their boats aground along the Patuxent River to prevent their capture, and British forces landed to march on the capital. Two days later British troops routed the Americans at Bladensburg, and the next day they entered Washington. At the navy yard Captain Thomas Tingey ordered the newly built frigate *Columbia* and the new brig *Argus* and other naval supplies burned; to the northwest he could already see flames as the British set fire to the Capitol and the president's house. Madison and his cabinet escaped into Maryland and Virginia; the city of Alexandria surrendered to the enemy.

Madison's flight inspired the Federalists to new heights of ridicule, as one newspaper crowed that a future heroic poem, "Madison, or the Battle of Bladensburg," would conclude, "Fly, Monroe, Fly! Run Armstrong, Run! Were the last words of Madison."[6] The Connecticut and Massachusetts legislatures called for a conference of the New England states, known as the Hartford Convention, to decide if it was worthwhile to maintain the crumbling Union. When a Republican paper in Boston printed a notice that James Monroe was offering to send fifty thousand "Virginian troops . . . to put down the Tories of Connecticut," a Federalist paper, asked, "Where were those 50,000 men when a British army of only two thousand, sacked the city of Washington, and not a Virginian either killed or wounded[?]"[7]

The country was rapidly falling apart as Federalists and Republicans blamed each other. "The government was in a state of distraction," Philadelphian William Shaler wrote to a friend. "Our finances were so deranged as to offer no hope of again raising the public credit, and the convention at Hartford was seeking the favorable moment to give the *coup de grace* to our expiring union."[8]

Washington Irving was on the steamboat from Albany to New York City when a passenger came aboard at Poughkeepsie.[9] In the dark cabin Irving could see only the shadows of other passengers as the stranger told them the news: Washington had fallen. The president's house, the Capitol, the Treasury, the navy yard, the War Office had all been burned. The passengers listened in silence and remained silent after the man finished. After a moment a voice filled with "complacent disdain" asked what "Jimmy Madison would do now?"

Washington Irving knew this tone of voice. He had long expressed the same "complacent disdain" in his own satires on the foibles of the Republican administrations. But hearing it now, he lost his temper.

"Sir, do you seize on such a disaster only for a sneer? Let me tell you sir, it is not now a question about Jimmy Madison or Johnny Armstrong," the mocking names Federalists used for the president and his secretary of war. "The pride and honor of the nation are wounded; the country is insulted and disgraced by this barbarous success, and every loyal citizen would feel the ignominy, and be earnest to avenge it." The cabin remained silent. When the boat docked in New York City, Irving sought out Governor Daniel D. Tompkins and volunteered to serve in any capacity. Tompkins sent Irving as his military aide and secretary to the frontier counties, to organize the state's defense once the British smashed through Chauncey's fleet. While in New England some arch-Federalists were seizing the moment to rebel, others, like Irving, threw themselves into the work of defense. Shaler later remembered this period after the British struck Washington as the time when the "spirit of the sound part of the nation was rising. . . . Mr. Adams says we shall ever be victorious."[10]

Before the Federalists could emerge victorious, however, the British would have to defeat the U.S. Navy. On Lake Champlain, Lieutenant Thomas Macdonough commanded the American forces. As a midshipman he and Decatur had once chased robbers through the streets of Syracuse. Now he faced one of the largest military forces the British had ever sent to North America. Eleven thousand men on sixteen ships commanded by Sir George Prevost prepared to take control of Lake Champlain. MacDonough and his men, on their four ships and ten gunboats, watched as the British squadron rounded Cumberland Head. He had his men kneel on the deck and pray.

Macdonough had taken a position between Cumberland Head and a shoal to the south. The British could not get around him; they would have to smash through his line. Macdonough knew the British could do this. With more firepower, they could batter away at the American ships with their broadsides. But Macdonough had attached hawser lines and springs to his ships so he could turn them. When enemy fire disabled his starboard guns, Macdonough ordered his ships turned around to fire their larboard (port) guns. His ingenuity gave Macdonough firepower to match the enemy, and his smaller squadron destroyed the British fleet. The invading army retreated to Canada.[11]

Two days later the British tried but failed to take Baltimore. The small naval force there prevented the British from closing in by sinking their smaller vessels in the shipping channels; the land and naval forces held off the invading force, which pounded Fort McHenry for twenty-five hours, beginning at seven on the morning of September 13. The fort did not fall, and the British fleet turned away. These two events—Macdonough's victory at Plattsburgh and the British failure at Baltimore—restored faith in the survival of the republic. Had the Americans lost, their republic would have fallen.

The nation had been given a reprieve, but neither Decatur nor Secretary Jones was ready to rest. Fulton launched the *Demologos* on October 29; when Jones heard the news, he sent Decatur a confidential letter. Could Fulton's steam warship be prepared for Lake Ontario? Decatur called on the inventor and also on Governor Tompkins, who had long experience with steamboats. Tompkins was not hopeful. "I do not believe . . . that vessels of this description would be formidable on the ocean, or in broad waters, or that they would be the most advisable for Lake Ontario," he reported. "Ships of the Line and Frigates, form the Naval Force upon which alone I should place reliance wither for blockading the enemy's fleet on that lake, or for conquering it in open fight." Fulton was more optimistic. He was just then finishing a new model "to carry not more than Three or Four guns of heavy metal, and to apply Torpedoes." This new ship would cost between fifty and sixty thousand dollars; if construction began by the first of December, he could have it ready in March. Until then, Lake Ontario would be frozen, anyway. With two steam warships, Chauncey could destroy the British fleet on the lake, and New York City could batter down the British blockade of its harbor.[12]

CHAPTER 17

"Let us go down like men"

WITH NEW YORK spared from a British invasion, Decatur prepared to take the war to sea. He suggested to the secretary of the navy that he lead a small squadron to attack British trade in the Mediterranean or in the Indian Ocean and Bay of Bengal. Decatur preferred the second plan, which followed the route and strategy Edward Preble had used fifteen years earlier in the French war, taking a squadron around the Cape of Good Hope, prowling against British ships off Bengal, Sumatra, and the Malacca Straits.

How to provision a fleet so far from home? Fighting ships needed to be light and maneuverable; weighing them down with enough freight to feed their crews on an extended voyage would defeat their purpose. Decatur had a ready solution. Just as he had earlier proposed setting up a "merchant" in St. Iago, this time he would charter a private vessel to carry the squadron's nonmilitary supplies. Decatur found an available merchant ship, the *Tom Bowline*, which he and his officers bought for $13,800. They filled it with enough provisions for the three ships in the squadron—the *President*, the *Peacock*, and the *Hornet*, which Biddle had brought down from New London. The *Tom Bowline* was a private vessel, chartered like any other merchant ship to carry freight. The fact that it was chartered by officers and crew aboard American naval vessels was a technicality. Once all its cargo had been delivered to the three warships, the *Tom Bowline* could stay in the Indian Ocean as a privateer. In mid-January the squadron prepared to sail.[1]

On January 14, two days after the nation observed a day of fasting and prayer called for by President Madison (New Englanders used the day to pray for peace; others prayed for victory), the squadron dropped down to Staten Island, waiting for an opportunity to slip out of the Narrows. Delays there aboard the *President* kept Decatur in port, so he sent the *Hornet* and the *Peacock* ahead, with orders to meet him in Tristan da Cunha. Then the *Tom Bowline* ran aground and had to be unloaded. Decatur, who was anxious to leave, ordered the *Tom Bowline* delivered to David Porter, in command at the navy yard. If the ship could not be repaired, Porter was to arrange another merchant ship for the squadron.

Saturday evening January 14, a gale blew in, which Decatur knew would force the British fleet away from the harbor mouth. He anticipated that they would choose the safety of the New Jersey coast, leaving Long Island's southern shore clear for him to sail. If he could sneak out of the Narrows under cover of the storm, then sail east along the coast of Long Island far enough to evade the British blockaders, he could be heading south across the open Atlantic by Sunday. Untying from its Staten Island anchorage at eight on the stormy January night, the *President* headed for the channel leading out of the harbor.

Suddenly, a jolt shuddered through the great ship's hull. It stopped dead in the channel. Either human error or, as some thought, deliberate sabotage had caused the pilot to misjudge the depth of the channel. The *President*'s keel was stuck on the bottom. For two hours the storm pounded the decks and masts and waves battered the hull as the ship lay on a bar. The rudder braces broke, the masts sprung, the false keel was displaced. After two hours of pounding, the tide began to lift his ship off the bar, and Decatur had to decide quickly where he would steer his damaged vessel. The *President* was in no condition to sail, he knew, but the wind howling out of the west prevented him from returning to New York harbor. He had not been so close to the open sea in twenty months; he would not turn back now. If he could get away from the blockaded coast, he was confident that he could reach Tristan da Cunha, where he could repair the ship. As the hull finally lifted clear of the bottom, Decatur steered out of the channel and into New York's lower harbor and then along the Long Island shore. Fifty miles east of the Narrows, he turned the wounded *President* south toward the open Atlantic.

The storm had abated in the night. At five the next morning Decatur saw three ships to the south. He changed course, steering the *President* northward. The ship did not sail well. As the sun rose, Decatur found himself surrounded by four British warships. The British squadron had guessed correctly that Decatur would seize the gale as an opportunity, and he had guessed wrong that the British would prefer the safety of the shore to the capture of an American commander. They had waited for him east of the Narrows, and now he sailed into their midst in a crippled ship. The frigate *Endymion* and fifty-six-gun razee *Majestic* were off his stern, the *Pomone* and *Tenedos* off his bow.

But luck still seemed to be on his side. A strong wind was allowing him to keep his distance from *Endymion* and *Majestic* but would have brought the *President* up to *Pomone* and *Tenedos* if they had not mistaken each other for American ships in the early morning light and raced off in pursuit of each other. As Decatur evaded the ships at his stern, exchanging ineffective fire with the *Majestic*, he ordered his men to lighten the ship, dumping provisions so it would sail more quickly. He realized now how inexperienced and exhausted his crew were. These were not the well-drilled men of the *United*

States. Some of them had first set foot on the *President* on the day they sailed, and had spent the night fighting the gale that battered their ship in New York harbor. Some of the officers and midshipmen were also new: Decatur had just promoted the eighteen-year-old Edward F. Howell to acting lieutenant; Jack Creamer, the boy who had asked to have his name entered on the *United States*'s roster just before the *Macedonian* battle, was on board as a midshipman; and the young midshipman George Hollins had never set foot on a ship until the day before. Now they struggled to keep their crippled ship under full sail while lightening its load and fighting a pursuing enemy. By mid-afternoon *Endymion* had gained enough to fire on the *President* from its bow guns. The *President* returned fired from its stern, but by 5:30, twelve hours after the chase began, *Endymion* was close enough to send a broadside into the *President*'s starboard quarter.

Decatur saw the broadsides coming. But now the enemy's strategy had given him a plan. "My lads," he announced, "that ship is coming up with us. As our ship won't sail, we'll go on board of theirs, every man and boy of us, and carry her into New York. All I ask of you is, to follow me. This is a favorite ship of the country. If we allow her to be taken we shall be deserted by our wives and sweethearts. What, let such a ship as this go for nothing! 'T would break the heart of every pretty girl in New York!"[2]

The exhausted men had not sailed with Decatur long, but they knew his reputation. He would fight and lead them to victory. They gave three cheers and prepared to take the *Endymion*. Decatur had a cannon aimed down to blow a hole into the *President*'s hold; he would destory the frigate, just as he had done eleven years earlier with the *Philadelphia*. "We will leave them the ashes of the President to take care of," Decatur said as he ordered the crew to quarters.[3]

Midshipman Hollins was so far having a miserable first day at sea. He had been home in Baltimore helping out with the defenses back in September when Oliver Perry passed through town, and the fifteen-year-old was so stirred by the chance to go to sea that he prevailed on his parents to find him a berth. Now his first sea voyage, which began in a gale, was going to end with the captain sinking the ship. Glory's allure had faded for Hollins. As the *Endymion* draw near, he worried aloud that he'd never be able to climb aboard. Why had he left home? "A huge fat old quartermaster" told him, "Never mind Mr. Hollins you hold on to my jacket & I'll take you aboard. We're not going to leave you here." Hollins thought this "rather consoling to one whose first day's experience of sea-going, was that sprightly days work."[4]

As the *Endymion* approached, Decatur had pike poles and pistols distributed to the boarding parties. But instead of closing, the *Endymion*'s captain kept slightly astern of the *President* and fired another broadside. Decatur ordered his men to the guns and to sails. They would fire back and try to outsail the enemy and escape under cover of darkness. At close range the two ships exchanged a series of devastating broadsides. Aboard the *President*, Lieutenant Fitz-Henry Babbit fell down the hatch, his leg blown off by the shot. Babbit survived for two hours. One comrade promised to deliver his watch to his brother; another took the miniature of his fiancée from around his neck to deliver home to Babbit's mother in Massachusetts.

Another British shot shattered the leg of Midshipman Richard P. Dale, son of the first commodore in the Tripolitan war. Decatur thought that young Dale would survive, but he died soon after Babbit. Lieutenant Archibald Hamilton—who had carried the *Macedonian*'s flag to Washington—was ordering his gun crew to "carry on boys! Carry on!" when a twenty-four-pound cannonball smashed his chest and "cut him in pieces."[5]

Oak splinters tore into Decatur's chest and face, knocking him to the deck. The men panicked when they saw their commander fall, but Decatur rose up, blood streaming from his face, and ordered them back to their guns. They fought on, broadside for broadside, for two hours. Lieutenant Howell (one of only two uninjured lieutenants on the *President*) was heard to say, "Well, we have whipped that ship, at any rate!" At that instant Midshipman Christopher Emmett saw the *Endymion*'s guns flash. "No, there she is again," Emmet said at the same instant Howell fell dead on the deck.[6]

By now it was 8:30, and there were "intervals of minutes, when the ships were broadside and broadside" but *Endymion* "did not fire a gun."[7] Even when the *President* turned its stern to the *Endymion*'s broadside, the British ship did not fire. Its guns were disabled, its sails and rigging so badly cut it could not sail. Howell had been right, *Endymion* was whipped. But the three other British ships were in sight. *Pomone* and *Tenedos* had recognized each other as British and now were coming to join the fight. His head bloodied and his chest aching, Decatur ordered the men to repair the rigging. The darkness and cloud cover offered a chance to outrun the enemy ships.

It was now 10:30 at night. Midshipman Hollins was racing from the quarterdeck to his station when he stopped short. The light from the binnacle shone on two halves of a man cut in two during the battle. Hollins was frozen in horror. His first day at sea could not get worse. Suddenly he felt a hand on his shoulder and heard a calm, steady voice: "Young gentleman have you nothing else to do than to be looking at such things as that, go and attend to your duty."[8] Hollins quickly snapped out of his shock and climbed aloft to fix the rigging. Later when he reflected on the horrific scene, he recognized the calm voice as Decatur's.

Darkness might have given cover to escape, but at eleven the clouds cleared and the moon revealed the crippled American ship. The *Pomone* pulled into cannon range on the larboard side. The *President* fired a broadside; the *Pomone* held its position and returned fire. For ten minutes the two ships exchanged broadsides. Decatur knew that he could hold off the *Pomone*, just as he had defeated *Endymion*, but now he saw *Tenedos* drawing up on his starboard quarter and *Majestic* covering the *President*'s stern. His options were running out. His ship crippled, twenty-five of his men including three lieutenants dead, sixty others wounded (including himself), and surrounded by the enemy, Decatur told his men that they had no choice but to surrender to the British squadron. He ordered all the men below; he alone on the quarterdeck would hand over the ship. There would be no dispute at the court-martial over responsibility. No American sailor would see Stephen Decatur surrender to the enemy.

As the *President* ceased firing, an officer called from the *Pomone*. Had Decatur surrendered? "I surrender to the squadron," Decatur called back. The British officer did not respond, but Decatur saw the men on *Pomone*'s gun deck moving toward the cannon. Were they going to fire? "To your quarters," he called below to his own men. I see they're bound to sink us, let us go down like men." The Americans readied their guns as *Pomone*'s captain called again, "Do you surrender?" Again Decatur answered, "I surrender to the squadron."[9]

The *Pomone* lowered a boat. Decatur waited as its men rowed toward his ship. A British lieutenant came aboard, and Decatur gave him command of the *President*. Then he went below to check on his own men. The surgeons busy with the wounded and dying in the cockpit looked up briefly when they heard Decatur's voice. His face was caked in blood. The surgeons immediately left the sailors they were attending to care for their wounded captain. Decatur shook them off, telling one, "When you have attended to these brave fellows, Doctor, I would thank you to look at my chest; it is very painful, and I believe I have been hurt."[10]

By two in the morning the *Majestic* and the crippled *Endymion* had drawn up to the *President*. By this time Decatur's broken ribs were bandaged and his face cleaned. He had changed into on his dress uniform. At three a boat took him to the *Majestic*, where he met the squadron commander, Captain John Hayes. For twenty-three hours the *President* had eluded the British squadron, had devastated one British ship and fought another until it became hopeless. Decatur solemnly took his sword and presented it to Hayes.

Hayes recalled Decatur's generous treatment of Carden after the *Macedonian* defeat. As Decatur handed him the sword, Hayes refused it, telling Decatur that he was proud to return "the sword of an officer, who had defended his ship so nobly."[11] With his sword, Decatur returned to the *President.*

In calm weather the next day his men and their captors began repairing their ships. On the *President*'s deck Decatur presided over funerals for his three lieutenants and twenty-two sailors. Then he and his surviving men were taken as prisoners to the British fleet. The boat carrying Decatur to the *Endymion* nearly foundered in a sudden squall; he made it through the storm and was taken aboard to lodge in Captain David Hope's cabin. During the night the squall turned into another gale, separating the squadron. *Endymion* had been repaired sufficiently to sail for Bermuda, while the *Majestic* sailed for New York to deliver Decatur's letters to Secretary of the Navy Benjamin Crowninshield and to Susan.

The storm continued, finishing the work the *President*'s guns had begun, destroying *Endymion*'s bowsprit, fore and mainmasts, and mizzen topmast. As Decatur watched *Endymion*'s men drop their upper-deck cannon overboard to lighten their load and ease their sailing in the blizzard, he worried for "the safety of our wounded left on board" the *President.* His ship had been badly damaged leaving New York and in the battle, and he did not think that its own masts would survive the voyage to Bermuda. But his men had done their work well, he noted, as he inspected *Endymion.* Early in the battle they had aimed for the masts and rigging, to cripple *Endymion* but not destroy it, so they could escape in it. As the plan changed, they had aimed more for the hull, but few of their shots had penetrated. For years he had suspected that American gunpowder was inferior; he had complained to the secretary of the navy of its poor quality. Now he was convinced that he had been right.[12]

Endymion brought Decatur to Bermuda on January 26, and his captured frigate arrived two days later. The British newspapers were triumphant. "The Yankees have a lame President on shore, had a crippled one on the ocean, now lost to them by the valor of a British frigate," a Montreal paper reported. "Their *Constitution* is still afloat; if she could be captured, what will become of the Union! Who knows but the *President* may, before long, sink the *Constitution*!" The day Decatur reached Bermuda, New York learned of his defeat. American newspapers put the best possible face on the loss. "The brave Decatur lives," a Maryland paper noted. "He fought until he was overpowered," and though the enemy had captured the *President*, "let him fit her out and place her by the side of the Constitution, and Capt. Stewart will restore her to his country."[13]

Just as the two sides predicted different outcomes, each reported the battle differently. The British and American officers agreed that Decatur had lost to the squadron. Captain Hayes suggested that the *Endymion* might even have defeated Decatur "had none of the squadron been in sight," but he knew that *Endymion* would have had to sink the *President* to defeat it. Vice Admiral Sir Alexander Cochrane, who had bottled Decatur up in New London for most of the war, hosted a dinner now for his former foe and his officers, and explained his defeat: Decatur "was completely mobbed."[14]

When Bermuda's *Royal Gazette* praised *Endymion* for capturing Decatur alone, the British captains Hayes and Hope demanded that the publisher, Edmund Ward, retract the claim. Ward did so, but after Decatur left Bermuda, he rescinded his retraction, claiming that the retraction had been printed only to "smooth it over" with Decatur. Fifteen of Decatur's midshipmen had stayed on in Bermuda, renting a house in the country. When they read Ward's denial, two of them decided to have it out with him. They found the publisher in King's Square, talking with a British lieutenant—who did not interfere as one of the Americans proceeded to whip Ward with a cane "in the most ample and satisfactory manner." Ward would not fight back in the street, but he did get the law on the midshipman, who left Bermuda that night.[15]

By this time Decatur was already home. He had sailed from Bermuda on the British ship *Narcissus*, which arrived at New London on February 21, 1815. One year earlier he and a small squadron had been blockaded in New London, and many of the town's citizens had made it clear that they would have welcomed the sight of Decatur being taken away on a British ship. Would the "blue light Federalists" of New London jeer him when he arrived as a British prisoner?

Before he had time to experience this humiliation, he received a note from Admiral Sir Henry Hotham, still blockading Long Island Sound. Hotham thoughtfully enclosed a letter to Stephen from Susan, sent in care of the British fleet. She had barely slept during her husband's month-long absence. In his own letter, Hotham congratulated Decatur on the fact that their two nations were now at peace.

Indeed, the war was over. Neither side had actually won, but both had agreed to stop fighting. American diplomats—John Quincy Adams, Albert Gallatin, Henry Clay, and James Bayard—had negotiated a settlement with the British, who pledged not to keep any of the American territories they had gained (by now the British occupied much of coastal Maine and Nantucket), and their ships would no longer harass Americans at sea. On paper the balance tipped toward the United States. Almost equally astounding, the British troops sent to take the Mississippi River had been utterly repulsed at New Orleans by General Andrew Jackson and his combined forces of Kentucky and Tennessee militia, Choctaw warriors, gunboat sailors, free Creoles from New Orleans, and Mississippi River pirates. Decatur arrived home to find that the war had been won by others.

February 22 was a high holiday for New London's Federalists: Washington's Birthday. This year all New Londoners—Federalists and Republicans—joined together to celebrate peace. Decatur stepped ashore into a New London he had not known during the months he had protected it. He expected to be received in disgrace; instead he was hailed as a returning hero. New Londoners crowded the docks to greet him, and as he stepped cautiously into a waiting carriage, the citizens cheered. He was alarmed when he saw a group of men unhitching the horses. What mischief did they now plan to embarrass him? But then the men of New London, Federalists and Republicans, took up the tongue and yoke and lines on their shoulders and pulled Decatur triumphantly through the streets, which were all lined with cheering crowds hailing their hero. Decatur rode silently through this spectacle of triumph and celebration. The citizens had planned a ball that night for Admiral Hotham and his British officers, who had blockaded their town for more than a year. Some of these officers were well known in the Federalist homes of New London, according to Republican rumors. This night Stephen Decatur was also an honored guest.[16]

Decatur left the strangely festive atmosphere of New London for New York, arriving there on February 26, four days too late for that city's even more fervent peace celebrations. There were fireworks and illuminations, and the French band he had brought home from the *Macedonian* had led a parade. His business partner Fulton had died two days after the peace, and Decatur had missed the funeral by one day; their *Demologos* would not have a chance to prove its value against an enemy attack. Nor would Decatur have a chance to redeem himself after losing the *President,* or being blockaded in New London. In Stephen's absence, Susan had written to Secretary Crowninshield requesting that her husband not be sent to sea. But the carpenters of New York City pledged a total of sixteen hundred days' work to build Decatur a new frigate. They wanted him to return to the sea and to glory.

CHAPTER 18

"Emerging from the cloud"

THE CELEBRATIONS in New London and New York were a painful reminder to Decatur that he had not returned home a hero. Hoping to clear his name, he requested that Secretary Crowninshield call a court of inquiry into the *President*'s surrender. British officers, eager to clear their own wounded reputations, were spreading an "infamous statement published in Bermuda" that *Endymion* alone had captured the *President.* Decatur wanted the truth established. He also requested that Crowninshield grant him "an active & conspicuous employment" as a way to prove "in Europe . . . that my statement had been satisfactory to my Government."[1]

Crowninshield "cheerfully" summoned a court of inquiry—consisting of Alexander Murray, Isaac Hull, and Samuel Evans—confident that they would see the "bravery and skill" of Decatur and the *President*'s men. He assured Decatur that the result would be "honorable to your high character as an officer" as well as a "credit to the navy" and "the honor of our National Flag." The court convened in April and found that the *President*'s capture had resulted from the ship's striking the channel bottom when it left the harbor. The court could barely restrain its admiration for Decatur—his "judgment and skill, perfect coolness, . . . determined resolution and heroic courage"— and his crew, who deserved the country's warmest gratitude: "They fought with a spirit, which no prospect of success could have heightened, and if victory had met its common reward, the *Endymion's* name would have been added to our list of naval conquests." The British had "gained a ship, but the victory was ours."[2]

Cleared by the navy, Decatur wanted to return quickly to action. The war with England was over, but the United States was preparing a fleet to strike at Algiers. In 1812 Algiers had declared war on the United States, assured that the British would sweep the U.S. Navy (which was no larger than the navy of Algiers) from the seas and Algiers would be free to take American merchant ships as prizes. Algiers had expected either a quick profit from captured American vessels or a lucrative treaty from Americans ready to buy peace. The American consul in Algiers was none other than Tobias Lear, architect of the 1805 Tripolitan treaty, regarded in Algiers as a "liberal man" eager to maintain peace. In short, the Algerians expected an easy time squeezing $2 million out of the Americans.[3]

Lear, however, had left Algiers rather than buy peace, and the British navy had failed to sweep the Americans from the seas. Now, with the British war over, the Madison administration was prepared to act. The administration's quasi-official paper, the *Richmond Enquirer*, thundered in February 1815 that "the day of Peace with England, ought to be the day of War against Algiers." The Tripolitan war had "brought great talents to light," most notably Decatur's, and "war with Algiers would be productive of the same benefits." The *Enquirer* urged, "We could not wish a finer school for our navy." The United States would send a greatly expanded school of sailors to Algiers. Commodore William Bainbridge was in Boston supervising construction of the *Independence*, at seventy-four guns the largest warship the country had yet built. Under Bainbridge's command, *Independence* would be flagship of the greatest American force yet sent to sea.

Unlike the just completed war against England, the new war against Algiers enjoyed support from both political parties. "This, at least, is a war which nobody objects to," a Federalist paper in Georgetown wrote. When construction on the fleet was delayed, the paper sarcastically asked if the Republicans were "determined not to have a war, unless they are sure of its being disliked by their political adversaries?"[4]

Even while her husband was still a prisoner, Susan had worried that on his return he would try to angle for an appointment to this expedition. She understood his need for redemption but could not bear another separation. Her downstairs neighbor Washington Irving recalled how Susan "would sometimes walk her room whole nights," "incapable of sleep," while her husband was at sea.[5] Even the peace treaty that lifted everyone else's spirits failed to buoy Susan. She unburdened herself to Secretary Crowninshield, confiding that she had been "so harrass'd and perturb'd during the last two or three years, that I really long for a little rest." The war had been a trial, and since Stephen had sailed she had been "so anxious about my husband's safety, that I have not yet been able to enjoy the glad tidings of Peace." Knowing that Stephen would seek a place in the Algerian expedition, she reminded the secretary that her husband had "already had a very arduous tour of duty in that quarter." She asked Crowninshield as a personal favor not to send Stephen to the Mediterranean, adding that "he has no wish to go there again unless it shou'd be deem'd indispensably necessary."[6]

Stephen was not happy when he learned of Susan's request. This was "the second time she has suffered her feelings to get the better of her judgement," he wrote to Crowninshield. While "her solicitude" for his safety touched him, "I cannot permit her to interfere in any way with my official duties." Crown-

inshield had naturally assumed that Susan spoke for her husband, but Decatur advised the secretary to consider any letters from Susan as written "without
my knowledge." If he had any favors to ask, he would ask them himself.[7]

Stephen Decatur assured the secretary that it was his wish to go to Algiers,
but he also needed Crowninshield's help in finding him a place in the fleet.
Bainbridge had been given overall command of the Algerian expedition, and
he needed this sign of official support much more than Decatur did. He did
not have to be reminded that he had surrendered the first two navy ships lost
in battle. Bainbridge's victory in the U.S.S. *Constitution* over the *Java* had
begun to restore his pride (though the *Constitution*'s sailors, who had been
victorious under Isaac Hull, tried to desert when they learned that Bainbridge
would be their new captain). Now Bainbridge would finally secure his reputation by leading the largest American fleet ever assembled into the Mediterranean.

Despite the wishes of his wife and of William Bainbridge, Decatur was
determined not just to go to Algiers but to lead the campaign. Crowninshield
proposed that Decatur take command after Bainbridge had accomplished
the mission. He could sail with Bainbridge—on the new frigate *Guerriere*,
being built in New York—and when Bainbridge returned home take command of the remaining ships in the fleet. Or he could sail later in the year
and relieve Bainbridge. His housemates at Mrs. Bradish's—particularly the
writers Washington Irving and James Kirke Paulding—had a different idea.
Irving suggested that Decatur sail to Algiers before Bainbridge. This was "a
chance for a brilliant dash," Irving told Decatur; by beating Bainbridge to
Algiers, he could "whip off the cream of the enterprise." Irving urged his
friend not to "lose the opportunity of emerging from the cloud which had
come over his celebrity."[8]

Decatur framed this suggestion carefully in a letter to Crowninshield. If he
sailed as Bainbridge's subordinate, the public might perceive this as "evidence of the confidence of the Government having been withdrawn from
me." He wanted "active & conspicuous employment" but would "prefer remaining on shore to taking a situation as second in the Fleet now going to
the Mediterranean." To solve this problem of public perception, he proposed
a slight change in strategy. Bainbridge would be the overall commander of
the squadron; but he could not leave for the Mediterranean until the flagship
Independence was fit to sail, and Crowninshield wanted to "send out the first
division immediately." The ships in New York were nearly ready, and since
"some one must command" the smaller flotilla, why not Decatur? He could
take the frigate *Guerriere* and the other nine ships—the frigates *Macedonian*
and *Constellation;* the sloop *Ontario;* the brigs *Epervier, Firefly, Flambeau,* and

Spark; and the schooners *Spitfire* and *Torch*. When Bainbridge arrived, Decatur could turn these ships over to him and sail home on a sloop.[9]

Crowninshield liked the idea. He was eager to get the squadron to Algiers, and also to keep his most illustrious captain happy. Bainbridge was furious when he realized that the navy was diverting supplies from his fleet being built in Boston to Decatur's in New York. Even men intended for his command were being sent to New York instead. Bainbridge had been told to offer new recruits a signing bonus of two months' wages; he learned that Decatur was offering three months' wages plus twenty dollars. The veterans of the Great Lakes fleet who were supposed to be making their way to Boston were going to New York and signing on to Decatur's squadron. Bainbridge's friend Henry Dearborn, former secretary of war, protested to Crowninshield that Bainbridge felt "pushed from the wall" by this treatment. Dearborn warned that with this kind of shabby favoritism, "the best men become disgusted & the favored crowd them from their stations." By exalting Decatur, the navy was humiliating Bainbridge, who after all "was a post Capt. when the former [Decatur] was only a Lieut."[10]

Bainbridge tried to hurry his construction along, but Decatur moved more quickly. By the time the court of inquiry had cleared him, Decatur had ten ships preparing to sail, the largest naval force the United States had ever sent to sea. On May 20, 1815—barely three months after he had returned home as a redeemed prisoner of war—Decatur sailed his fleet out of New York. He had tried to enlist Washington Irving as a passenger on the expedition (Irving was planning a trip to Europe anyway), but the writer, not believing that Decatur could have his ships ready so soon, had booked passage on a passenger ship; he wound up sailing five days after Decatur. (Paulding's nephew Hiram, just back from serving on the Great Lakes, sailed as a midshipman on the *Constellation*; years later he would rise to the rank of vice admiral.) Irving and his circle saw another opportunity for Stephen Decatur's glory; Susan was distraught.

Decatur's fleet reached Cádiz in just over three weeks, then touched at Tangier before sailing through the straits to Gibraltar. Crowds gathered on the waterfront in Britain's Mediterranean fortress when Decatur's fleet entered the harbor. With "elegant style" Decatur led *Guerriere* in a parade of American ships, "his broad pendant, and all his flags flying." A British naval officer watching through his spyglass called over an American merchant. Could the American identify these ships for him? The visitor looked out into the harbor, then politely began calling the roll, beginning with the ships the United States had captured from the British. "That, Sir, is the *Guerriere*. That, Sir, is the *Macedonian*. That, Sir, is the *Epervier*. The next, Sir, is—"

"O damn the next," the British officer said as he stormed away.[11]

Decatur paused in Gibraltar only long enough to show his fleet and flag, then quickly sailed on. In Cádiz and Tangier he had learned that the Algerian admiral Hamidou Ra'is was near Cabo de Gata in the forty-four-gun frigate *Meshouda*, specially built for him by a Spanish naval architect, waiting to collect Spain's half-million-dollar payment to Algiers. A fearless and able commander, Hamidou was admired at home and respected abroad. The son of a tailor, he had been at sea since the age of twelve, and a captain in the Algerian navy since 1798. He mainly preyed on merchant ships, counting captures from Genoa, Naples, Spain, Sweden, the Netherlands, and the United States. In 1798, the same year Decatur had joined the navy to fight the French, Hamidou had captured two French warships and the French military base at La Calle. He had once taken a Portuguese frigate off Gibraltar at high noon, and in 1810 had taken two larger Tunisian vessels, but because the Tunisians surrendered after his fleet had surrounded them, Hamidou would not claim sole credit for the captures. James Kirke Paulding contrasted Hamidou's modesty with the arrogance of the British commanders who claimed that *Endymion* alone, and not their entire squadron, had taken Decatur in the *President.* Paulding hoped that "other nations would take example from the mountain Arab" and not credit victories "to a single ship, that were gained by a squadron." The Italian poet and scholar Filippo Pananti, who had once been Hamidou's prisoner, later recalled the admiral's hospitality and civility. Decatur's biographer A. S. Mackenzie called Hamidou "the Decatur of Algiers."[12]

Two days after his dramatic entrance into Gibraltar, Decatur's fleet was off Cabo de Gata, where it found the *Meshouda*. The *Constellation* reached Hamidou's vessel first, with *Epervier* close behind. The Americans flew the British flag until they were practically within range, and Hamidou was fooled. But once he realized that he was being approached by Americans, he turned toward Cartagena to the northeast. The *Constellation* fired off two rapid broadsides. The first cut Hamidou Ra'is in two. His sailors panicked and rushed for the safety of the hold. From the masts the Algerian marines continued to fire, bravely fighting on as American cannon shredded the sails and rigging around them.

Charles Gordon on the *Constellation* and John Downes on *Epervier* knew that they were close to victory. But they were stunned to see Decatur signaling from the *Guerriere,* "Cast to starboard." He was ordering them to pull away. Why? What was his plan? They stopped firing as *Guerriere* drew nearer, and were absolutely astonished when the flagship sailed coolly between the *Constellation* and *Meshouda* and delivered two broadsides of its own at the nearly defeated Algerian. The first broadside killed five Americans and wounded thirty when a deck gun exploded. The *Meshouda*'s marines, firing from their fighting tops, wounded five of *Guerriere*'s men as Decatur brought his ship under the lee of *Meshouda*, continuing to fire at close range. *Constellation*, falling behind, fired a broadside into *Meshouda*'s stern. The Algerian sailors mustered their courage to return to the deck and lower their flag.

As Decatur sent a boat to take possession, the Algerian sailors and marines busily threw their dead overboard; Hamidou had asked that his body not be allowed to fall into the hands of infidels. While Decatur was preparing to claim his prize, the officers and crew on *Epervier* and *Constellation* vented their outrage. They had all but completed the capture, and now their commander was snatching it from them. He was, as Washington Irving suggested, whipping the cream off every enterprise. *Constellation* midshipman John Causten wrote that the officers of the squadron "detested" their prima donna commander, so intent on his own glory that he denied victory to others.

A tense group of captains gathered the next afternoon in Decatur's cabin, still fuming about Decatur's stealing the glory. "Such fighting would never take an Englishman," warned Gordon, and Downes of the *Epervier* had been heard to say that "he never saw a ship so shamefully maneuvered, & so miserably fought in all his life as the Guerriere."[13]

Decatur worked to win back their confidence. He had the table in his cabin piled high with scimitars, pistols, and knives taken from the *Meshouda*. To Downes, who had said he'd never seen a ship so poorly handled as *Guerriere*, Decatur replied that he had never seen a ship so skillfully handled as *Epervier*. He insisted that Downes have first pick of the captured weapons. As each officer in turn chose a trophy, the anger abated. They may have been swayed by Decatur's charm; they certainly were aware of his growing power in the navy. Gordon wrote an account of the battle to his brother-in-law, Congressman Joseph Nicholson, but warned, "Do not Publish my letters, As you will find the Comm'dr. takes the Capture to his Ship." Gordon did not want to be caught in a public dispute with Decatur. "Whatever Opinion the officers of the Navy may have of Commodore Decatur," Midshipman Causten wrote, "none are so inconsiderate as to war against his *popularity*."[14]

His officers for the moment appeased, Decatur led his fleet further into the Mediterranean. Two days after taking the *Meshouda*, they spied the twenty-two-gun Algerian brig *Estedio*, with 180 sailors, off Cape Palos. The Algerian quickly sailed toward the shallow coastal waters, where *Guerriere* and *Constellation* could not follow. Decatur sent his smaller ships—the brig *Spark*, the schooners *Torch* and *Spitfire*, and Downes on the *Epervier*—after the *Estedio*. The Algerians tried to escape to shore, but a shot from an American cannon sank an escaping Algerian launch. The four American vessels finally caught the *Estedio*, finding twenty-three dead men on board and taking eighty prisoners. No Americans were killed or wounded in the fight. Sending the two prizes, *Estedio* and *Meshouda*, and the Algerian prisoners into Cartagena under the *Macedonian*'s escort, Decatur turned toward Algiers.

Leaving the rest of his fleet blockading the harbor, Decatur sailed *Guerriere* into Algiers on June 28.[15] From the foremast he flew the white flag, a signal for peace; from the mainmast he flew the Swedish flag, a signal for Sweden's consul, Johan Norderling, to come aboard and act as intermediary. The Americans had not had a diplomatic representative in Algiers since Lear had left in 1812; William Shaler had come along on *Guerriere* to handle negotiations and then stay on in Algiers once peace was secured. Norderling boarded *Guerriere* the next day, escorted by the Algerian captain of the port. Decatur asked the captain where the Algerian fleet was. "By this time," the captain said, "it is safe in some neutral port."

"Not the whole of it," Decatur answered. Hamidou Ra'is was dead; *Meshouda* and *Estedio* were prizes in Cartagena. The captain did not believe him. Decatur had *Meshouda*'s lieutenant brought to the cabin. When this officer confirmed that Hamidou was dead and the frigate lost, the captain of the port "rushed at him, seized him by the beard & was about to jerk him down to his feet when Decatur interfered & prevented it." With this news confirmed, the captain told Decatur he must come ashore; they could not negotiate on the ship. Decatur refused; he remembered how the hapless Captain Morris had been arrested in Tunis. The treaty had to be negotiated on board the *Guerriere*, and Decatur would not agree to a truce until the treaty was signed. The captain protested: Decatur was flying a flag of truce; he could not attack Algerian ships while under the white flag. Decatur answered that the *Guerriere* was indeed under a white flag, but the other American ships immediately outside the harbor were not, and they would do as they pleased.

The captain and the Swedish consul returned to Algiers. The regency's situation had changed since Dey Ali had declared war. Ali had been murdered in a March coup d'état, whose leader had ruled for only a few weeks before his own murder. The new Dey, Omar, hoping to avoid the fate of his predecessors, was trying to consolidate his own power, and the news that the American fleet was blockading his capital and had already taken two of his ships encouraged him to act quickly. The next day he sent Norderling and the captain back to the *Guerriere* with a treaty. He would free the ten Americans taken in 1812; he would compensate Americans for property seized and never take any more American ships. Decatur and Shaler also insisted that the United States would no longer pay annual tribute to Algiers.

No nation had ever demanded so much of Algiers. Omar had declared "that he would not have agreed to such terms for any power in the world, except the man who went in a dark night, and burnt the Philadelphia—that there was no knowing what such a person might do; and it was better to make peace upon his own terms."[16]

But with his own political position tenuous, Omar worried about setting a precedent by waiving tribute. Why would any other nation pay if the United States did not? The captain tried to move Decatur and Shaler on the question of tribute. Perhaps the United States could make an incidental or symbolic annual gift, such as a barrel or two of gunpowder?

"You can have the powder," Decatur replied, "but you must have balls with it."[17]

The captain then asked for a truce to give Omar and his government time to discuss the treaty. Decatur and Shaler refused. Could the Algerians have just three hours? No, Decatur and Shaler said, "not a minute." They knew as well as the captain and Omar that the rest of the Algerian squadron might arrive at any moment. "If your squadron appears in sight before the treaty is actually signed by the Dey, and the prisoners sent off, ours would capture them," the Americans warned.[18]

Seeing that he could not have more time, the captain shifted to a different course. The two captured ships—*Meshouda* and *Estedio*—could be of little use to the Americans, whom he could see were much more skillful builders of ships than the makers of the Algerian fleet. But it would greatly "satisfy the people" of Algiers if the Americans gave them back. This would convince the Algerians that Omar could exact concessions from the Americans, even as the treaty conceded much to the United States. Decatur and Shaler considered the value of allowing Omar to save face with his people, weighing it against the expense of repairing the two ships and sending them across the Atlantic. If Omar signed the treaty as it was, they agreed, with no mention of *Estedio* and *Meshouda*, then Decatur would return the ships as "a favour conferred on the Dey by the United States."[19]

Back to Algiers the captain went, warned that until he returned to the *Guerriere* with a signed treaty and the ten American prisoners, Decatur would attack any Algerian ship entering the port. As Omar and his advisers discussed the treaty, Britain's consul stopped in to see how the negotiations were proceeding. The Algerian prime minister angrily informed him that Algiers was accepting the Americans' demands. "You told us that the American Navy would be destroyed in *six months* by *you*," he complained, "and *now* they make war upon *us* with *three* of *your own vessels* they have taken from you."[20]

On the *Guerriere*, Decatur dressed to receive the final treaty. In his gold-laced coat and hat and his cassimere pantaloons, wearing the badge of the Cincinnati, he "looked the very ideal of the hero."[21] As he waited for the Algerian emissary to return, he saw an Algerian warship enter the port. The Algerians might be signing the treaty, or they might be tricking the Americans into complacency. Decatur would take no chances. He ordered his men to quarters; they would run the Algerian aground and board it in its own home port. He had taken gunboats and a frigate in Tripoli harbor; he would now take an Algerian vessel in the harbor of Algiers. Ordering the saber and pistol taken from the *Meshouda* brought to the capstan, Decatur steered *Guerriere* toward the Algerian warship. From the dock the frantic captain of the port signaled to stop the attack. He had the treaty! He had ten prisoners he was bringing in a boat to the *Guerriere*! Decatur ordered his men to stand down. He had led his men to battle for the last time.

The relieved Algerian captain arrived aboard the *Guerriere* with the ten Americans and a new treaty. Decatur had the Americans and the treaty taken aboard *Epervier* to return to the United States. Lieutenant Commander Downes came aboard *Guerriere* to take command of Decatur's ship. If Midshipman Causten had a correct reading of the dynamics, this was a strange choice. Downes, according to Causten, loathed Decatur. But was this promotion part of a strategy to win over the lieutenant commander, or simply a recognition of his abilities? In any event, Decatur brought Downes aboard *Guerriere* and sent Lieutenant Commander John Shubrick to bring *Epervier* home. Shubrick had been a lieutenant with Decatur on the *President*; he had hoped for a shore assignment when he returned from captivity in Bermuda. Decatur had persuaded him to come on the Mediterranean expedition, and now, at the first opportunity, he sent Shubrick home. Tragically, after stopping in Gibraltar with the ten American prisoners and the new treaty, *Epervier* was never seen again.[22]

Forty-eight hours after arriving in Algiers, Decatur sailed away, leaving Shaler "as Consul General in the most dreary residence on this Earth."[23] Their peace treaty was the first in recent memory with the Algerian regency that did not require the payment of tribute to Algiers. John Quincy Adams, the American minister in London, expressed his hope that Decatur and Shaler's peace "may prove as permanent as it is glorious." The "lesson" Decatur had delivered to Algiers, Adams told him, "will make a durable impression on its future policy; and I most ardently pray that the example, which you have given, of rescuing our country from the disgrace of a tributary treaty, may become our irrevocable law for all future time."[24]

CHAPTER *19*

"Without the assistance of Bainbridge"

A FTER A BRIEF visit to Italy, Decatur sailed on to Tunis. That regency was at peace with the United States, but during the war it had allowed the English to take from its neutral port two British merchants ships captured by an American. The privateer *Abaellino* had sent the prizes to Tunis knowing that Tunis was bound by treaty to protect them. The British warship *Lyra* happened to be there when the ships arrived. Under international law, this should not have mattered. But the *Lyra*'s captain put his own prize crew aboard the vessels and sent them to Malta.

The American consul, Mordecai Manuel Noah, demanded that the Bey of Tunis pay the United States the $46,000 the ships were worth. The Bey stalled, and Noah was on the verge of leaving Tunis when Decatur's fleet arrived on July 26. Through Noah, Decatur sent a message to the Bey: Either pay up in twelve hours or face the consequences.

Noah had longed to deliver a message like this one. But Decatur also brought Noah a shocking letter from Secretary of State James Monroe. The administration, Monroe wrote, had not realized "at the time of your appointment" that "the RELIGION which you profess would form any obstacle to your consular functions." But "recent information" had proved to Monroe that Noah's religion—the consul was Jewish—would have "a very unfavorable effect" on his ability to negotiate in Tunis. On receipt of the letter, Noah should consider himself "no longer in the public service."[1] Noah was stunned. More than a month earlier he had decided to return home because he had been unable to force the Bey to pay compensation for the two prizes. Now that the fleet had arrived with sufficient power to make the Bey pay up, he was told he had been fired because he was Jewish.

Noah showed Decatur the letter from Monroe officially relieving him of his duties. Legally, Decatur should not have consulted with Noah on American strategy. But Decatur knew that he and Noah had similar views on North Africa and the Mediterranean. Like Decatur, Noah had long argued against the idea of buying peace, and both men were puzzled that Noah was being ignored while Tobias Lear, who had thought "we might possibly purchase a peace for $300,000," was heeded.[2] Now they learned that their government had dispensed with Noah not because of his opinions but because of his faith.

Decatur and Noah chose to ignore Monroe's orders. Although they knew

169

that Monroe had fired Noah, the Bey of Tunis had not. Noah went ashore to demand payment within twelve hours.[3]

"Tell your Admiral to come ashore and see me," the Bey told Noah.

"He declines coming, your highness, until these disputes are settled, which are best done on board ship."

"But this is not treating me with becoming dignity. Hamuda Pacha of blessed memory, commanded them to land and wait at the palace, until he pleased to receive them."

"Very likely, your highness," Noah said. "But that was twenty years ago."

"I know this Admiral." The Bey grew thoughtful. "He is the same one who in the war with Sidi Yusef, of Trablis, burnt the frigate."

"The same."

"Hum! why do they send wild young men to treat for peace with old powers?" Decatur, the wild young man, capable of sailing beneath the guns of Tripoli to destroy the *Philadelphia*, was capable of anything. But the Bey still challenged Noah. "Then you Americans don't speak truth," the Bey said. "You went to war with England, a nation with a great fleet, and said you took their frigates in equal fight; an honest people always speak truth."

"Well, sir, and that was true," Noah told him. He pointed out into the harbor, and as the Bey followed with his telescope, Noah identified the American ships. "Do you see that tall ship in the bay, with a blue flag [the *Guerriere*]? That was taken from the British; that one near the small island [the *Macedonian*] was also captured on equal terms; that sloop near Cape Carthage [the *Peacock*] was also taken in battle."

The Bey laid down the telescope, reclined on his cushions, "and with a small tortoise shell comb set with diamonds, combed his beard." As he combed and thought, he and Noah watched two small boats from the American fleet easily navigate the harbor. One small boat sailed just beneath the batteries of Tunis; a crew of American sailors rowed a pinnace while one sailor sounded the harbor's depth. Looking through his telescope, Noah recognized the sailor making the soundings as Commodore Decatur. Perhaps it was another scientific expedition; Decatur had occupied himself ten years earlier by collecting animal specimens as he awaited the Bey's decision on peace or war. Now with an air of calculated indifference—or was it meticulous preparation?—Decatur was exploring the Bey's harbor.

"Tell the Admiral to land," said the Bey, "and all shall be settled to his satisfaction."

Once again Decatur changed into his full dress uniform, with the gold lace on the hat and the badge of the Cincinnati on his chest, and landed in Tunis. He and Noah met at the American consulate to wait for official word from the Bey. The British consul, Richard Oglander, joined them, though, like his counterpart in Algiers, he may have come to wish that he had stayed home. The prime minister's brother arrived with the payment for the two American prizes—a bundle of $46,000 in cash. He threw the bundle at Decatur's feet, then turned to the British consul: "You see, Sir, what Tunis is obliged to pay for your insolence. You should feel ashamed of the disgrace you have brought upon us. I ask you if you think it just, first to violate our neutrality, and then leave us to be destroyed or pay for your aggression."[4] Both Algiers and Tunis had now made peace with the United States, and in doing so each blamed its misfortunes on the British.

Decatur left Noah in Tunis. The following year Noah returned to the United States, where he had an unsatisfactory meeting with Secretary of State Monroe, though President Madison was more sympathetic. Noah wrote a defense of his conduct as American consul in Tunis and called for an end to the kind of religious bigotry that he felt was behind his recall. He went on to write patriotic plays and edit a newspaper in New York, all the while trying to create a new homeland for Jews on the Genesee River in western New York State. To the end of his long life, Noah would remember how Stephen Decatur had relied on him at the very moment when his own government had tried to cast him off.

Decatur sailed into Tripoli on August 5. Eleven years earlier he had become a hero in America for his exploits here; now his name was again beginning to be heard throughout the Mediterranean. Like Tunis, Tripoli had allowed the British to take American prizes out of its harbor during the war. Decatur demanded that Tripoli pay $30,000 for this violation of neutral rights. Yusuf Pacha Qaramanli—still in power—called for twenty thousand of his subjects to man Tripoli's batteries against an American attack. He also sent an official to the *Guerriere* to negotiate. Learning that Tunis and Algiers had made peace, and seeing no benefit in another American war, Qaramanli agreed to pay $25,000 and to release ten hostages—eight Sicilians and two Danes. Decatur did not go ashore, but sent his band to play "Hail, Columbia!," "The President's March," and "Yankee Doodle." Yusuf's cannon fired a twenty-one-gun salute as the American flag was raised over the U.S. consulate. On August 9, having secured peace with all three Barbary States, Decatur sailed from Tripoli.[5] How Preble would have relished this moment.

Decatur now steered the fleet toward Syracuse, Preble's base during the Tripolitan war. Quarantine kept him from visiting the town he had known ten years earlier. He sailed around to Messina to deliver the Sicilian hostages. Facing contrary winds, the local pilot refused to take the responsibility of bringing the *Guerriere* into port. Decatur, who had learned to speak Italian fluently during his first stationing in Sicily, asked if the harbor charts were accurate. Assured that they were, and eager to bring the eight Sicilians home quickly, Decatur took the *Guerriere*'s helm and steered his frigate against the wind into the harbor at Messina.

The people welcomed Decatur as a "Champion of Christendom." He stayed ten days in the city he and Eaton and Preble had visited ten years before, making a greater impression than he had as a young captain traveling through the Sicilian countryside. He had now accomplished what Preble had hoped to achieve in Tripoli, and what no other nation had been able to do in Algiers. A Sicilian newspaper reported that "that brave officer," Decatur, "has the glory of having, after 35 days' absence from the *New World*, concluded the most honorable peace for the GREAT NATION which he represents, and very much to the advantage of the Commerce of his Country."[6]

From Messina, Decatur sailed on to Naples. After visiting the ruins of Pompeii and Herculaneum and the tomb of Virgil, he was received by the king of Naples and the Two Sicilies, who formally thanked Decatur for the safe return of the Sicilian hostages. Decatur insisted that his action was but a small token of thanks for the support Naples had given the United States during the American war against Tripoli.

Americans would not learn of Decatur's victories until the fall, as the *Epervier* had been lost at sea. But around the Mediterranean and Europe the news was spreading. Washington Irving wrote happily from England to his family in New York that "friend Decatur has had a successful recontre with the Algerines," and that the "triumph will completely fix Decaturs reputation." Decatur could now "repose on his Laurels" while his victories gave him the financial means to "solace himself under their shade." He had done what Irving had known he would. The writer told a friend in New York to congratulate Susan and assure her "that now I am willing she shall have" her husband to herself.[7]

Decatur sent the rest of his fleet to find William Bainbridge, who by this time must have reached Gibraltar or Málaga. Bainbridge had sailed from Boston on July 2; by that time Decatur and Shaler had made peace with Algiers. By the time Bainbridge reached Gibraltar, Decatur had resolved U.S. differences with Tunis. Bainbridge realized that although he commanded the largest American ship ever built, and that once all the squadron arrived he would be in command of the largest American fleet ever assembled, he had nothing to do. Worse, he was stricken with measles.[8] Bainbridge sailed from Gibraltar to Algiers but did not stop. He remained off Algiers only long enough to send Shaler a message that "he was bound up the Mediterranean," then he passed on "at a great distance without stopping."[9] He was hoping to

get to Tripoli in time to resolve the problems with that country before Decatur arrived, but he was too late. Decatur had already been there. Bainbridge
stayed overnight August 26–27 in the city where he had been a prisoner for
seventeen months, then sailed for Tunis. While Decatur was being received
by the king of Naples and thanked for his efforts in Tripoli, Bainbridge was
learning that Decatur had also resolved American differences with Tunis.

Measles and Decatur: how much more could Bainbridge endure? This
mission was to have secured his reputation, making up for so many other
moments of infamy. But Decatur seemed to turn up everywhere, lurking in
the shadows of Bainbridge's low points and hovering above his peaks. Decatur's father had captured the *Retaliation* from the French; Bainbridge surrendered it to the French. The younger Decatur became a hero in 1804 because
Bainbridge had surrendered the *Philadelphia*—a ship built for the senior Decatur—in 1803. For his *Philadelphia* triumph Decatur was promoted to captain—the youngest man ever commissioned captain in the U.S. Navy. Did
anyone remember that Bainbridge had once been the youngest man to be
commissioned captain? Bainbridge destroyed the *Java*; Decatur defeated the
Macedonian and then brought it home. Now Decatur had gone ahead and
completed Bainbridge's mission almost before the senior commodore had
reached the Mediterranean. With nothing to accomplish—though he assured Secretary of State Monroe that "had occasion demanded, or an opportunity offered . . . the Gallant officers and men under my command, would
have proved that devotion to their Country, which our small Navy has so often
exhibited"—Bainbridge took the fleet back to Gibraltar to return home.[10]

As Bainbridge scratched his measles and nursed his wounded pride, Decatur was finding another opportunity for his men to prove their own devotion to country. As he sailed from Naples to the coast of Spain, Decatur on
the *Guerriere* ran into the rest of the Algerian fleet. Four frigates and three
sloops swiftly closed in around the American frigate they found sailing alone
in the Mediterranean. Decatur ordered his crew to quarters, cleared the gun
deck for action, and, when preparations were complete, mustered the crew
on the quarterdeck.

"My lads," he told them, "those fellows are approaching us in a threatening
manner; we have whipped them into a treaty, and if that treaty is to be broken,
let them break it. Be careful of yourselves. Let any man fire without orders at
the peril of his life. But let them fire first, if they will, and we'll take the whole
of them."[11] Decatur's crew returned to their primed and loaded guns—being
careful not to get too close—and waited for the Algerian fleet.

The flagship approached on *Guerriere*'s leeward side—a sign of peaceful
intentions, though Decatur would take no chances. As the frigate drew along-

side, the Algerian admiral called through his trumpet in Italian, the lingua franca, "*Dove andate*?" Where are you going? Taking his own trumpet Decatur answered slowly and clearly, "*Dove me piace*," Where I please.[12]

The American frigate, going wherever in the world it pleased, sailed on for Gibraltar.

Bainbridge had found the rest of Decatur's fleet in Gibraltar and was waiting there for *Guerriere*. Finally he could wait no longer. On a clear October morning Bainbridge prepared to sail home. He would leave John Shaw and three ships to maintain the American presence in the Mediterranean. Bainbridge ordered his fourteen other ships—one ship of the line, three frigates, and his sloops and brigs and schooners—to unfurl their sails and parade out of the harbor. It was a magnificent procession, more inspiring than Decatur's arrival with ten ships back in June. As Bainbridge's *Independence* cleared the harbor, another American frigate rounded Europa Point and sailed in. It was the *Guerriere*! As the frigate passed each ship in Bainbridge's procession, the sailors could barely control their joy. *Guerriere* fired salutes, and the sailors saluted and cheered back as *Guerriere* and Captain Decatur sailed on toward the *Independence*.

Midshipman Alexander Slidell Mackenzie on the *Chippewa* was transfixed. As *Guerriere* drew near to the *Independence*, Mackenzie saw an "officer of distinguished mien" appear on deck and climb into a boat. It was Stephen Decatur! Every sailor in the fleet cheered as the launch brought Decatur toward the flagship. Their thoughts turned back to "the burning of the Philadelphia, the hand to hand encounter in the gunboats, the capture of the Macedonian, the desperate defence against the attack of the British squadron"—the U.S. Navy's greatest triumphs. And now Decatur had won peace in the Mediterranean! They hailed him as he was carried in triumph to the *Independence*.

But the *Independence* did not slow down. Under full sail it pressed ahead as Decatur's oarsmen struggled to catch up. Decatur had so far orchestrated a dramatic entrance into the harbor and received the ovation he deserved; now Bainbridge was turning the moment into a race. Decatur's men rowed harder and faster, and finally caught the *Independence*. Mackenzie felt a "thrill of patriotic pride"—he could still feel it thirty years later—as he watched Decatur climb aboard. Bainbridge felt a different sensation.[13]

Decatur's tumultuous welcome died away as he stepped onto the ship. Bainbridge received him like "a *total stranger*" and then demanded that he take down his commodore's pennant from the *Guerriere*. Stung by this rebuke, Decatur refused to take down the banner, which he had "worn . . . at the mast head of the Guerriere from the time of his leaving America, and should return home with it flying from the same place." Decatur "had completed the work for which he had been sent to the Mediterranean, without the assistance of Bainbridge or his vessels; but still, if that officer had arrived before peace had been made, he should have given up the command to him."[14] Decatur returned to the *Guerriere*; Bainbridge sailed on. The two men would not speak for five years.

Bainbridge continued to lead his fleet out of Gibraltar, and Decatur steered *Guerriere* back in. But he would not stay long. Bainbridge was justified in his resentment, but Decatur would not let the matter simply drop. He decided to set out for home as quickly as he could. With Bainbridge traveling in a fourteen-ship convoy and Decatur sailing alone, Decatur knew that he could beat Bainbridge back to America just as he had beaten him to Algiers. One day after Bainbridge's snub, Decatur and *Guerriere* sailed from Gibraltar. "As the sun rose" on November 12, New Yorkers "beheld . . . nearly twenty sail of square rigged vessels approaching with a fair wind and flood tide; coming, as it were, under the protection of the elegant frigate Guerriere, Commodore Decatur." The ships—including vessels named for a Massachusetts Federalist (the *Fisher Ames*) and for a Republican (the *Lady Gallatin*)— came "all from foreign ports, with full and valuable cargoes." Two days later— Tuesday, November 14—would be the busiest day on record for the New York Custom House, taking in nearly double the amount of revenue ever entered in one day. "This is a proud day for New York," the collector said. The National *Intelligencer* commented that this was one of the "pleasant scenes which result from an unrestricted commerce." This commercial boom had been brought about by the Madison administration—and Commodore Decatur.[15]

Bainbridge and his fleet arrived in Newport the next day. Once again, Decatur had beaten him.[16]

Decatur had been gone only six months. As one of his sailors wrote to an uncle at home, "We, in the space of ninety days, settled with three of the Barbary powers, whipped one, and made peace on our own terms—and exacted tribute from two others."[17] They had captured an Algerian frigate and brig, made a treaty with Algiers—the first Algiers had ever signed that renounced tribute—secured peace with Tunis and Tripoli, returned hostages to Sicily and to the Danes, been welcomed by the king of Naples, and demonstrated to Europe and North Africa the skill of Americans at building ships and taking them into combat.

Secretary Crowninshield sent Decatur an effusive note of welcome, congratulating him on his "safe return, to your Country, your family & your friends," promising that "due attention" would be paid Decatur's "meritorious officers," and begging him to accept the secretary's "respect and regard."

Three days later Crowninshield sent Bainbridge a much shorter note, acknowledging his return but neither congratulating him nor mentioning how delighted his country, family, and friends must be on his arrival. Worst of all for Bainbridge—after Decatur had upstaged him in the Mediterranean and then beaten him home across the Atlantic with the news—he now found himself out of a job. To take command of the *Independence*, he had given up his post as commandant of the Charlestown Navy Yard in Massachusetts. He had expected that the post would be waiting for him on his return, and on the same day that Crowninshield was composing his curt welcome, Bainbridge had written the secretary about his Charlestown post. Now Crowninshield informed him that in his absence his position had been given to Isaac Hull.[18]

CHAPTER 20

"Honor to the Name of Commodore Decatur"

"WE HAVE NOT titles or stars to reward you," the *Richmond Enquirer* apologized in an editorial addressed to Decatur. "We have no Garters to adorn you, no lordly-sounding names, or munificent pensions to bestow" on the "hero, who returns covered with glory, only to share it with his countrymen." Decatur had been summoned to war "by justice and not by ambition," not to "make conquests, but to set the captive free" and to deliver his country from being a tributary to Algiers. On the Barbary Coast he had "revived the terror of the American Nation" among the Algerians "and compelled them once more to pay respect to our flag." European nations might be content to pay tribute, but Decatur's "chivalrous munificence" had freed the captives while "relieving the losses of the conquered!—Hail then to the Hero who has achieved these successes! Honor to the name of Commodore Decatur!"[1]

President Madison's annual message to Congress begins like an adventure story. "The squadron," he related, "under Commodore Decatur, lost not a moment after its arrival in the Mediterranean in seeking the naval force of the enemy, and capturing two ships, one of them commanded by the Algerian admiral." In this battle the "high character of the American commander was brilliantly sustained," as was the "accustomed gallantry of all the officers and men." After giving this "demonstration of American skill and prowess," Decatur had "hastened to the port of Algiers, where peace was promptly yielded to his victorious force." Against Algiers he had secured the "rights and honor of the United States" against that regency's "pretensions" to demand American tribute. Madison praised Decatur for securing the freedom of Americans to trade in the Mediterranean. Almost as an afterthought the president mentioned Bainbridge and his "subsequent transactions" with his "larger force" in Decatur's wake.[2]

Decatur had whipped the cream off the enterprise and was again the nation's idol. Americans knew what they could expect from him. The *National Intelligencer* reported in early September that although the details of the Algerian treaty were still unknown, "we learn, generally, that they are such as Commodore Decatur thought proper to dictate." The treaty itself bore this out, as the *Baltimore Patriot* reported: "Peace was concluded with the Dey of Algiers on the 12th of July—and on our own terms."[3]

The ovation Decatur received in 1815 would be even louder and more sustained than in 1805 or 1812. "How must a man feel," *Niles Weekly Register* wondered after a year of applause, "to receive the caresses of a whole people!" The celebrations had begun as the first news of the treaty arrived in early September. "Commodore Decatur, and our negociations in the Mediterreanean" was one toast offered at a September 5 dinner at Tammany Hall honoring Albert Gallatin and Henry Clay, two of the negotiators who had won peace from the British at Ghent. Decatur was once again the toast of New York—and of the nation. Decatur arrived in New York in time for the city's annual celebration of the 1783 British evacuation. He was the guest of honor at the dinner, along with Oliver Hazard Perry, the artist John Trumbull, and various military and political dignitaries. Joseph Bonaparte—whose brother had once courted Susan Wheeler—had been invited but declined to attend.[4]

As the nation had time to reflect on what Decatur had accomplished, its wonder grew. In Washington, the *Daily National Intelligencer* noted that the sloop *Peacock*, its commander unaware that the War of 1812 was over, did not return from its cruise against the British until October 31. Decatur had concluded the Algerian war well before this, making for "an unprecedented historical fact, to wit, *the declaration, prosecution, and successful termination, of one naval war, before all the cruisers of a previous naval war had come in.*" The *Intelligencer* asked rhetorically, "What nation on the globe can say this?"[5]

The *Boston Gazette* reported that the "Algerines, Tunisians, and Tripolitans, have been reduced to humiliating terms by this chivalric commander." Decatur had delivered "an *electrick shock* as was never before discharged from a christian battery. DECATUR may well be termed the 'Champion of Christendom.' " His treaty had earned "a Glory which never encircled the brows of a Roman Pontiff; nor blazed from an imperial diadem."[6]

Baltimore's newspapers were perhaps the most effusive. The *Patriot*, calling Decatur "the favorite of the navy, and honored by the voluntary and unanimous applause of his countrymen," suggested that he "had a fair claim to be made a knight of the order of St. John of Jerusalem." Of course, Americans were against all such noble titles; but "if the knights of Malta should ever come into vogue again," the American sailors would be "represented in the institution." For who had "done more against the Barbary pirates than the Americans, and Decatur in particular?" The only objection the paper could make to a knighthood for Decatur was that "it would too much detract from the merit of a *Republican Commodore*."[7]

Decatur had not returned home to a country completely at peace with itself. While his success in Algiers was a national triumph, the partisan press also made clear that his victories had political import. At the beginning of the

year New England Federalists, meeting at the Hartford Convention, had opposed Madison's policies in general and the ongoing war in particular. The
Baltimore Patriot reported that now "tory-federalists" everywhere were "de-
sponding" over "Decatur's triumphs" and his treaty with Algiers, as this was
further evidence "that President Madison and his cabinet know how to man-
age national affairs very well."[8] The Republican press would not allow its
readers to forget that earlier that year extreme Federalists had wanted to
break the Union apart; more moderate Federalists simply wanted Madison to
resign. Now Madison had been fully vindicated, thanks to the heroism of
Decatur.

Federalists would not simply accept this charge. Georgetown's *Federal Republican* recalled that it was the Republicans who had been the "opposers of
the navy" in the 1790s, but the Federalists had fortunately overruled them.
"This is history. 'Tis done. They cannot alter it." The paper asked: "What
triumphed over the British on Lake Erie? Federal policy—What on Lake
Champlain?—Federal policy—What on the ocean? Federal policy—What
over the Tripolitans?—Federal policy—What over the Algerines?—Federal
policy—What over the Barratarians?—Federal policy. What now enables a
man, in any part of the world, to hold up his head and say—*I am an American?*
Federal policy." While suggesting that the Republicans be forgiven their earlier opposition, since they had learned from their mistakes, the paper declared that the navy's most important victory was "that over the democrats."[9]

Federalists and Republicans alike used any convenient issue to savage each
other. Decatur was en route to a testimonial dinner in Baltimore, where the
issue of the moment was the recent election of a new U.S. senator. The
Decaturs' friend, Federalist Robert Goodloe Harper—who had been practic-
ing law in Baltimore since his retirement from Congress in the Jefferson
revolution of 1800—had been elected to succeed Samuel Smith, the powerful Republican, and brother of the former navy secretary. Republicans falsely
charged Harper with stealing the election; then, when the *Patriot* published a
letter that had fallen out of Harper's pocket, the Federalists countered by
referring to the Republicans as "pick-pockets." Harper would serve barely a
year before resigning, though in 1816 he would become the Federalist candidate for vice president. It was men like Harper—smart, capable, honest—
who were the Federalist Party's only hope for revival. Unlike other Federalists
tainted by association with the Hartford Convention, Harper had served with
distinction in the war. The rival Republicans nevertheless spared no epithet
in denouncing him. Throughout the week of Decatur's visit, Stephen and
Susan stayed in the Harpers' home, as the Baltimore papers took turns vilify-
ing the senator elect and lauding the naval hero.

What most impressed participants at Baltimore's testimonial dinner for Decatur on the day after Christmas was the fact that men "of different political sentiments"—who spent most of their public moments damning one another and warning the public about the horrors that awaited should the other party get an ounce of power—had come together with "great harmony and good humor" on Decatur's behalf, for "to do honor to the gallant officer who was invited, appeared to be the object in which all were anxious to unite."[10]

Only a year or so earlier Baltimore had provided another lesson in civic cooperation. The British raid on Washington in September 1814 had alerted Baltimore to prepare its defenses, and the people of Baltimore made good use of the time. Citizens of all political opinions had joined together to defend the city; the navy had prevented the British from closing in on Fort McHenry by sinking its gunboats; the army had held the fort; and the militia, commanded by General Robert Smith, had held off the British army. Decatur could not help but imagine that if the people of New London had been this engaged, or the military forces around Washington so ably led, the war might have turned out differently.

Now the city united again to applaud "the man whom the country delights to honor," as one toast put it. Decatur was presented with a silver serving set, inscribed with a Latin motto: "Rebus gestis insigni—ob virtutes dilecto" (Distinguished for his heroism; admired for his virtues); one toast at the banquet asserted that Decatur's valor had "illustrated the brightest page of our history," and another thanked his "gallant squadron" for teaching Algiers to "respect the laws of nations." The *Baltimore Patriot* wrote of the "genius and chivalric cast of mind" that distinguished a hero like Decatur from the "phlegmatic fighting officer" and noted that it was "the manner of achievement more than the achievement we admired." His "genius accomplished what his cannon would have been found inadequate to effect!" Decatur might have said, the paper concluded, in the "language of Caesar," "I came, I saw, I conquered."[11] Called on to deliver his own toast, Decatur had raised his glass to "Citizens of Baltimore: Their patriotism and valor defeated the veteran forces of their enemy, who came, saw, and fled."[12]

From Baltimore, Stephen and Susan traveled to Washington. Just sixteen months earlier the capital had been burned, the nation's survival thrown in doubt. Now, with survival sure, Washington was rebuilding quickly. The *National Intelligencer* noted the "spirit and enterprise of those" who were building the new Capitol, which would house Congress much more comfortably than the building burned by the British. Most important, the British had failed "to break the spirit or cramp the energy of a free people," who would "rise with elastic spring from every effort of this kind."[13] The national mood had been despondent in January 1815; by the turn of the New Year 1816, the mood was euphoric.

Decatur was part of the "unusually large" crowd that spent New Year's Day calling on President Madison.[14] The next week Pennsylvania's congressional delegation hosted a gala dinner at McEowen's Hotel on Capitol Hill to honor Decatur as well as Charles Stewart and James Biddle. Though only a few hundred men could gather at the dinner, all across the country people could read about the event in their newspapers and even sing the new songs written for the occasion. One song, to the tune of "Anacreon in Heaven," had Neptune telling two Prince Regents—English and Algerian—to send the "impudent" American sailors to the ocean's bottom. The American tars in their "cock-boats" chase the British from the sea, and then the Algerian "fell on his face while he swore by his beard" that "Decatur had threaten'd to cut off his ears." Neptune tells the Dey:

> Go! Make peace, if you can! With these same Yankee devils . . .
> If their power be so great
> Your prayer is too late.
> For I, though immortal, am govern'd by Fate.

And fate now decreed, thanks to these impudent Yankees, that the seas will be free.[15]

The "Yankee tars" who had freed the seas were also celebrated in a song to the tune of "Yankee Doodle" written for the Pennsylvania dinner:

> Whene'er the tyrants of the main
> Assault Columbia's Seamen,
> They'll find them ready to maintain
> The noble name of freemen.
> *Chorus*:
> Toast the brave, for they will save
> Columbia's fame from sinking;
> The honor'd spars of Yankee Tars
> Are glorious themes for drinking.

Sailors had long been regarded as lawless men outside the pale of society; now they were fierce defenders of "the noble name of freemen"; their bravery prevented Columbia's fame from sinking; their "spars" were not only honored but also "glorious themes for drinking." Each of the next fifteen verses celebrated a different naval hero of the war—not only Pennsylvanians, and not only officers. Gallant tars were honored along with their captains: Hull and Jones, Bainbridge and Lawrence and Macdonough, as well as the guests of honor. For Decatur the company sang:

> Then quickly met our nation's eyes
> The noblest sight in nature—
> A first-rate frigate as prize
> Brought home by bold DECATUR.

The final verse brought the story forward to Decatur's mission to Algiers:

> Our Yankee Tars, to Afric's shore,
> Our heroes, lastly, lead 'em—
> And Turkish banners bow before
> The starry flag of Freedom.[16]

Decatur's toast was relatively simple: "The State of Pennsylvania: Powerful and Patriotic." Stewart and Biddle had more complicated ideas. Stewart gave a toast to the "foreign and domestic enemies of the United States," with the explanation, "May their machinations be restrained within just limits by Constitutional and Common Law." Biddle hoped that the "local distinctions of our Country" would be "remembered only for the purpose of . . . mirth and festivity."[17] All men were hoping to maintain the nation's fragile unity; all knew the dangers of internal discord but recognized that civil disagreement was essential to free government.

Decatur was becoming used to this parade of ceremonial banquets. In Philadelphia, New York, Baltimore, and Washington, committees of loyal friends organized these gala events on short notice, selling tickets to other friends and strangers eager to honor him. Those who could not attend, men and women living in distant towns and villages, read about the event in their newspapers.

From Washington the Decaturs traveled to Norfolk, where they had first met. Old friend and lawyer Littleton Tazewell, along with John Nivison and R. B. Taylor, organized another testimonial dinner for Decatur.[18] More than 120 men sat down to dinner on April 4, and after the tables were cleared, the drinking, toasting, and singing began. The men sang two more new songs, both to the tune of "Anacreon," in celebration. "Decatur's Return" welcomed the "gallant son of COLUMBIA" who had "directed the torrent of fire" at the "rude savage," who retired in dismay, and gave the nations of Europe "a sample of how all our tributes shall flow."

> Columbia and Fame, shall emblazon the name,
> Of Decatur, who nobly her rights did maintain.
> And whenever a nation of Freemen is found.
>> With the full flowing bumper thy name shall go round.

One new song began "See Decatur our hero returns from the West" and recounted how that "insolent Moor," the "haughty Dey" of Algiers on "Afric's bleak shore," had demanded tribute

> From American freemen . . .
> But Decatur draws nigh,
> His name strikes like lightening—in terror they fly,

and the "proud Crescent falls to the American star." All of these songs undoubtedly made a deeper impression when men had been drinking for several hours. Men would continue to write patriotic songs to the tune of "Anacreon"; but Francis Scott Key's version—a revision of the song he had written in 1805, when Decatur first returned from Tripoli, and rewritten after he watched the British bombard Fort McHenry—had already entered the national consciousness. At the Norfolk banquet one citizen toasted "The Star Spangled Banner: Long may it wave, 'O'er the land of the Free and the home of the Brave.' "

The Norfolk celebration concluded, as usual, with toasts: to the Mediterranean, "the sea not more of Greek and Roman, than of American glory"; to naval enterprise and the militia which had "triumphed over the conquerors of the conqueror of Europe"; to national glory, General Jackson, and the governor of Virginia; and finally to the women of America: "Their smile is the richest reward of patriotism."[19]

Then it was Decatur's turn. He had learned perhaps from his rather stilted New York toast to the "liberality" of New Yorkers to keep it brief and simple, and to focus on praising the people at hand. He had so far said nothing profound or even particularly memorable, but toasts were not meant to be either. Still, he could not help but be reminded of his father's toast back in 1806: "Our children are the property of their country!" The old man, barely literate, had shouted it out as though he'd been challenged. Seven years later Stephen saw those words emblazoned above his head at the New York banquet honoring him for bringing home the *Macedonian.* The old captain's words had lived after him. Would Stephen ever say anything so memorable?

He rose and lifted his glass. An expectant silence settled as the crowd waited for his toast—to them? to Virginia? or Norfolk? No. Decatur spoke clearly: "Our Country!" All raised their glasses.

"In her intercourse with foreign nations may she always be in the *right.*" All in Norfolk would remember that back in 1798, many Virginians had questioned the "rightness" of the war against France, and in 1812 New Englanders had protested the war against England; the nation had been divided over its role in the world since the Washington administration. Men and women had argued and fought over whether the nation was in the right. Without giving his audience time to reflect on the many meanings of this statement, Decatur concluded, ". . . and always *successful, right* or *wrong.*"

Decatur had experienced the bitter consequences of failure. The loss of the *Philadelphia* in 1803, the *Chesapeake*'s disgrace in 1807 and Lawrence's death on board *Chesapeake* in 1813, the embargo and the gunboat policy, his own capture barely a year earlier, by the British fleet: these were the consequences of failure, but not necessarily of national folly. The country's leaders could be wrong, as Madison and Jefferson had argued in 1798, and as New London's Federalists had argued in 1814. But there would be no way for Americans to set their country to rights without victory.

Decatur and the company drank. After Decatur left the room, his friend and lawyer Tazewell offered toasted him: "Most admired where best known." We cannot know if the men present immediately recognized that Decatur had said something profound or memorable. But he had. *Niles Weekly Register* called his toast a "stroke" against the Massachusetts senate, still smarting from the War of 1812 and Madison's improbable escape from both the British and the Federalists, which had declared such celebrations of American victories *"immoral* and *irreligious."*[19]

But not all would agree with the toast. In Europe, John Quincy Adams, who read accounts of the toast in the newspapers, wrote to his father: "I can never join with my voice the toast which I see in the papers attributed to one of our gallant naval commanders. I cannot ask of Heaven success, even for my country, in a cause where she should be in the wrong. Fiat justicia, pareat coelum. My toast would be, may our country always be successful, but whether successful or otherwise always right. I disclaim as unsound all patriotism incompatible with the principles of eternal justice. But the truth is that the American union, while united, may be certain of success in every rightful cause, and may if it pleases never have any but a rightful cause to maintain."[20] Twenty-six years later, long after Decatur was dead, Adams would make this same argument in a speech to Congress. The United States was preparing to go to war with Britain and with Mexico, and the result would be expansion of the nation and, Adams feared, of slavery. The Americans had sufficient power, as he had said, always to succeed. Now, in the 1840s, the republic was using its power not for the cause of justice but for the cause of greed and self-interest. The nation did not deserve to succeed, because it had chosen the wrong path. Decatur, seeing the burned capital and recalling the political dissensions that allowed it, had wished for national success, right or wrong. Adams, fearing the consequences of power without morality, again disagreed.[21]

Decatur did not live to see the war with Mexico or the question of slavery come to dominate American public life. Samuel Taylor Coleridge, recalling his conversation with Decatur in Malta just after the Louisiana Purchase, wrote that Decatur feared his country was growing too fast, too soon, that Americans would be weakened by the greed and complacency of those to whom success comes without struggle. But for Americans in 1816, these problems were in the future; for now, Decatur had issued a ringing toast to inspire and provoke them.

At Petersburg, Virginia, Decatur sat down to dinner with three hundred citizens gathered to honor him. After the preliminary toasts to the Constitution, and to Washington and Franklin ("The lightnings of heaven could not withstand the sage, the powers of earth could not corrupt the statesman"), one of the guests proposed Decatur's own toast: "Our Country—in her intercourse with foreign nations, may she always be in the right; but always successful, right or wrong." Three guns fired in salute, and the company gave six cheers. Decatur toasted the "citizens of Petersburg," who "honor . . . others, for services which they themselves have exceeded."[22]

CHAPTER *21*

"You will have to pass over my dead body"

NOW A PUBLIC HERO, Decatur had already considered his future role in the American service. Even before sailing for the Mediterranean, he had written to Secretary Crowninshield that on his return he "should be glad to have some situation on shore," deferring to his wife's wishes. Having experienced the climates, political and otherwise, in New England and in Norfolk, his preference now was to be stationed "in the middle states any where between Washington & New York (should a vacancy occur)." New York, Philadelphia, or Washington would be "more congenial to my health than an Eastern or a Southern station."[1]

Crowninshield had a position for Decatur, on the newly created Board of Naval Commissioners. Congress voted in 1816 to expand the navy—its first peacetime expansion. Decatur and the other commanders had demonstrated the navy's value to the republic, and especially the value of bigger ships rather than the small gunboats. Congress planned to spend a million dollars every year for the next eight years building frigates and even larger vessels.[2]

A bigger navy, Decatur believed, needed better administration. The civilian secretaries of the navy, intended to prevent the military from overriding the elected branches of government, had such a "deficiency in practical nautical knowledge" that they tended to "encrease the expense of our establishment infinitely beyond what it ought to have been." Each individual captain was responsible for outfitting his own ship. This system of autonomous captains had worked in the 1790s, when the navy consisted of only six ships; but now that the service had grown, it needed tighter constraints to prevent running up "enormous unnecessary expences." Decatur knew that the survival of the navy depended on public support, and that wasteful spending in the past had "in a great degree contributed to its unpopularity."[3] To keep the navy popular, its officers must be efficient as well as heroic. The public would not support heroes who wasted their money.

Administrative problems had hampered the navy's efficiency during the first months of the war. The abrasive but competent naval secretary, William Jones, had resolved these problems; his successor, Benjamin Crowninshield, had experience in running merchant fleets (his family was one of the leading mercantile powers in Massachusetts) but spent much of his time at home in Salem managing the family business, delegating much of the navy's daily administration to his clerk, Benjamin Homans. In 1815, Congress created the Board of Naval Commissioners, composed of three captains appointed by the president, to take on the department's administration. The board would also give the senior captains a role in governing the navy and ease communication between the military officers and their civilian supervisors.

John Rodgers, David Porter, and Isaac Hull, the first three commissioners, met for the first time in April 1815. They clashed almost immediately with Secretary Crowninshield about whether they or he would run the navy. Rodgers, Porter, and Hull, men of ability and strong opinions, used to commanding others, believed that they had been charged with setting naval policy. Crowninshield saw their roles reversed: he and the president would make policy, and the commissioners would follow their direction.

In the most fundamental sense this was a struggle for power. The main political obstacle to building a navy twenty years earlier had been Republican fears of military control. Now, though the officers and men had demonstrated their fealty to republican principles, it was not difficult to imagine naval officers using their military might to overwhelm elected officials. This was the ideological issue. Rodgers, Porter, and Hull were not attempting to stage a coup; but the fairly recent example of Aaron Burr's conspiring with disaffected officers showed the danger of irresponsible use of power. President Madison decisively backed Crowninshield, restricting the commissioners to advising the secretary and carrying out civilian directives.

Barely a month after arriving in Washington, Hull lobbied for and received command of the Charlestown Navy Yard, vacated by William Bainbridge. His position as a commissioner remained vacant until December, when Decatur returned from the Mediterranean and accepted Madison's nomination to the board. The Senate confirmed Decatur unanimously, and on January 2, 1816, he took his seat at the table with Rodgers and Porter.

Although the commissioners would not set naval policy, overseeing the navy's expansion gave them more than enough to do. They had new ships to build, older ones to repair, weapons to purchase and test, food and supplies to procure, sailors to recruit, future officers to train, and new technology to develop. They met together on Mondays, Wednesdays, and Fridays, and were in the office from ten to three every day but Sunday. In December 1818 they would divide their responsibilities: Rodgers would handle ship construction and repair and ordnance, Decatur would be responsible for supplies and contracts, and Porter would oversee the organization of navy yards and deal with the reports sent in by naval officers. In the meantime, though, the three men worked together on all these problems, a process that gained in joint expertise what it lost in efficiency.[4]

With the memory of the British invasion still fresh in their minds, the commissioners made it a priority to improve the Chesapeake's defenses. They unanimously agreed that the Chesapeake, with its mild climate and central location on the east coast, would be the best site for a base of naval operations. In the spring of 1816 Decatur and Susan traveled to Norfolk to survey various sites along the bay. Porter and Rodgers joined them in June. Since the commissioners could not agree on a specific location, each wrote his own report. Decatur forcefully argued that the "present Navy yard at Norfolk (independent of the protection it would afford the Chesapeake) is in all respects incomparably the best place for a naval depot."[5]

He noted the distinct disadvantages of the other sites—Hampton Roads, the York River, Tangier Island, St. Marys on the Potomac, and the Patuxent River. A naval depot, he explained, required two essential sets of features. First, it must have a steady supply of fresh water, it must be contiguous to the ocean, and it must be connected to timber reserves and other naval stores. Second, it should be close enough to a population center that labor and provisions could be "commodiously drawn," and the depot should have a large, safe, and well-defended harbor.[6] Decatur believed that Norfolk was better suited on all these counts than any of the other sites. Perhaps the most worrisome factor to the civilians in placing the nation's central naval facility so close to the entrance of the Chesapeake was that it would expose the fleet to attack. Decatur argued that keeping the fleet near the bay's mouth in a place as easily defended as Norfolk (during the war a small militia force on Craney Island had effectively prevented a British landing) would actually protect the rest of the Chesapeake. An enemy would want to stay at the entrance to the bay either to blockade the fleet or to destroy it. There would be no military objective farther up, so by fortifying Norfolk at the bay's entrance, this point which at the moment was "the most vulnerable part of the coast, would become the strongest. It would become itself a defense of our seaboard."[7] The secretary of the navy agreed, and Norfolk became the navy's central supply depot.

The commissioners also did not entirely agree on the future of a steam-powered navy. Rodgers and Porter still had little use for steam-powered fighting ships, but they knew that steam engines could saw wood and pump water in the navy yards. The commissioners did recommend that "some competent person" be engaged to put a steam engine into a frigate, an assignment New Yorker Henry Ogden took on in February 1819. In November the commissioners contracted Thomas Vinson of Martha's Vineyard to build a live oak frame for a steam battery.[8] When an inventor named Bailey proposed an improved steam pump, the commissioners told him to experiment at his own expense; he could bring it to them when it was perfected.[9]

The expanding navy drew in contractors and inventors, and the commissioners spent much of their time studying improvements in ships and weaponry. In May 1817 they saw a demonstration of Pierre Dupont's gunpowder, and in August "an ingenious man" named Andrew Ochley explained his new type of shell. Rodgers recalled one inventor pitching his new gun to the commissioners. After he and Decatur interviewed the inventor in the commissioners' meeting room, Rodgers went upstairs to his own office. Apparently the inventor took the opportunity of Rodgers's absence to suggest a private arrangement with Decatur: if Decatur would use his influence to get the navy to buy his weapon, the inventor would split the profits. Perhaps the inventor recalled that Decatur and Robert Fulton had been business partners, or perhaps he had worked similar deals with other captains. But times had changed. Rodgers rushed down from his office when he heard Decatur shouting—something he had never heard before—and in the meeting room he found the inventor on his knees, Decatur standing over him with his sword at the inventor's throat "commanding him to ask his pardon" for insulting Decatur's honesty and beg for his life."[10] The navy did not buy the new weapon.

The commissioners also took responsibility for overseeing promotions. Crowninshield sent them a list of his candidates for promotion to lieutenant in 1817, but the commissioners protested. He had mainly selected sailing masters, men responsible for technical expertise aboard ships, rather than the midshipmen, who were generally treated as officers in training. Once the commissioners had explained the distinction, Crowninshield relented, asking them to provide their own list of candidates. Some of the men whose names had been on the first list and had heard they were to become lieutenants now wondered why they had been passed over. One disappointed sailing master personally appealed to the commissioners, believing that they had mistaken his character. He provided the board with character references, exonerating himself from charges that, it turned out, had never been made. Rodgers assured him that the commissioners appreciated his good character and had passed over him not for personal reasons but because he was a sailing master.[11]

The commissioners also grappled with broader questions of politics. Merchants and farmers on the eastern seaboard had long known that naval contracts were lucrative. The commissioners were also aware of this, and knew that the navy needed to convince Americans in the interior—along the Ohio and Mississippi rivers—that the expanded navy benefited them. They were determined to buy beef and pork from the interior, though doing so would present its own difficulties. Intent on finding provisions across the Alleghenies, the commissioners wrote to William Child in Baltimore that they "have no occasion, at this time, to purchase his pork."[12] Instead, they contracted with Colonel James Johnson of Great Crossing, Kentucky, to supply 2,700 barrels of pork and 1,400 barrels of beef, most of it intended for the Mediterranean squadron. But little of it crossed the Atlantic.

While it made economic and political sense to bring Ohio and Kentucky farmers into the navy system, new contractors such as Colonel Johnson did not know the navy's specifications. He had already shipped the meat by the time the commissioners explained that the "whole of the head of the Hog, the jowl as well as the scull," was to be "excluded in the Navy pork." He had included too much that sailors would not eat. In addition, the sheer distance his barrels of pork and beef had to travel increased the chances that the meat would spoil in transit. When the first 336 barrels of beef arrived in New Orleans, a naval inspector attested to "the excellence of it's quality," but by the time the beef reached Boston, only 54 barrels were still edible. Certain that the 669 barrels of beef still at sea would be spoiled when they arrived, Hull refused to receive them. He had the Massachusetts inspector general examine the beef, which not only was rotten but also had not been cut to the navy's specifications.[13]

The commissioners told Captain Daniel Patterson at the New Orleans station to find a new meat inspector; they were expecting an additional 2,000 barrels of Johnson's beef and wanted to make sure it was carefully inspected. They warned Johnson that he was ruining the chances for other western farmers to deal with the navy. Although they had hoped to "distribute the benefits of naval expenditure" throughout the nation by buying meat "from the Western Country," if Johnson failed to supply unspoiled beef and pork at a reasonable price, he would force the commissioners "to look in future to the seaboard for supplies."[14]

The commissioners knew that more was at stake than several thousand barrels of beef and pork; they were establishing the navy as a national institution. Working in Washington as the national capital was being rebuilt and the republic's future identity was being redefined, Decatur and the other commissioners were conscious that their success depended on cultivating relationships with the civilians who governed the nation.

Decatur, Rodgers, and Porter also were living on land for the first time in many years. Each man now needed to buy or build a home in Washington, where the British attack had depleted an already insufficient supply of lodging. Stephen and Susan had lived with her father in Norfolk and in boardinghouses in Newport and New York; they now had the opportunity to own their own home. Stephen had not had a home to live in since he left Front Street. While the Decaturs were in Norfolk, an officer at the Bank of Columbia wrote to ask if Stephen was interested in buying one of the "Seven Buildings," a 1796 development on Nineteenth Street, west of the Executive Mansion on Pennsylvania Avenue. The price was $3,600. The Decaturs promptly agreed; housing in Washington was scarce, and the Seven Buildings were a prestigious address. For a time the Department of State had been housed there, and now President and Mrs. Madison were renting the largest; their home was nicknamed the "House of 1000 Candles" for the frequent parties the first couple hosted.[15]

Although Decatur found the house "in many respects out of repairs," he sent the bank $2,200. Wanting to have the house ready by the time he and Susan returned to Washington, he asked Secretary Crowninshield "if it would not be asking too much from you, if you had leisure, to take a look at it & direct it to be put in comfortable & decent order & painted (inside white)." If Crowninshield could oversee the painting, Decatur assured him, "the papering I can attend to myself on my return to Washington."[16]

Decatur had come a long way from Front Street. He now had the president as a neighbor (until March 4, 1817, when the president's term expired) and the secretary of the navy to decorate his home. The war had made him not just a hero but a wealthy man. His salary as a commissioner was $10,500 a year, but he had also received much more prize money—$30,000—than any other captain in the U.S. Navy. In addition Congress had authorized $100,000 to the captors of the *Meshouda* and *Estedio*, which Decatur shared with the other officers and men in the squadron. Now he had this capital to invest, and he did so wisely. He sensed that with the nation at last secure in its boundaries, the capital city would grow, so Stephen invested in Washington real estate, as well as in steamboats and other technological advances. His father-in-law, Luke Wheeler, pressed him to join his investment schemes (Wheeler and Commodore Thomas Truxtun had bought Washington real estate years earlier). Although Stephen tried unsuccessfully to find Wheeler a position with the Bank of the United States ("induced," he said, by "the wishes of Mrs. Decatur to locate her Father in Washington"), he wisely avoided his father-in-law's business advice.[17] Decatur had his own sense about investments, though he was not infallible. Many years later Richard Rush recalled the two Georgetown lots he had bought in 1816, which Decatur had assured him "would of themselves be a little fortune for . . . my children." "Alas for those Washington delusions!" Rush wrote.[18]

Washington presented new opportunities, new possibilities, and new dangers. As a young midshipman, Stephen had marked out the names of lines on the deck of the *United States*; he now found himself in a new career and needed to learn quickly. After the Tripolitan war he had turned to Benjamin

Rush to tutor him; now he approached his neighbor James Madison for instruction on the workings of the American political system. He could not have had a better mentor. Madison was the principal architect of the United States Constitution. More than that, he had won the Constitution's ratification in Virginia (out-debating Patrick Henry in a stormy convention) and been the most effective member of Congress in the 1790s, first as a key ally of the Washington administration (the vivacious young Philadelphia widow Dolley Payne wrote of her excitement that "the great little Madison" was to be introduced to her; they later married), and then as the leader of the Republican opposition. Madison had organized Thomas Jefferson's presidential campaigns in 1796 and 1800, led the opposition to the Alien and Sedition Acts during the Adams administration, and for eight years served as secretary of state. A small, scholarly man, Madison was the republic's most profound political theorist, as well as its ablest practical politician. James Kirke Paulding, Washington Irving's literary partner and now the navy commissioners' secretary, compared Madison to a college professor—curious about the world around him, and able to discuss ideas and issues with insight. "Quick, temperate, and clear" was how one New York politician described Madison (contrasting him with the "slow, passionate, and dull" Monroe)."[19]

When Decatur approached the president for instruction on how the political system operated and how it was designed to work, Madison produced a copy of *The Federalist*, the eighty-five essays that he, Alexander Hamilton, and John Jay had written to explain the Constitution (and urge its ratification) in 1787–88. Although Madison and Hamilton would later disagree sharply about the Constitution's meaning, they had written these essays under the single pseudonym of "Publius," and for all public purposes had been in complete accord on the Constitution's limits and possibilities. Madison now took the time as he set Decatur on his course of reading to mark off in his copy which author was responsible for which essays.

Washington was a small community filled with influential and interesting people. As the city began to rebuild, Stephen and Susan became centers of its society. The British ambassador was struck by Stephen's "soldierly grace," and his knowledge of naval lore impressed all. One evening after dinner Decatur demonstrated Nelson's victory in the Battle of the Nile, using nutshells to represent the French and British ships. His point was that Nelson owed his victory to superior gunnery. While an American captain could be expected to be an authority on seamanship and maritime history, Attorney General Richard Rush was impressed with Decatur's "great resources of native intelligence and propriety upon all subjects."[20]

Rush and Decatur had been boys together in Philadelphia, though they had not known each other well. But in Washington, Rush found himself spending more time with Decatur. When he left the administration (he stayed on briefly after James Monroe became president) to become American minister to London in 1817, Rush gave up his Washington home and found himself spending even more time with Decatur, not in the formal dinner parties Susan and Stephen hosted but informally. Decatur "opened his door to me at all hours," wrote Rush, recalling their "little dinners at five minutes notice, with none but himself and wife, walks together in the summer evenings, &c. &c." Rush, one of the most intellectually accomplished men of their generation, found Decatur to be "a man of ten thousand."[21]

Rush really came to appreciate Decatur when it was time for him to sail to England. He was to depart from Annapolis on the navy's new ship, the *Franklin*. Rush had left Washington believing that the government that was sending him to Europe was paying for his passage. But the *Franklin*'s captain had not been told this, and expected passengers to provide their own meals and supplies while at sea. The navy was not running passenger ships, and traditionally ambassadors did supply their own food and drink (certainly few would wish to share the rations of sailors). Rush had just enough money to buy provisions, but then would have nothing to live on when he reached England. Saying nothing of his difficulties to President Monroe (whose confidence in an ambassador unable to feed himself would be limited), he wrote frantically to relatives and friends for help. He asked his brother to lend him $100 or $150, and explained his embarrassing situation to Secretary of State John Quincy Adams.

Adams saw two options. As secretary of state he could formally request the Navy Department to issue an order to cover Rush's expenses, beginning a chain of paperwork and interdepartmental reimbursements; or he could simply ask Stephen Decatur to go to Annapolis and "exercise his diplomatic skill." Five days after Rush sent his desperate requests for loans, he was able to report that his "embarrassments" over his sea stores were "all removed" and that "neither side" even had "any recollection of them." How had this bureaucratic nightmare been resolved? "Commodore Decatur" had made a quick visit to Annapolis and "at a word, put all right."[22]

The Decaturs' role in Washington social and intellectual circles became more prominent as the Monroe administration refused to engage in the kind of entertaining that had made the Madison presidency a political success. Monroe was more formal and less socially adept than Madison, and Washington society suffered for it. Instead of frequent dinner parties and social engagements, Monroe revived the formal receptions that President Washington had favored; guests came, were introduced to the president and first lady, then stood awkwardly trying to make conversation. The Monroes had got off to a bad start when Mrs. Monroe insisted that the wives of ambassadors should make the first call on the president's wife, whereas the wives felt that as new arrivals in Washington, they should be called upon by residents, such as Mrs. Monroe. As a result of this diplomatic impasse, neither the wives nor the ambassadors would call at the White House. Other Washington women— Louisa Catherine Adams, Floride Calhoun, and Susan Decatur—became the capital's popular hostesses.[23]

The Decaturs tried to improve local society by bringing friends to the capital. Stephen attempted to coax Washington Irving out of his European exile. When Benjamin Crowninshield resigned in 1818, Decatur and the other commissioners took the opportunity to try to force out the imperious chief clerk, Benjamin Homans, as well. Decatur persuaded Rodgers and Porter to hold the clerk's position for Irving, whose literary partner, James Kirke Paulding, was already in Washington as the naval commission secretary. Having both Paulding and Irving on the navy's payroll—in positions that did not require long hours—promised to enliven the capital's social life. "It is a berth highly respectable—very comfortable in its income," Irving's brother William wrote to the writer. The pay was about $2,400 a year, on which Decatur said he could "live in Washington like a prince," and the job was "light in its duties, and will afford you a very ample leisure to pursue the bent of your literary inclination. It may also be a mere stepping-stone to higher station, or may be considered at any rate permanent."[24] Despite this lucrative offer and Decatur's lobbying, Irving chose to remain in Europe to write his novels, and Homans managed to hold on to his job. In the long run perhaps Irving and the nation benefited by his singular devotion to his fiction; but Washington society and the navy suffered. (The navy administration did attract other writers: Paulding later became the clerk and ultimately secretary of the navy, a position also held by the historian George Bancroft and novelist John Pendleton Kennedy.)

Madison's retirement also threatened to remove from Washington Decatur's architect friend Benjamin Henry Latrobe. Latrobe had been given the contract to oversee the rebuilding of the Capitol and Executive Mansion; he moved easily in Washington society, but fell out of favor in the new administration. Monroe's commissioner of public buildings did not like Latrobe and was determined to fire him. Unhappily for Latrobe, Samuel Lane had the president's ear (he "breakfasts, dines, and sups with him," Latrobe told Robert Goodloe Harper). Lane chastised Latrobe in a way "no schoolboy could have borne patiently" for spending too much time in Baltimore (where he was overseeing construction of the new Roman Catholic cathedral) and not enough in Washington. Latrobe turned to friends such as Harper and Decatur to use their influence with the president, but to no avail. Latrobe resigned on November 20, 1817.[25] Stephen and Susan had bought land on President's Park (now Lafayette Park) north of the Executive Mansion. Almost immediately on Latrobe's resignation, they hired him to design a new home for them.

Latrobe had become one of the new nation's most accomplished architects, but his first job on arriving in America in 1796 had been tuning Luke Wheeler's pianoforte. A bet in Norfolk led to Latrobe's first commission to build a house. Captain William Pennock, who owned an odd-shaped lot, challenged Latrobe to design an elegant house to fit into it. To win the bet, Latrobe's design had to meet with Luke Wheeler's approval. Latrobe designed a house, Wheeler approved the plan, and with his winnings Latrobe went off to seek his fortune. Two months later Latrobe overheard in a Richmond tavern the story of "a Frenchman" in Norfolk who had produced "the most preposterous design" for a house. Latrobe was astonished that Pennock had been "mad enough to attempt to execute" his plan, but not that the workmen were unable to build beyond the ground floor. The contractor was "wedded to the heavy wooden taste of the last century" and did not see how to finish the structure without its collapsing. The American builders blamed the French architect. On overhearing a detailed description of his design "interlarded with many oaths and imprecations against the Frenchman," Latrobe went back to Norfolk to oversee completion of the Pennock House.[26]

Even if Susan did not remember Latrobe tuning her pianoforte, she would have known the Pennock House. She and Stephen wanted their home to be the center of Washington society. It was to be one of the capital's most elegant social settings, second only to the White House. And if President and Mrs. Monroe chose not to entertain in their mansion, then the Decaturs would provide venues for the parties that made political life in the capital bearable. But while the Decaturs planned to entertain in their home, they would also live in it. Latrobe prided himself on his closets and kitchens. No American lady—particularly one like Susan Decatur—could have enough closets, he told her. He was also appalled by the dark and smoky kitchens where Americans prepared their food. He would not relegate the Decaturs' kitchen to the basement or the back of the house, or to a separate building, but would place it right off the entryway. Although guests would not see the kitchen, they would appreciate the quality of the food that was prepared in this clean and well-lighted space.[27]

Decatur bought materials for the house from the network of navy agents. From Boston he ordered "250 cask of Thomas Town Lime, & 10000 feet of 3 inch curled maple, seasoned or if the three inch can not be obtained 1400 feet of plank that will work 2 inches, & of good width," and "200 feet 2 inch birds eye maple" for the elegant home Latrobe had designed.[28] Latrobe undoubtedly enjoyed working on this showplace in sight of the White House. The house still stands, though by the time the Decaturs moved into it in January 1819, Latrobe had gone to New Orleans to design a waterworks and hospital.

At dinner one evening with the Decaturs, Latrobe mentioned his son John, who had just entered West Point. The previous year West Point's cadets had mutinied, and Latrobe "loosely and jocosely" said he had warned his son "that no folly could be greater, than that the Cadets, right or wrong, should expect to succeed in any attempt against their officers." Latrobe hoped that John was smart enough to stay "always . . . on the side of the strongest." Latrobe expected Decatur to agree. Decatur had twenty years of military experience, knew the importance of discipline, and had quite forcefully made the point about supporting his country "right or wrong." But Decatur surprised him. Although Decatur knew that, "practically as well as on principle," the "necessity of severe discipline in all military bodies, he should despise a young soldier or Cadet at West point, who on no other grounds than prudence, took sides against his Comrades." The cadets must understand that "their brother cadets are their contemporaries, and their teachers are going off the stage while they are coming on." Young officers should therefore develop "a character of firmness and independence among those with whom they are going to spend their lives" rather than remain subservient to "those who will be dead when they might be useful."[29]

John H. Latrobe must have been confused when his father changed his advice. Shortly after John's arrival at West Point, some of his fellow cadets circulated a petition against an abusive commanding officer. Taking his father's earlier advice, John stayed out of the dispute and supported the academy's hierarchy. But now his father counseled him differently. Adopting Decatur's position, Latrobe advised his son against "sticking to the side of Government" in the hope of advancing in rank, for "no policy can be better for your advancement, and none worse." His loyalty must be to his fellow cadets: "sticking to your comrades when they appear to be right" was the prudent course.[30]

Decatur could not forgive all disobedience. He refused to attend services at the elegant St. John's Episcopal church, just across President's Park from his new house. Decatur had been raised an Episcopalian and been wed by a Presbyterian. He did not disagree with Episcopal doctrine, and if he were to attend a church, he could not have found one closer than St. John's. But during the war, while studying in a New York seminary, St. John's minister, the Reverend Dr. William Hawley had been named captain of a volunteer militia company. When the company was ordered to the Niagara frontier, Hawley and his men refused to go; they believed that they would be more useful to the defense of New York City. Decatur would not attend Hawley's church because the minister had "refused to obey orders."[31]

Decatur could forgive other offenses. In 1809 he had indulged Dr. William P. C. Barton's request to be appointed surgeon on the *United States*. Barton, however, had been a disaster, and Decatur had had him arrested the following year for striking the sailing master in the presence of the crew. Sent back to an assignment on land, in March 1813 Barton was again posted to the *United States*. Much to Decatur's annoyance, Barton tried to get out of the assignment, not wanting to go to sea. Secretary Jones denied his request, telling Barton that if officers "were suffered to decline active & honorable service at such a crisis as this in order to enjoy a sinecure on shore, the good of the service would be rendered subservient to personal interest & indulgence."[32] Fortunately for all, Barton eventually retired from the navy. He was now a professor of botany at the University of Pennsylvania. Decatur was flattered when Barton sent him a copy of his lavishly illustrated, two-volume *Vegetable materia medica of the United States, or Medical Botany*. Decatur insisted, however, that he be "considered as a subscriber to the work," paying for it rather than receiving it as a gift, though declaring himself still "as much indebted to you for your kind intentions, as tho' I accepted" a complimentary copy.[33]

Obeying orders while remaining loyal to one's comrades: Decatur and his fellow naval officers were working out the role of professional fighting men in a society governed by elected leaders. Burr's conspiracy just ten years earlier revealed how fragile the American political system could be. The experience of the recent war had proved that a citizen militia was not always effective for defense, but the alternative of a permanent military force seemed worse. Now with the navy expanding and being governed in part by uniformed men, Decatur and the other commissioners were deeply conscious that their role was not to govern but to protect their fellow citizens. Commanding at sea was easy, compared to the difficult roles of political leaders such as Madison. Decatur had spent his childhood in Philadelphia when it was the new republic's capital; now he lived in Washington, where he was getting an insider's view of the political process. His reading of history and political theory impressed on him how tenuous a hold republican liberty had in any society, and how easily a nation could turn from liberty to despotism. He had seen it happen in Sicily and Naples.

Decatur and the other navy captains, more so than officers in the U.S.

Army, were aware of how closely connected American security was to events across the sea. Decatur's career had begun during the war with France; he had earned his greatest victories in the Mediterranean and off the coast of West Africa. During his last voyage to the Mediterreanean, he had set in motion a chain of events there that had nearly led to war in North America and imperiled the civil government of the United States. When the Spanish refused to release the Algerian ships *Meshouda* and *Estedio*, which Decatur had captured, some Americans saw this as an opportunity to declare war on Spain. The Americans who were eager for war were not concerned with the fate of the ships; they coveted Spanish Florida, particularly the ports of Pensacola and Mobile, which would give farmers in Georgia, Alabama, and Mississippi access to the sea. During the war General Andrew Jackson had tried to take Pensacola after a British force staged a demonstration there to divert him from the defense of New Orleans. Now, in 1818, as rumors of war with Spain circulated, Jackson, commander of the U.S. Army in the South, crossed the Spanish frontier into Florida and occupied Pensacola. After much discussion in the cabinet, the Monroe administration formally apologized to Spain for Jackson's invasion (Secretary of State John Quincy Adams alone felt that Jackson had acted properly.) The nation avoided war with Spain by buying Florida (including the gulf coast of Alabama and Mississippi) in 1819.

Though war had been averted, the Senate launched an investigation into Jackson's conduct. Senator Abner Lacock of Pennsylvania presented his report to the Senate in February 1819, castigating Jackson for exceeding his authority and recklessly risking war. Lacock made no outright mention of the fact that several of Jackson's friends had reportedly speculated in real estate near Pensacola, but he did include affidavits attesting to this as an appendix. The Senate did nothing more than print the report and ignore it. With Florida now in U.S. hands and the nation at peace, there was no need to take action.

But Jackson was furious. He was enormously popular as a result of his victory at New Orleans and his capture of Pensacola, and he regarded Lacock's report as an attempt to smear his reputation—which it may have been. The rumor reached Washington that Jackson was on his way to the capital to "cut off the ears" of various members of Congress—perhaps Lacock or perhaps Senator John Eppes of Virginia.[34] After Secretary of the Treasury William Crawford advised Lacock to be "on his guard" against Jackson, Lacock received permission from a Washington justice of the peace to carry a pistol in self-defense.

Jackson reached Washington on the evening of March 2, 1819. The next morning he took a carriage to the Capitol. Everyone had heard that he intended to assault Lacock, or perhaps Eppes—or at least to chastise them for attacking "not only my public acts but my private character." But when Jackson arrived at the Capitol, he found Stephen Decatur blocking the door. (It is not clear which door Decatur was blocking—the door to the building or to the Senate chamber. According to Lacock, Decatur met Jackson "near the door of the Senate," though Jackson claimed later that he was never "in the walls of either House of Congress, and not at all in the Senate.") When he demanded the right to enter, Decatur told him to get back in his carriage. Jackson again insisted he would enter the Senate. "If you do, General," Decatur replied, "you will have to pass over my dead body."

Could any other public figure have stopped Jackson? Word spread throughout Washington of this dramatic confrontation between the two heroes of the War of 1812. One would use physical force against elected officials; the other would use force to prevent it. Years later Benjamin Ogle Tayloe speculated about what might have happened if Jackson had tried to force his way past Decatur into the Senate chamber. The outcome would have been deadly, Tayloe knew, but it "might have saved the country from the disastrous consequences of Jacksonism."[35]

CHAPTER 22

"A duty I owe to the service"

T HE NAVY'S effectiveness as a fighting force and the public's faith in its integrity depended on the good character of its officers. Decatur had advised Secretary Crowninshield to publish court-martial verdicts and other reprimands of officers, "else an innocent man might be supposed to have been guilty, & guilt . . . supposed to be innocent."[1] The public relied on these men and had a right to know their character. The public also had a right to expect that incompetent officers would not be tolerated in the service. And so it was with some alarm that the commissioners learned James Barron was applying to be restored to the rank of captain.

Suspended for five years in the wake of the *Chesapeake* disaster, Barron had been in Copenhagen when the war broke out in 1812. He had not returned to the United States until after the war, and in the spring of 1818 came to Washington to secure his reappointment. If he were reinstated with his seniority as of 1807, he would be senior to both Decatur and Porter. But for them, keeping Barron out of the navy was more than a matter of protecting their own status. The three naval commissioners had judged Barron back in 1807—both Decatur and Porter serving on the court-martial, which Rodgers had chaired. The Barron brothers' failure to fight in the Tripolitan war had disgusted Rodgers (he and the Barrons had threatened to duel at the time), and Decatur had made up his mind about Barron during the preliminary court of inquiry.

But Barron's Virginia relatives had been lobbying their congressional representatives to reconsider his case, and there was now some public pressure to do so. The *Daily National Intelligencer* printed a letter from a Williamsburg correspondent working to clear Barron's name, who wrote, "I remember the impression made on me by the trial of that officer; and have always regretted for his sake, as well as for the great bulk of the people, that the facts and testimony which were submitted to the court-martial were never established." The writer "never saw the true point of blame" in Barron's actions other than "that he did not foresee, or foretell, what was to happen on the passage to sea."[2]

In this case, the officers on the court of inquiry and on the court-martial understood that Barron was responsible for his ship, and that any captain should be ready to fight when a ship from another nation approaches. Barron had not fulfilled his responsibility. His suspension for five years was to serve as a lesson to other captains to be prepared.

Decatur, Rodgers, and Porter were not being vindictive. They had heard troubling rumors in the ten years since Barron's suspension. According to Captain William Lewis, one of the men Decatur had freed in Algiers, Barron had told the British consul in Pernambuco, Brazil that even if the *Chesapeake* had been prepared for action, he would not have ordered his men to resist the *Leopard.* Barron knew that he had deserters on board, and so did the U.S. government. In fact, according to the story, Barron believed that President Jefferson had deliberately sent him out "in a defenceless state"; he wanted the *Chesapeake* "attacked and disgraced" so he could "attain his favorite object" of involving the United States in war with Great Britain. It was a shocking admission, and it enraged Decatur and every other captain who heard of it. The fact that Barron had said this to a British consul made it unforgivable. By this time Lewis was gone—he had sailed from Algiers on the *Epervier* and disappeared with that ship—but Captain Thomas Ridgely reported hearing the same story from his brother-in-law, who had heard it from the consul himself. The navy captains all agreed with Lewis, who had told Decatur in Algiers "that Barron is a traitor, for I can call by no other name a man who would talk in this way to an Englishman, and an Englishman in office."[3]

Worse stories emerged. Barron, who had returned to sea as a merchant captain after his suspension from the navy, had been sailing between Europe and South America. It was said that once war was declared against England in 1812, he sailed under a British license carrying goods to British ports. When Barron's suspension expired in early 1813, he had written from Denmark to inform the secretary of the navy that he was available to return home. But Barron did not return; instead he waited for the secretary to answer his letter. For three years Barron waited—while men such as Lawrence and Allen were giving their lives, while the British occupied coastal New England, invaded the Chesapeake, and burned the capital.

Barron finally arrived in Washington in the spring of 1818. It was not a pleasant visit. Secretary Crowninshield refused to reinstate him; some members of Congress were sympathetic, but were not prepared to go further than that; and his former colleagues in the navy shunned him. One day Barron saw John Rodgers on the street. Putting behind him the fact that he and Rodgers had challenged each other to a duel in 1806, and that Rodgers had presided over his court-martial in 1807, Barron hailed Rodgers as an old colleague whom he had not seen during his ten years of exile. But Rodgers stared through him and walked coldly by. As for Decatur, he believed that by keeping Barron out of the navy, he was "performing a duty I owe to the service; I was contributing to the preservation of its respectability."[4]

The commissioners knew that the future of the navy rested with them. The Madison administration had been prepared to expand the navy; but would the Monroe administration agree? Would the public support a service in which incompetence—if not outright treason—was rewarded so long as the culprit had seniority? Reinstating a discredited officer, Decatur believed, despite evidence of treason would be disastrous for the navy, signaling that it neither rewarded merit nor punished incompetence. In discussing Barron's case with other navy officers, Decatur had met only "one who did not entirely concur with me."[5]

Barron's name certainly came up at the navy office and at the Decaturs' elegant dinner table. Decatur may also have spoken of Barron during the weeks he was in Norfolk in March and April 1819. He did not see Barron—who lived in Hampton—at this time, but Barron heard reports of what Decatur was saying about him and felt compelled to write Decatur in June to demand an explanation. "I have been informed," he complained, "that you have said that you could insult me with impunity, or words to that effect."[6] If Decatur had in fact said this, it would be grounds for a duel. Decatur had to take responsibility for his words, and Barron had to demonstrate that he could not be insulted.

"Whatever I may have *thought, or said, in the very frequent and free conversations I have had respecting you and your conduct,*" Decatur wrote back, "I feel a thorough conviction that I never could have been guilty of so much egotism as to say that 'I could insult you' (or any other man) 'with impunity.'" Decatur then chastised Barron for failing to show the "frankness which ought to characterize our profession" by withholding the name of the person who was telling him such stories.[7]

"Several gentlemen in Norfolk, not your enemies," Barron replied, had told him of Decatur's alleged statement; the story "was in circulation" throughout Norfolk but "could not now be traced to its origin." But Decatur's answer now, that he had not said what he had been accused of saying, relieved Barron's "mind from the apprehension" that Decatur had degraded his character.[8]

Decatur could have let the matter rest. But he wanted Barron "to understand distinctly" that he had "meant no more than to disclaim the *specific* and *particular* expression" that "I could insult you with impunity." Decatur was as indifferent to the identities or "motives of the 'several gentlemen of Norfolk'" and the various "rumors which 'cannot be traced to their origin'" on which their information was founded" as he was to Barron's "motives in making such an enquiry upon such information."[9]

Here the correspondence ended. The commissioners busied themselves with building ships and provisioning the fleet, and Barron sought other ways to support his family. The whole matter might have ended as well if not for a completely improbable event on the Orinoco River: Oliver Hazard Perry died of a fever two months later, in August 1819.

Decatur had been Perry's friend and mentor ever since they first met in Newport after the Tripolitan war. After languishing on the Newport gunboats when the War of 1812 began, Perry volunteered for the more sickly climate of the Great Lakes so as to have a chance at seeing action. He had succeeded brilliantly. His victory on September 10, 1813, on the *Lawrence* and the *Niagara* had made Perry a hero on a par with Decatur. Although some officers grumbled that Jesse Elliott—commander of the *Niagara*—had deliberately kept his ship out of the action, Perry had endorsed Elliott's case for earning a gold medal for the battle. Privately Perry wrote that it was "better to screen a coward than to let the enemy know there is one in the fleet."[10]

But now that the war was over, Perry reconsidered. He too was concerned about the future of the navy. Like Decatur, he knew what kind of character was required of naval officers, and Elliott had clearly been incompetent. Perry drafted an account of the battle of Lake Erie questioning Elliott's role and discussed with Decatur having the matter brought before a court of inquiry and a court-martial. Perry had given Decatur his written statement before sailing for South America. When Perry died on August 23, his death evoked the kind of public mourning that had followed the death of James Lawrence. He was buried in Trinidad (his body would be returned to Newport in the 1840s) as his own nation honored him as a hero.

Elliott knew what this meant to his career. Perry alive was formidable; dead he was infallible. Worse, Perry's charges would be presented by Stephen Decatur, whose influence in the navy—and in the nation's mind—seemed to grow daily. Elliott had been under a cloud since 1807, when he alone had defended James Barron. Now he turned to Barron to help clear his own name. Elliott visited Barron (he may have been the source of the stories Barron had heard about Decatur) and provoked a renewal of the correspondence. Elliott now hoped to destroy Decatur's reputation by forcing him into a duel with Barron. It was unlikely that Barron could kill Decatur, but if Decatur were to kill or even wound Barron, the public would see their great hero as an arrogant bully.

Meanwhile, a friend from Norfolk wrote Decatur in late August that a lady from Hampton, possibly a relative of Barron's, had come to town expressing concern about a "correspondence" between Decatur and Barron, which she feared "would end in a meeting," or a duel, between the two men. Decatur's friends in Norfolk thought her fears exaggerated. But since word of the correspondence was circulating in Norfolk and Hampton, his correspondent suggested that Decatur send copies of Barron's letters to Littleton Tazewell, Decatur's lawyer, in Norfolk.[11]

"I had supposed that the measure of your ambition was nearly completed," Barron wrote angrily to Decatur when he learned that the letters were now circulating in Norfolk, and after Elliott had repeated more of Decatur's slights, "and that your good fortune had rendered your reputation for acts of magnanimity too dear to be risked wantonly on occasions that can never redound to the honor of him that would be great." Barron vented all his anger, frustration, and humiliation in this letter, which is longer than all the notes the men had exchanged in June combined. Barron saw all his misfortunes springing from Decatur's "rancor towards me," which had not been satisfied by the "cruel and unmerited sentence" of the court-martial or his "nearly seven years" of exile from family, friends, and country. For thirteen years Barron had been "oppressed," "chiefly by your means," and now had had enough. He had come home at last to nurse his "lacerated feelings" in the solace of his family, until Decatur's "malignant spirit" rose to ruin his reputation. Decatur, he charged, was showing the letters to Barron's "particular friends" in Norfolk with the aim "of alienating from me their attachment." Barron had also heard that Decatur, "tauntingly and boastingly," had expressed the hope of fighting a duel—that Decatur had said he wished Barron "would yet act like a man." Barron took this as a challenge, and accepted it as such. Since Decatur had issued the challenge, Barron would choose the place, weapons, and distance, though he knew Decatur's "personal courage" would make him "disdain any unfair advantage, which your superiority in the use of the pistol, and the natural defect in my vision, increased by age, would give you." Barron asked that Decatur not put his name on the envelope when he replied, "as, I presume, you can have no disposition to give unnecessary pain to the females of my family."[12]

Decatur received this remarkable letter during a busy time. Rodgers was in New York attending to the construction of ships, leaving Decatur as acting chair of the Board of Commissioners. Decatur was also indirectly overseeing ship construction in Baltimore, Washington, and the Chesapeake, lobbying Congress, and leading the Washington social scene. New family responsibilities also arrived that fall, when his sister, Ann, died on September 25 and Stephen went to Philadelphia to take charge of his nieces. Since his brother-in-law was in declining health (he would die the following August), Stephen brought the three girls with him. Priscilla, then seventeen, he took as far as New Castle, Delaware, where she would continue her education. Her older sisters, Mary and Anna, he brought to Washington, hoping to introduce them into the city's society.[13]

Stephen was also trying to learn what had happened to their brother, Stephen Decatur McKnight. He had been a lieutenant under Porter on the *Essex*, and was captured by the British in Valparaiso, but had not been seen since he boarded the Swedish brig *Adonis* in Rio in 1814 for the passage home. Decatur asked Secretary of State John Quincy Adams to inquire through diplomatic channels. (Ultimately it would be learned that the *Adonis* had met the American sloop *Wasp* near the Cape Verde Islands; McKnight had gone aboard the American sloop, which was never seen again.)[14]

Decatur reviewed his June correspondence with Barron before answering the latest letter.[15] If those letters had "alienated your friends from you," he told Barron, it was owing to the letters themselves. Decatur had said nothing about them to Tazewell. Nor would he treat the men who had court-martialed Barron "with so much disrespect" as to review the sentence they hand handed down. Barron called it "cruel and unmerited," but the nation and the president had accepted it. Decatur reminded Barron that he had tried to excuse himself from the panel, as he had not only "formed, but expressed an opinion unfavorable to you," and he had given Barron an opportunity "to protest against my being a member" of the court. Decatur made it clear that his opposition to Barron was purely professional: "Between you and myself, there never has been a personal difference: but I have entertained, and do still entertain the opinion, that your conduct, as an officer, since the affair of the Chesapeake, has been such as ought to forever bar your admission into the service."

Still, Decatur assured Barron that he had not issued a challenge. Barron's first letter in June had been provoked by "'rumors' which could not be traced" and which turned out to be false; Barron should have learned by now to be cautious about acting on such rumors "as if they were true." Reports that Decatur had boasted and taunted Barron to "act like a man" were also unfounded. Although Decatur had not issued a challenge, he had been told before they began their correspondence that Barron was on his way to Washington "with the intention of calling me out." Decatur repeated what he had said then: that if Barron "made the call, I would meet you—but that, on all scores, I should be much better pleased, to have nothing to do with you."

Decatur knew that fighting a duel would not "raise the reputation of any man" and was no test of personal courage. But he had chosen to make "arms his profession" and so did not feel that he could decline a challenge. Other officers had told Decatur that Barron was beneath his notice and not entitled to face Decatur on the field of honor; but Decatur disagreed. If Barron insisted on a challenge, Decatur would allow their seconds to decide "weapons, place, and distance," and would yield to Barron "any little advantage of this kind." As to his relative youth, Decatur thought that their age difference could not have been "more than five or six years." (It was eleven.) As for Decatur's allegedly superior eyesight, "it would have been out of the common course of nature, if the vision of either of us had been improved by years." Barron had also mentioned Decatur's supposed skill with a pistol; that, said Decatur, "exists more in your imagination than in reality—for the last twenty years I have had but little practice." In fact he had not fought a duel since 1799.

Perhaps recalling how the Barron brothers had challenged and then dodged John Rodgers after the Tripolitan war, Decatur believed that James Barron had "come to the determination to fight some one, and that you have selected me for that purpose." He would have preferred that Barron had "made his decision [to fight] during our late war, when your fighting might well have benefited your country as well as yourself."

Barron received this letter on November 9. It took him three weeks to draft a reply, as he would not write while his family was in the house. In the meantime, Decatur learned that Barron had not in fact sailed under a British license during the war; he sent a brief note to Barron telling him he now knew that story was false. Barron, however was concerned not with the small points but the "accumulated insults" that Decatur, "above all my enemies," had been heaping upon him "in every shape in which they could be offered."[16] Decatur's lengthy letter of October 31—it may be the longest letter Decatur ever wrote—was "sufficient proof" for Barron of Decatur's "rancorous disposition" toward him. "Every word you have uttered, and every line you have written in relation to me," he charged, was a mark of "personal hostility" and "personal enmity."

Barron then refuted each of the specific charges Decatur had made. The charge that Barron had told the British consul at Pernambuco that he would not have fired back at the *Leopard* was such a "ridiculous, malicious, absurd, improbable falsehood" that no one could believe it unless that person were trying to convince "the public that I am an ideot." Barron admitted that he knew the consul well, but he did not know Captain Lewis, from whom Decatur had heard the tale. The story itself rested on flimsy evidence, "weaker even than second-handed testimony," and if Lewis believed the story, insisted Barron, it must have been because he had "imbibed a prejudice against me" from "your acquaintance with him."

Barron had come to detest Decatur not only because the younger man was blocking his readmission to the navy, but also because he believed that Decatur was showing an astonishing ingratitude. Did Decatur not remember how Barron had written to the secretary of the navy in 1803 to urge that the young lieutenant be given command of his own vessel? Did Decatur not recall how Barron had persuaded him not to resign from the service "in a pet, because you were removed from the first lieutenancy of the New York, to that of second of the Chesapeake"? Decatur might have forgotten Barron's kindness and mentoring, but "the history of your conduct to me will outlive you, let my fate be what it may." Barron rejected Decatur's claim that he bore him no personal ill will, insisting that the entire dispute was indeed personal, not professional. Decatur's "inflated pride" had led him to believe his own influence "greater than that of any other officer of the navy," making him "more tenacious of its honor and 'respectability' than the rest of the officers were." Decatur claimed to have met only one officer who did not share his views of Barron. This was hardly surprising to Barron, since Decatur was "most commonly attended by a train of dependents" constantly "revolving around you like *satellites*," seeking the "sunshine of your favour" and deriving their own importance "from the countenance you may *condescend* to bestow upon them."

Decatur received this letter just as he was bound north to Philadelphia. When he got back to Washington, he turned to other officers for advice. Charles Morris—the first man aboard *Philadelphia* in 1804—told Decatur to ignore it. Rodgers—a recipient of similar challenges from Barron—also felt that Decatur had much to lose and nothing to gain by dueling Barron. If he ignored the challenge and Barron called him a coward, what of it? Who would believe James Barron—who had counseled buying peace with Tripoli and then surrendered the *Chesapeake* without firing a shot—over Stephen Decatur? Porter had the same reaction. Decatur listened but decided that he should face Barron. He wanted a senior officer, however—another commissioner—to act as his second. This would signal that the feud was not between Barron and Decatur but between Barron and the U.S. Navy. But both Rodgers and Porter saw the duel as futile and declined to serve as Decatur's second.

Decatur was sensitive to his need for a capable second. He still had in mind the last duel in which he had been involved, in 1818. Perry had been challenged to fight by Marine Captain John Heath, whom Perry had punched during a Mediterranean cruise. Deeply embarrassed at losing his temper,

Perry had asked for a court-martial, which found both men at fault—Heath for disobeying an order, Perry for punching him. Both men were reprimanded privately. After returning to America, Heath had spread the story that Perry—the hero of Lake Erie—had hit a marine captain. With Heath feeling that public support was behind him, he challenged Perry to a duel. Perry reluctantly accepted. As an officer, Heath was entitled to reclaim his battered honor on the dueling ground. Perry had asked Decatur to serve as his second.

Decatur had tried to avert the duel—planned for October 8, 1818, just across the District of Columbia border in Bladensburg, Maryland—by taking a trip to New York. Heath and Perry followed him there, and on October 19 they all rowed across the Hudson to Weehawken, New Jersey, to the same dueling ground where Aaron Burr had killed Alexander Hamilton fourteen years earlier. Perry had told Decatur he knew that Heath was in the right. He was determined to let the marine restore his honor; he would not fire back. Perry wrote this in a letter for Decatur to read aloud after the duel. By the terms of the *code duello* the principals could not speak to each other until after all shots had been exchanged. The men stood back to back. At Decatur's order, each took five paces and turned. Heath fired and missed; Perry did not shoot. Decatur stepped forward then and took from his pocket the letter Perry had written to explain his conduct. After Decatur read it aloud, he asked Heath's second if he was satisfied. He was. They all rowed back to New York.[17] Decatur had acted as a second should: he had tried to avert the duel, and then at the earliest moment had stepped in to make sure each party retained both his honor and his life. He wanted a second who would do the same.

As Decatur mulled over this problem during a daily walk in Washington, he was startled when a carriage stopped and out bounded William Bainbridge. He and Bainbridge had not seen each other since their unpleasant meeting in Gibraltar. Now Bainbridge apologized. "I behaved like a great fool," Bainbridge told him, and asked Decatur to forgive him. In a joking way Bainbridge reminded Decatur, "You always contrive to reap laurels from my misfortunes." Bainbridge's sudden appearance and change of heart puzzled Decatur. Bainbridge was in the area to build another seventy-four-gun ship, the *Columbus*, under construction at St. Marys, Maryland, and undoubtedly realized that his own naval career would not be helped if he continued to feud with Stephen Decatur. Decatur invited Bainbridge to come to his home for a glass of wine. Bainbridge came for a drink and stayed for two or three weeks.[18]

Susan was shocked when Bainbridge walked through the door and again when he did not leave. This was the man who had treated her husband like a stranger the last time they had met. How could Stephen welcome him in so easily? Her husband had a more forgiving nature—forgiving of anything but a breach of duty. Decatur had trouble grasping "the universal sinfulness of man's nature," as he once confessed to John Randolph of Roanoke, the brilliant but mad congressman from Virginia. Decatur was surprised "that the best people in the world," including his own mother, "should always speak of themselves as sinners." He apparently did not. Randolph understood why sin seemed so "dark and unintelligible" to Decatur, but predicted a time would come when he would be "self-arraigned and self-condemned," not of "cowardice, falsehood, or any mean and dishonorable act," but of having received "great and innumerable favors" and repaid the divine "Benefactor with ingratitude. This will be guilt enough to humble you, and you will feel and own that you are a sinner."[19] Forgiveness of others came easily to Decatur; the idea that he himself needed to be forgiven did not.

Susan did not know when Bainbridge came through the door that her husband was preparing to fight a duel; nor did she know that Bainbridge, unlike Rodgers and Porter, had agreed to act as his second. After listening to but not heeding the counsel of Morris, Rodgers, and Porter to ignore Barron's last letter, Decatur replied on December 29. He had a different recollection of his own early days in the navy from the one Barron had described. Barron could not have persuaded Decatur not to resign in 1803, since "I have never, since my first admission into the navy, contemplated resigning," and Isaac Chauncey could vouch for the fact that Decatur had not been transferred out of the *New York* in 1803 but had been forced to leave the Mediterranean to escape arrest for his role in the duel between Joseph Bainbridge and James Cochran. As for the suggestion that Decatur had barred Barron's reinstatement to preserve his own relative rank, Decatur noted that every junior officer in the navy must then feel equally resentful. And if Decatur really was "disposed to kill out of my way . . . those who interfere with my advancement, there are others, my superiors, who I consider fairly barring my pretensions—it would serve such purpose better, to begin with them." Decatur did not regard Barron as a threat to his career. "You never have interfered with me in the service," he said, "and, at the risk of being esteemed a little vain, I must say, I do not think you ever will."[20]

Decatur did not intend to mollify Barron. He closed by saying that he would ignore any further communication from Barron except a direct challenge. On January 16 Barron wrote back that Decatur was "at liberty to view this as that call." Decatur replied that he was "at a loss to know what your intention is." But if Barron "intended it as a challenge, I accept it," and referred Barron to Bainbridge to make the arrangements.[21]

Barron's second would be Jesse Elliott. Other naval officers had told Decatur that Elliott was trying to provoke the duel, that it was he who had instigated the renewal of the correspondence, and that he would do his best to prevent any peaceful resolution. Barron had wondered in his November 30 letter to Decatur who the "intermeddling gentleman was" who had told Decatur that Barron had been bound to Washington the previous spring to challenge him. "If I may be allowed a conjecture, I think I can recognize in him the self-same officious gentleman who . . . originated the report of your having made use of the gasconading expressions you have disowned."[22] Barron and Decatur were both beginning to realize now that Elliot had manipulated them into this position. He had pushed Barron to issue a challenge, and had relayed back to Barron Decatur's hostility. Barron may have believed Elliott's assurances that once he had arranged the duel, he would be able to negotiate a settlement that would lead to his reinstatement. Certainly the example of the Heath-Perry duel would have been in their minds.

Stephen and Susan attended President Monroe's Wednesday afternoon reception on March 8. It was their fourteenth wedding anniversary. Susan did not know that while they were at the White House, Elliott and Bainbridge were meeting on the *Columbus* to work out terms for Stephen's duel with James Barron. Bainbridge and Elliott agreed that the two principals would meet at Bladensburg on the morning of Wednesday, March 22. They would use pistols fired at eight paces. This was a short distance—about twenty-four feet, two yards shorter than in the Perry-Heath duel—to which Bainbridge had agreed as a concession to Barron's purported failing eyesight. When Decatur read over the terms, he saw that Bainbridge had conceded an advantage to Barron, and began to put his affairs in order. Once his second had agreed to the terms, Decatur could not change them.

The weather in Washington turned rainy and raw over the next two weeks. Telling Susan that, against his wishes, he might be sent on another sea voyage, Stephen explained his various real estate and investment portfolios to her. Although he hoped that she would not rely on her father's financial advice, he suggested she invite Luke Wheeler to come and stay; and with their friend Robert Goodloe Harper already in the household, Stephen suggested that Kitty Harper join the family as well. With all three nieces at home, the house was full of life as Washington officially welcomed spring and celebrated the recent wedding of Maria Monroe. Susan reveled in being Washington's social queen. For two weeks Decatur kept his secret. Susan did not know, and the family did not know. He happened to run into Thomas Macdonough outside the Willard Hotel on March 21, and though Stephen embraced his old midshipman and the two had one of their deep conversations, he did not tell the devoutly religious Macdonough that the next morning he would duel Barron.

CHAPTER 23

"I never was your enemy, sir"

SUSAN WAS still asleep when Stephen left the house on the clear cold morning of March 22. He did not wake their guests—her father, their nieces—as he slipped out the door. He walked briskly across President's Park, past the White House, then quickly up Pennsylvania Avenue to Capitol Hill. At Beale's Hotel, Bainbridge and navy purser Samuel Hambleton met him. Hambleton would recall Decatur's animation and appetite as the three men ate a large breakfast. Decatur reminded them that he had brought his will for them to witness, but during their conversation he forgot all about it. After breakfast they climbed into the carriage Bainbridge had hired to take them across the District line into Bladensburg, where the militia forces had scattered in 1814, allowing the British to enter Washington. The carriage reached the crest of a hill overlooking a creek feeding the Potomac. Jesse Elliott appeared and told them to wait. He would fetch Barron from his hotel.

The two men returned shortly. Decatur and Barron now regarded each other with curiosity as Bainbridge and Elliott reviewed their agreed-upon rules. They had not seen each other since the *Chesapeake* court-martial thirteen years earlier. Barron had gone gray in his years of exile; his kind face was now grim and lined with worry. Decatur, no longer a slender young hero, was now distinctly middle aged, heavier, and trying to disguise his thinning hair by combing locks up from the sides.

As they studied each other, Elliott paced off the distance. Barron asked Bainbridge, who would do the counting of "One, two, three," to speak the numbers now as he would during the duel. Neither man could fire before "One" or after "two." Bainbridge, he knew, corrected for a slight stammer by beginning sentences with "uh-to," which a nervous duelist might mistake for "One, two," and Barron wanted to hear how Bainbridge would sound. Bainbridge had already told Hambleton that he planned to count as quickly as he could. Now he slowly and nervously intoned, "Present—One—Two—Three."[1]

Bainbridge was now so nervous he could not load the pistols, so with Elliott's permission, Decatur took the pistols and loaded them himself. Returning to his place, he studied Barron across eight paces of ground. In a fleeting moment of silence Barron blurted out, "Now, Decatur, if we meet in another world, let us hope that we shall be better friends." Decatur answered, "I never was your enemy, sir."[2]

They had spoken directly to each other—violating the code of the duel. Now Hambleton thought they were stepping toward each other. Was this a reconciliation? The duel had been worked up by rumors and innuendo; it could be resolved by a direct conversation. Barron, who had issued the challenge, was now offering Decatur a chance to resolve their conflict without shooting, and Decatur embraced the chance; he was not Barron's enemy. This was the moment for their seconds, Elliott and Bainbridge, to resolve their differences and complete the reconciliation.

But Elliott would not have it. He ordered them "back to your places," and Bainbridge, unsure perhaps of his own role, began his carefully practiced recitation. "Present—One—"

At "One," a shot was heard, and Barron immediately fell to the ground. Decatur lowered his right hand to his side. His pistol slipped from his grasp. Then he collapsed.

Each man had fired at the same instant, aiming for the other's hip—to wound but not to kill. Decatur's shot knocked Barron to the ground as it tore into his right hip. His pelvic bone stopped the bullet. Barron's shot hit Decatur's right hip but then passed left through his groin, tearing through his intestines and lodging in his left hip. His rigid self-control had kept him standing, apparently unhurt, until he collapsed.

Decatur lay as if dead. Barron thought that he too was dying, but called out to the others to cover Decatur with his own coat. Then Decatur revived, and Bainbridge and Elliott carried him closer to Barron. Barron told Decatur he forgave him from the bottom of his heart.

Struggling for breath Decatur asked, "Why did you not return to America when the war broke out?"

"I had not the means," Barron confessed. During his lonely years in Copenhagen he had barely supported himself—and could do nothing for his family at home—by devising inventions. Out of pride he had concealed his poverty from every other soul since his return; he told Decatur now only because it seemed that both men would soon be dead. There was nothing more to hide from each other.

Decatur asked sadly, "Why did you not inform me of your situation? I would gladly have furnished you with the requisite funds."[3]

By now the field was becoming more crowded with men who had known about the duel. Bailey Washington was reminded of "the closing scene of a tragedy" when he saw Decatur and Barron lying on the ground like Hamlet and Laertes.[4] These men instinctively gathered near Decatur, they may not even have recognized Barron. Robert Goodloe Harper knelt by Decatur's side as captains came out of the woods. When David Porter arrived and saw Barron lying alone on the cold grass, he propped him up and wondered where Elliott had gone. He could not understand why Barron's second had deserted him. After comforting Barron, he took off after Elliott, thinking that Decatur was already dead. Porter was in a rage when he caught Elliot a mile down the road. Trembling, Elliott asked how things fared on the field. "They fare so badly, sir, that you left your friend weltering in his blood upon the bare earth; go back and do what you can to lessen the mischief you have aided in committing; go back and do your duty to your wounded friend."[5]

Porter turned back to the field and arrived before Elliott had mustered his courage to return. Barron was no longer alone; John Rodgers stood over him. Rodgers had tied his horse to a tree and marched across the field to see what help he might give Decatur. For a few steady seconds he had looked Barron in the eye then crossed to Decatur. Seeing how little could be done, Rodgers turned back to Barron and asked in tone of voice that Barron found irritating, "Are you much hurt?" Barron lay on the ground believing that he was dying, but could still muster the dignity to reply, "The last time I saw you I touched my hat to you; you did not return the compliment, and you must apologize for that before any questions of yours will receive an answer from me."[6]

Porter prevented Rodgers and Barron from exchanging any more harsh words. Now the surgeons were ready to move Decatur from the field. They lifted him into Rodgers's carriage. Lying still was excruciating; being moved was worse. Seeing Barron alone on the ground—Elliott was still nowhere in sight—Decatur called out that Barron should come back to Washington in his carriage. The other men shook their heads. As the carriage doors were being shut, Barron called out, "God bless you, Decatur." Decatur called weakly, "Farewell, farewell Barron."[7]

Porter commandeered a passing carriage and lifted Barron into it. The captains who had snubbed Barron now wrapped him in their coats to keep him warm, and Porter set out with him to Washington. Porter leaped out when they came across Elliott, still making his way slowly back to the dueling ground. Enraged, he forced Elliott to get in with Barron and sent them on their way.

Rodgers's carriage arrived at the Decaturs' house 10:30. Stephen insisted on waiting in the carriage until Susan and his nieces had been sent upstairs; they were not to see him in this condition. Then he was carried across the sidewalk and up the front steps and laid down on a sofa in the front parlor. He knew the doctors could do little for him, so he sent them upstairs to care for Susan, who was beside herself with anger and grief. From his pocket he produced the will. Rodgers witnessed it. The will gave all his property to Susan. He had mentioned the need to provide for his nieces, but certain that Susan would be even more generous than he, he simply left everything to her.

Stephen endured, wondering how a person could endure such pain. Again and again he cursed his foolishness. Why had he not died in the service of his country? As the news spread, President Monroe canceled his weekly reception; Congress suspended its business. Official Washington—cabinet officials, naval officers, members of Congress—came to President's Park to look into the parlor and offer help to the dying man and his family. On the street outside, neighbors and strangers gathered in the cold clear afternoon. They shared stories of Decatur—not the valiant naval hero but the neighbor who had bought them wood in the winter and groceries when times were hard. His niece Priscilla heard one of these strangers exclaim, "I have lost my best friend."[8]

Quiet whispers circulated of more ominous meetings: Elliott and Porter were to duel the next day, it was said. Barron—lying wounded at a hotel near the Capitol—would duel Rodgers if he recovered. Washington waited, wondering what would become of the navy, what would become of the nation. Upstairs, Susan remained secluded with Catherine Harper, unwilling, unable to look at another face. Her suffering would go on for another forty years. Stephen's ended shortly after ten that night.

Afterword

THE TWO SURVIVING navy commissioners reconvened on Saturday, March 25. Their only business was to cancel the board's subscription to *Niles Weekly Register*. Rodgers and Porter found that morning's account of "the late unhappy occurrence near this city" to be "so destitute of even the color of truth that the confidence hitherto felt" in the *Register*'s veracity "no longer exists."[1] In his account of the duel Hezekiah Niles falsely reported that Barron had "recently claimed the command of the Columbus 74, as the senior of com. Bainbridge, which claim was resisted by all the navy board," particularly Decatur.[2] This made the duel appear to be an official act rather than a private matter between Barron and Decatur.

Decatur's death was a tragedy for the navy. In the days that followed, speculation mounted that other duels were in the works: Rodgers versus Barron, Elliott versus Porter. Macdonough and other officers managed to quell these feuds, but the damage to the navy's reputation had been done.[3] Congress briefly considered a bill to prohibit dueling but took no action. Decatur and Barron were the last navy captains to fight a duel. Others had learned from their ghastly example and decided to duel no more.[4]

Niles did not retract his statement, but on April 8 he began printing the correspondence between Barron and Decatur that led to the duel. The correspondence made Barron, now recovering from his wounds, seem a more sympathetic character. In July 1821 the navy convened a court of inquiry to examine Decatur's charges against Barron. The court could find no proof that Barron's reported conversations at Pernambuco had ever taken place but was not satisfied with Barron's explanation for his failure to return home during the war. After publishing the full record of Barron's 1807 court-martial, however, the navy reinstated Barron. He was given command of the navy yard in Decatur's home port of Philadelphia in 1824. He had won a measure of vindication, but he never lived down the disgrace of the *Chesapeake* or the notoriety of having killed the navy's greatest hero. Barron retired from active service in 1838, and died in 1851, the navy's senior captain, but after striking the *Chesapeake*'s colors in 1807, he never commanded another ship in the U.S. Navy.[5]

Susan and most of the navy's officers blamed Jesse Elliott for instigating the duel. The navy did not pursue its inquiry into the Lake Erie incident (inquiries into defeats move more quickly than inquiries into victories), but Susan began a public relations battle of her own in 1820–21 by publishing

Perry's account of Elliott's cowardice. Elliott and his supporters responded—most powerfully in James Fenimore Cooper's *History of the Navy of the United States of America*, which exonerated Elliott. Perry's nephew, Commodore Mathew Calbraith Perry, issued his own pamphlet on the controversy charging Elliott with cowardice and duplicity. Barron could earn sympathy, but Elliott's future in the navy was severely limited by the simple fact that the other officers hated him. He realized that their support was less essential than that of the secretary of the navy and the president. As commander of the Boston Navy Yard in the 1830s (he succeeded Bainbridge, who had finally won back the coveted position), Elliott demonstrated his fealty by ordering the *Constitution*'s eagle figurehead replaced by an effigy of President Andrew Jackson. It did not win Elliott any friends in either the navy or Whiggish Boston (Samuel Dewey rowed out to the ship one night and cut off the top of Jackson's head), but it helped Elliott survive in the navy.[6]

James Fenimore Cooper's account of the battle of Lake Erie in his monumental *History of the Navy* downplayed Perry's role.[7] Naval officer Alexander Slidell Mackenzie, who witnessed Decatur's dramatic entry into Gibraltar and had been able to supplement his military pay by writing well-received travel books, tried to correct Cooper's interpretation with a two-volume biography of Perry. When Mackenzie followed this with a biography of John Paul Jones, Harvard president Jared Sparks approached him to write a short life of Decatur for his series of American biographies. Mackenzie promised a sketch of about 150 pages to be completed by January 1845.[8] By December 1844 Mackenzie had the first hundred pages done but found that he was only up to the end of the Tripolitan war. Worse, he learned that his nemesis "Mr. Cooper is engaged in preparing a biography of Decatur for Graham's Magazine."[9] Mackenzie tried to hurry, but he kept finding more material and more people who remembered Decatur. He did not send his manuscript in until April 1846, and by then it had swollen to nearly four hundred pages. Mackenzie intended to write subsequent revised editions, but his own death cut short his plans.

One of the final corrections Mackenzie requested in the manuscript was to change a reference to Susan's "premature decay" after her husband's death to "premature decline" or "some other expression that may be less grating to female ears."[10] Susan had cooperated with Mackenzie, though her husband's papers had been scattered. She had remained in seclusion for months after her husband's death; for two weeks she could bear to see no one but Kitty Harper. Kitty had brought her friend out that April to spend the summer with her venerable father, Charles Carroll of Carrollton. Carroll wrote his son-in-law in June that Susan seemed to be improving: "I think the exercise & change of scene has greatly benefited Mrs. Decatur; her spirits are more composed, she dines with us, & converses more."[11]

Susan eventually went back to Washington. She stayed for a time at Kalorama, where Stephen was buried, then at a Georgetown cottage. Stephen had been the businessman of the family. Without him, Susan turned the portfolios over to her father. Within a short time Stephen's estate—estimated to have been worth $100,000—was gone. Susan rented out the house on President's Park, first to the Russian ambassador, then to Secretary of State Henry Clay and to his successor, Martin Van Buren, who admired its capacity for entertaining and its proximity to the White House. Susan continued to entertain at her cottage on the grounds of the Catholic college at Georgetown, hosting small dinner parties in her modest new home. Senator Edward Livingston's wife wrote that unlike most Washington parties, "where it matters little whether a man is a fool or not, provided he can fight his way through" the crowd, at Susan Decatur's "small evening parties," the fortunate guests "meet by turn every person of distinction in Washington—foreign ministers, charges d'affaires, etc., etc." Susan would not invite everyone. "To be admitted into her set is a favor granted to comparatively few, and of course desired by all."[12]

Susan did not remarry, but lived out her life faithful to her husband's memory. Washington gossip suggested that she had a romantic relationship with the British ambassador, Stratford Canning. She converted to Roman Catholicism in 1827, influenced by her long association with Georgetown and by her lifelong friend Kitty Harper, though some Washington gossips suggested that her real motive was to wed the ninety-year-old Charles Carroll of Carrollton, with whom she usually spent her summers.[13]

In recalling her husband's capture of the *Macedonian*, which had launched her brief career of opulence, Susan realized that he had never received any prize money for capturing the *Philadelphia*. She undertook a relentless campaign to have Congress grant her and other surivivors of that expedition their just compensation. Susan enlisted testimonials from men who had known her husband, from former prisoners in Tripoli, and from former crewmates, and published her assembled documentary evidence in pamphlet form in 1826.[14] Mordecai Noah wrote of the effect Decatur's exploits in 1804 had had in Tunis in 1815; Salvatore Catalano, the pilot, and others testified that Decatur could have brought the *Philadelphia* out of Tripoli harbor—which would have established beyond doubt that it was his prize—but had destroyed it on Preble's orders. Susan believed that her claim was "completely *hemm'd in* by precedents!" and she did not see "how an *honest* nation can depart from" precedent.[15]

Susan made Benjamin Crowninshield, returned to Washington as congressman and chair of the House Committeee on Naval Affairs, her chief but sometimes unwilling advocate on Capitol Hill. "Now just let me tell you what I wou'd like you to do," she wrote him when she learned that the claims committee was favorably disposed. He should propose giving her half of the prize money, dividing the rest among the officers and crew.[16] Although Susan mentioned in her pamphlet that as a woman she could not testify personally before the committee, she lobbied effectively and tirelessly without entering the Capitol. She invited Congressman to tea, and sent the pamphlet to Henry Clay and Daniel Webster, then told Crowninshield that she "shou'd like you to converse with Mr. Clay, about our Claim," since she was sure that Clay "wou'd like to be useful to me," and Webster had "always manifested very friendly feelings towards me."[17]

It took Susan more than ten years to receive her claim, an effort that required her to lobby Congress and three successive presidential administrations. When the money finally came, she donated it to the college at Georgetown. In return she was given a small annuity and a place to live out her years.

Susan had sent her nieces Anna and Priscilla home to Philadelphia when their uncle died. The inheritance Decatur had pledged to them never materialized; Priscilla charged that Susan had squandered it. The lost inheritance played a large part in the ugly relationship that developed between Susan and her husband's Philadelphia family, but not the only part. Priscilla was "disgusted" by Susan's conduct toward the sisters. Her uncle had taken the girls in and looked after their education, and Anna had lived with Susan in New York and New London, but once Susan was left in charge, she had allowed them to see only "such persons as were agreeable" to her. Even after Priscilla married Captain Levi Twiggs, Susan refused to allow his Washington friends into her home "as she was expecting other company."[18]

Losing their uncle was nearly as devastating to the girls as it was to Susan, but they recovered. Their family, though, continued to experience tragedy. Just a few weeks after Stephen Decatur's death, Secretary of State Adams received the confirmation that Stephen Decatur McKnight—Anna and Priscilla's brother—had been lost at sea in 1815. Later that summer Dr. William Hurst, the girls' stepfather, died, and during the 1830s Priscilla would bury five of her own children in Washington's Congressional Cemetery. In 1847 both her husband and a son died fighting in Mexico.

During his lifetime some captains had criticized Decatur for grandstanding, but others recognized that having a charismatic and dynamic leader was good for the service's public image. With his death and that of Perry in 1818, the navy lost its two least tarnished heroes. Decatur was able to win friends and influence Congress and successive administrations to expand the service; after his death the navy would suffer not because he was gone but because in the public mind it had become less crucial to the republic's survival. As a mourning sailor told Judge Henry Baldwin at Decatur's funeral, the navy had lost its mainmast. Naval officers would continue to justify their service's existence by pursuing scientific expeditions, as Decatur had done informally, and by acting as the nation's first diplomats, as he had done formally. (David Porter would be the first American ambassador to Turkey; James Biddle exchanged ratifications of the first American treaty with China; Matthew Calbraith Perry opened American relations with Japan.) But ninteenth-century America would expand on land rather than on the sea.

The navy had capable leaders, but in the public mind Decatur had been more than that. Richard Rush believed that greater things had lain in store for his friend; and it is easy to imagine, during the political transition of the 1820s from the genteel republicanism of Madison and Monroe to the turbulent democracy of Andrew Jackson, political leaders opposed to Jackson's ascendancy turning to Decatur as a candidate for the presidency. Decatur had worried in 1804 about the consequences of the Louisiana Purchase. With the United States in complete control of the North American continent, the American people, he feared, would not have the challenge of a nearby rival, and so would not develop the sense of "national honor" required to be a great country. Instead, he told the poet Coleridge, "we shall resemble a swarm of insects," consuming and corrupting the earth's fruits in a state of "shapeless anarchy."[19] Whether Decatur might have provided a different outcome became a moot point once his life was cut short.

George Decatur Twiggs was a marine major stationed at Philadelphia's navy yard in the 1840s when he decided to bring his great-uncle's body home. His father, Levi Twiggs, married to Decatur's niece Priscilla, had been a marine under Decatur on the *President*; now Levi was fighting in the Mexican War. George Twiggs contacted Susan, telling her that the tomb at Kalorama had been untended and was in disrepair. It would be fitting to have Stephen laid to rest at St. Peter's Church with his parents and sisters. Susan agreed.

Twiggs and other Philadelphians, perhaps inspired by the new monument in Trafalgar Square to honor Lord Nelson, planned a granite pillar; it remains the tallest in the burying ground, though far shorter than the one in London. Twiggs enlisted three friends of his great-uncle—Charles Stewart, Francis Gurney Smith, and Joseph Ingersoll—to oversee the Philadelphia ceremony. Secretary of the Navy John Y. Mason led a small group to Kalorama to bring Decatur's casket from its tomb. Accompanied by a military guard, the casket traveled by train to Baltimore. There the mayor and the commander of Fort McHenry escorted it to the steamboat *Constitution*. It was appropriate that

Decatur's body be carried home for the final time on a steamboat—he had pushed the navy to develop this new technology—named for Preble's flagship which Decatur had commanded briefly in 1804.

Stephen Decatur's oak and cedar casket lay in state in Major Twigg's residence at the Navy Yard. From there on the morning of October 29, 1846, the procession left for St. Peter's Church. It was a reminder of earlier times, when the nation was new and its future bright. Decatur would forever be young in the nation's imagination, but the men who had been young with him now were old. During the week of Decatur's second funeral, Salvatore Catalano died in Washington; he had piloted the *Intrepid* into Tripoli on that February day in 1804 that made Decatur a hero. Charles Stewart had been captain of the *Siren* on that fateful mission; now he was Decatur's chief pallbearer, leading the procession of military and civil officials, shipmasters, military pensioners, and citizens past Decatur's childhood home on Front Street, past the scenes of their childhood battles, turning from there onto Dock and then Walnut, from Walnut to Third, and down Third to St. Peter's Church. There the wooden casket was placed inside a metal box at the graveside. Navy purser Francis B. Stockton turned the key to lock Decatur's remains inside and handed the key to Major Twiggs. Then the box was placed in the ground.[20]

Stockton himself would one day be laid to rest next to Decatur. Stephen's Philadelphia family brought Susan to take her place by his side when she died in 1861. They also cleared up a mystery. For years Susan Decatur's age had been a matter of conjecture: the 1840 census taker thought she was born in the 1790s; twenty years later she gave her birth date as 1799. On the simple granite marker in St. Peter's churchyard were carved her name, the fact that she had been Stephen Decatur's beloved and devoted wife, and her date of birth, 1776.

As Stephen Decatur's body made its way from Washington to Philadelphia, the nation was at war with Mexico. George Twiggs and his father would both die there in 1847. New England opposed the Mexican War with nearly the same fervor as it had blocked the War of 1812. John Quincy Adams warned that it would be the death knell of the republic; Albert Gallatin saw alarming parallels to the 1760s, when English liberty had eroded when Britain expanded into an empire.

Stephen Decatur's second funeral may have been intended to remind Americans of a time when virtue and valor were joined and men could astonish the world with their heroic deeds. Decatur had embodied the astonishing possibilities of the American republic. As Secretary Mason entered the tomb, he could not resist a chance to look once more at the face of Stephen Decatur. The oaken lid was lifted. But the cedar-lined case held only a skeleton clad in a few fragments of dress blue uniform.

NOTES

Prologue

1. John Quincy Adams, Diary, March 14, 1820. Microfilm, P-54, reel 34, Adams Papers, Massachusetts Historical Society, Boston.

2. Margaret Bayard Smith, *The First Forty Years of Washington Society*, ed. Gaillard Hunt (New York: Charles Scribner's Sons, 1906), 150.

3. Mrs. Phoebe Warren Tayloe, *Benjamin Ogle Tayloe. In Memoriam* (Washington, D.C.: privately printed, 1872), 161.

4. Ibid.

5. Ibid.

6. General Solomon Van Rensselaer to Harriet Van Rensselaer, Washington, D.C., March 20, 1820, in Benson J. Lossing, *The Pictorial Field Book of the War of 1812* (New York: Harper & Brothers, 1868), 942n.

7. *Georgetown National Messenger*, March 24, 1820.

8. *Essex Register* (Salem, Mass.), March 29, 1820.

9. *Salem (Mass.) Gazette*, March 28, 1820

10. Louisa Catherine Adams to John Adams, March 23, 1820, Adams Papers, Letters Received and Other Loose Papers, reel 449.

11. John Adams to Louisa Catherine Adams, May 8, 1820, Letterbook, August 18, 1819–20 to February 1825, Adams Papers, reel 124.

12. *Essex Register*, March 29, 1820.

13. Catherine Allgor, *Parlor Politics: In Which the Ladies of Washington Help Build a City and a Government* (Charlottesville: University Press of Virginia, 2000), 79–80.

14. Smith, *First Forty Years*, 150.

15. John Sergeant to his wife, Washington, D.C., March 24, 1820, Society Small Collection, Box 33, Historical Society of Pennsylvania, Philadelphia.

16. *National Messenger*, March 27, 1820

17. *Essex Register*, April 1, 1820.

18. Undated ms., Decatur Family Papers, folder 22, Historical Society of Pennsylvania.

19. Josephine Seaton, *William Winston Seaton of the National Intelligencer: A Biographical Sketch* (1871; rpt. Arno Press and New York Times, 1970), p. 148.

20. Louisa Catherine Adams to John Adams, March 24, 1820, Adams Family Papers, reel 449.

21. John Quincy Adams, Diary, March 24, 1820, reel 54; Tayloe, *In Memoriam*, 163.

22. *Essex Register*, April 1, 1820.

23. Alexander Slidell Mackenzie, *Life of Stephen Decatur, Commodore in the U.S. Navy* (Boston: Charles C. Little and James Brown, 1846), 332n.

24. John Quincy Adams, Diary, March 22 and 24, 1820, reel 54.

25. Richard Rush to Charles Jared Ingersoll, London, June 4, 1820, Charles Jared Ingersoll Papers, Richard Rush Letters, Correspondence: March, Historical Society of Pennsylvania.

26. Louisa Catherine Adams to John Adams, March 24, 1820.

Chapter 1

1. James N. Arnold, ed., *Vital Records for Rhode Island*, vol. 10, *Town and Church* (Providence: Narragansett Historical Publishing Company, 1898), 445, 453, 496. The dates of Priscilla and Stephen's wedding (September 26, 1751) and young Stephen's baptism (June 6, 1752), suggest that Priscilla may have been pregnant at the time of the marriage, which was hardly unusual in this period. Most sources give the American-born Stephen's birth year as 1751, which would indicate that he was born well before his baptism date, even granting that until 1753 the New Year was celebrated on March 25, not January 1. Perhaps his parents neglected to baptize him at birth; or perhaps they waited a respectable time to give the appearance of legitimacy.

2. Stephen Decatur Sr. to Joseph Cowperthwait, February 27, 1774, Decatur Family Papers, folder 00, Historical Society of Pennsylvania.

3. Note of Priscilla Twiggs, niece, in Twiggs Family Notebook, folder 22, Decatur Family Papers.

4. Richard Rush to Susan Decatur, May 22, 1840, in Mackenzie, *Decatur*, 357.

5. Mackenzie, *Decatur*, 14.

6. Charles Lee Lewis, *The Romantic Decatur* (Philadelphia: University of Pennsylvania Press, 1937), 17.

7. William M. P. Dunne makes the case that the Barron-Decatur feud stemmed from remarks Barron made later about Decatur breaking his engagement to Mary King, Rufus King's granddaughter. Also during this time, Decatur may have had an altercation with a prostitute. According to a newspaper article in the *Wilmington (Delaware) Daily Commercial* of December 22, 1874, young Decatur argued with a prostitute and then killed her. His prosecution was prevented by two skillful lawyers, John Sergeant and a man identified only as Bedford, who also managed to keep word of this affair out of the newspapers, and indeed out of the historical record. Should it be believed? Neither Dunne, Decatur's most scrupulous recent biographer, nor Charles Lee Lewis, his only authoritative twentieth-century biographer, has been able to find any more substantiation apart from the 1874 news clipping. See Lewis, *Romantic Decatur*, 271n5; William M. P. Dunne, "Pistols and Honor: The James Barron–Stephen Decatur Conflict, 1798–1807," *American Neptune* 50 (Fall 1990), 245. I am indebted to Martin Zell, docent at the Stephen Decatur House in Washington, D.C., for sharing this information with me.

8. William Bell Clark, *Gallant John Barry, 1745–1803: The Story of a Naval Hero of Two Wars* (New York: Macmillan, 1938), 380.

9. Ibid., 387–388.

10. Ibid., 390, 392.

Chapter 2

1. Clark, *Gallant John Barry*, 411.

2. Christopher McKee, *A Gentlemanly and Honorable Profession: The Creation of the U.S. Naval Officers Corps, 1794–1815* (Annapolis: Naval Institute Press, 1991), 212.

3. Mackenzie, *Decatur*, 25.

4. Ibid.; Irvin Anthony, *Decatur* (New York: Charles Scribner's Sons, 1931), 45.

5. Clark, *Gallant John Barry*, 417.

6. Ibid.

7. Ibid., 417–18.

8. *Russell's Gazette*, July 23, 1798, in Martin Griffin, *The story of Commodore John Barry father of the American navy* (Philadelphia, 1908), 355.

9. Clark, *Gallant John Barry*, 419–20.

10. Thomas Wilkey, "Journal Kept On Board the United States Ship Delaware Stephen Decatur Esq. Commander," August 12, 1798, Library Company of Philadelphia.

11. Ann Decatur to Benjamin Rush, August 29, 1798, Ms. Correspondence of Dr. Benjamin Rush, vol. 23, 36, Library Company of Philadelphia.

12. Mackenzie, *Decatur*, 37.

13. Benjamin Stoddert to John Adams, September 21, 1798, and Adams to Stoddert, October 1, 1798, in Griffin, *Commodore John Barry*, 361; ibid., 364.

14. Clark, *Gallant John Barry*, 428–29.

15. Ibid., 439.

16. Mackenzie, *Decatur*, 32, 34.

17. Clark, *Gallant John Barry*, 443.

18. Ibid., 444.

19. Griffin, *Commodore John Barry*, 395.

20. Charles Oscar Paullin, "Dueling in the Old Navy," *U.S. Naval Institute Proceedings* 35, no. 4 (1909): 1155–87, esp. 1162; Mackenzie, 38–39.

21. For this account, see Mackenzie, *Decatur*, 34–36.

22. Paullin, "Dueling in the Old Navy," 1163.

23. Mackenzie, *Decatur*, 45.

Chapter 3

1. David F. Long, *Ready to Hazard: A Biography of Commodore William Bainbridge, 1774–1833* (Hanover, N.H.: University Press of New England, 1981), 56–58.

2. Ibid., 65.

3. Mackenzie, *Decatur*, 154.

4. For this account, see Lewis, *Romantic Decatur*, 192–93; Long, *Ready to Hazard*, 62–63.

5. Paullin, "Dueling in the Old Navy," 1158, 1159.

6. Thomas Truxtun to Secretary of the Navy, Norfolk, March 3, 1802, Captain Dudley W. Knox et al., eds., *Naval documents related to the United States wars with the Barbary powers*, 6 volumes (Washington, D.C.: U.S. Government Printing Office, 1939–1944), 2:76 (hereafter cited as BW).

7. Secretary of the navy to Truxtun, March 13, 1802, BW 2:83.

8. Secretary of the navy to George Harrison, Navy Agent, Philadelphia, February 5, 1802, BW 2:50; Truxtun to Aaron Burr, Norfolk, March 22, 1802, BW 2:94.

9. James Fenimore Cooper, *History of the Navy of the United States of America*, 2 vols. (Cooperstown, N.Y.: H. & E. Phinney, 1847), 1:205.

10. Dunne, "Pistols and Honor," 252.

11. Captain Daniel Carmick, USMC, to Lieutenant Colonel Commandant William W. Burrows, USMC, Leghorn, October 15, 1802, BW 2:293–94.

12. Ibid.

13. Captain Daniel Murray to Secretary of the Navy, November 7, 1802, in Lewis, *Romantic Decatur*, 277–78n84.

14. Nathaniel P. Willis to Secretary of State, September 15, 1802, BW 2:275.

15. Henry Wadsworth, Journal, September 13, 1802, BW 2:273–74

16. Ibid.

17. Ibid., April 2, 1803, BW 2:387.

18. Ibid., June 15, 1803, BW 2:453–54.

19. Ibid., May 22, 1803, BW 2:416.

20. Mackenzie, *Decatur*, 56.

21. For this account, see ibid., 58; Wadsworth, Journal, February 14, 1803, BW 2:362. The figure of twelve yards is from Paullin, "Dueling in the Old Navy," 1164–65.

22. Wadsworth, Journal, April 6, 1803, BW 2:388; Secretary of the navy to Edward Preble, May 27, 1803, and Secretary of the Navy to Decatur, May 27, 1803, BW 2:424.

Chapter 4

1. Secretary of the Navy Robert Smith to Decatur, May 27, 1803, BW 2:424.

2. Smith to Edward Preble, May 21, 1803, BW 2:411.

3. Decatur to Smith, Boston, July 11, 1803, Letters to the Secretary of the Navy from Officers below the Rank of Commander, 1802–1886, National Archives and Records Administration, Washington, D.C., Microfilm, M-148, reel 1.

4. Lieutenant Richard Somers to Secretary of the Navy, July 31, 1803, BW 2:502.

5. Decatur to Secretary of the Navy, August 1, 1803, BW 2:503–4.

6. Decatur to Secretary of the Navy, August 21, 1803, Letters to the Secretary of the Navy, 1802–1886, roll 1:23.

7. Preble to Secretary of the Navy, July 29, 1803, BW 2:501; Decatur to Secretary of the Navy, August 1, 1803, BW 2: 502–3.

8. Decatur to Secretary of the Navy, August 21, 1803, BW 2:516; Decatur to Secretary of the Navy, Nantasket Roads, September 6, 1803, BW 3:21,

9. Decatur to Secretary of the Navy, September 8, 1803, BW 3:24.

10. Decatur to Secretary of the Navy, Newport, September 19, 1803, BW 3:66; Joseph Blake et al. to Decatur, U.S. Brig *Argus* at sea, September 12, 1803, BW 3:28.

11. Decatur to Secretary of the Navy, off Rhode Island Light, September 27, 1803, BW 3:91.

12. John Gavino to Secretary of State, Gibraltar, November 15, 1803, BW 3: 222; Preble, Circular Letter, USS *Constitution*, Gibraltar, November 12, 1803, BW 3:215–16.

13. Preble to Decatur, Gibraltar, November 7, 1803, BW 3:203.

14. Preble to Secretary of the Navy, USS *Constitution*, Syracuse Harbor, December 10, 1803, BW 3:256.

15. Preble to Secretary of the Navy, December 10, 1803, BW 3:257.

16. Preble to Decatur, USS *Constitution*, Syracuse, December 1, 1803; BW 3:245.

17. Preble to Decatur, December 8, 1803, Letterbook, Historical Society of

Pennsylvania. What action did Preble take? What became of Boyd? Boyd seems to have had a troubled career. He had become a midshipman in 1800, served as second officer on Gunboat Number 9 in 1805–6, but his "disobedience of orders and unofficer-like conduct," in the words of one lieutenant, constantly caused trouble. Rodgers had him sent home under arrest in 1806; at the beginning of the War of 1812, Boyd was again or still, a midshipman. See Thomas Magruder to David Porter, *Enterprise*, Bay of Naples, February 6, 1806, BW 6:41; Lieutenant Samuel Elbert, Gunboat Number 9, Charleston, to Secretary of the Navy, July 22, 1806, BW 6:363; Secretary of the Navy Paul Hamilton to Samuel Smith, December 24, 1812, in William S. Dudley, ed., *Naval War of 1812: A Documentary History*, 3 vols. (Washington, D.C.: Naval Historical Center, 1985–), 1:629.

18. Washington Irving, *Journals and Notebooks*, vol. 1, *1803–1806*, ed. Nathalia Wright (Madison: University of Wisconsin Press, 1969–1985), 193;

19. Mackenzie, *Decatur*, 63.

20. Irving, *Journals and Notebooks*, 193.

21. Sailing Master Nathaniel Haraden, USS *Constitution*, extract from Logbook, December 23, 1803, BW 3:288; Edward Preble, Memorandum Book, December 23, 1803, BW 3: 289.

22. Salvador Catalano, deposition, February 2, 1804, BW 3:180–81.

23. Haraden, Logbook, December 24, 1803, BW 3:395; Edward Preble, Diary, December 24, 1803, BW 3:294; Christopher McKee, *Edward Preble: A Naval Biography, 1761–1807* (Annapolis: Naval Institute Press, 1972), 185.

24. Captain William Bainbridge to Preble, January 18, 1804, BW 3:347.

25. Preble to Decatur and Charles Stewart, January 31, 1804, BW 3:375–77; Mackenzie, *Decatur*, 68.

Chapter 5

1. Haraden, Logbook, February 3, 1804, BW 3:388; Ralph Izard to his mother, February 2, 1804, BW 3:382.

2. According to Charles Morris there were six midshipmen, but the official report listed seven: Ralph Izard, John Rowe, Morris, Alexander Laws, John Davis, Thomas Macdonough, and Thomas Anderson; see BW 3:423.

3. *The Autobiography of Commodore Charles Morris, U.S. Navy* (Boston: A. William & Co., published for the U.S. Naval Institute, 1880), 27.

4. Ibid., 28.

5. McKee, *Preble*, 197.

6. Lewis Heerman, quoted ibid.

7. Ibid.

8. Ibid., 198.

9. Morris, *Autobiography*, 29.

10. Bainbridge to ?, Tripoli, February 18, 1804, BW 3:433.

11. Bainbridge to Preble, February 16, 1804, BW 3:410; the italicized portion was written in lime juice.

12. Jonathan Cowdery, Journal, February 16, 1804, BW 3:532.

13. Nicholas C. Nissen to the Danish consul, Marseilles, February 29, 1804, BW 3:421.

14. Lieutenant Richard Somers to Preble, February 16, 1804, BW 3:411; Richard O'Brien to Tobias Lear, April 23, 1804, BW 4:60.

15. Quoted in Charles W. Furlong, "Finding the Frigate *Philadelphia*," *Harper's*, 111 (June–November 1905): 53.

16. McKee, *Preble*, 199.

17. Quoted in Furlong, "Finding the Frigate *Philadelphia*," 53.

18. McKee, *Preble*, 193–194.

19. Haraden, Logbook, February 19, 1804, BW 3:444.

20. Robert T. Spence quoted in Susan Decatur, *Documents Relative to the Claim of Mrs. Decatur, with her Earnest Request that the Gentlemen of Congress will take the trouble to read them* (Georgetown, D.C.: James C. Dunn, Printer, Bridge Street, 1826). 21–22.

21. Mackenzie, *Decatur*, 81.

Chapter 6

1. Preble to Decatur, February 20, 1804, BW 3:446.

2. Charles Stewart to Secretary of the Navy, June 4, 1803, BW 2:438–39.

3. Mackenzie, *Decatur*, 124; Samuel Taylor Coleridge, "Table Talk" (June 9, 1832), in *Collected Works of Samuel Taylor Coleridge: Table Talk I*, 27 vols. ed. Carl Woodring (Princeton: Princeton University Press, 1990), 14:300. There is some confusion about whether Coleridge was recounting a conversation with Stephen Decatur or William Eaton. Since Coleridge used a similar quotation in an 1818 essay (see note 4), two years after Decatur's triumphant return from the Mediterranean and seven years after Eaton had gone to his own unhappy reward, it seems more likely that he was either quoting Decatur or putting Eaton's sentiment in Decatur's more popular voice.

4. Samuel Taylor Coleridge, "On the Law of Nations" (1818), in *Collected Works of Samuel Taylor Coleridge: The Friend I*, ed. Barbara E. Rooke (Princeton: Princeton University Press, 1969), 4:297.

5. George Davis to Secretary of State, Tunis, March 26, 1804, BW 3:525.

6. Decatur to Preble, Messina, March 30, 1804, BW 3:546–47.

7. Crew of *Enterprise* to Preble, April 5, 1804, BW 4:11.

8. McKee, *Preble*, 231.

9. Edward Preble, Diary, Sunday, April 22, 1804, BW 4:53.

10. Samuel Sloan, Journal, 1803–4, April 20, 1804, U.S.S. *Constitution* Museum, Boston.

11. McKee, *Preble*, 231.

12. Frances Leckie to Preble, Syracuse, April 21, 1804, BW 4:46.

13. Marcello DeGregorio to Preble, [April 21, 1804?], BW 4:47.

14. Preble, Diary, April 23, 1804, BW 4:56.

15. Leckie to Decatur, October 12, 1819, in McKee, *Preble*, 232n.

16. Preble to Secretary of the Navy, USS *Constitution* off Tripoli, June 14, 1804, BW 4:187–88; Edward Preble, Diary June 13, 1804, BW 4:185–86.

17. Cooper, *History of the Navy*, 1:239.

18. Mackenzie, *Decatur*, 87–88.

19. John Darby, Journal on *John Adams*, August 7, 1804, BW 4:385.

20. Ibid. Blake resigned from the service in 1806. See Cooper, *History of the Navy*, 1:273, appendix, note C.

21. Decatur to Keith Spence, USS *Congress*, Tunis Bay, January 9, 180 [4] BW 4: 346.

22. Footnote to Preble's report in Charles W. Goldsborough, *United States Naval Chronicle* (Washington, D.C., 1824), BW 4:296–97n.

23. On December 7, 1805, Frazier was granted a pension of nine dollars per month. Although he suffered from his injuries until his death on or about April 22, 1833, he never collected his pension. He had entered the service in 1802, changing his name from James North to Daniel Frazier. Though his name is all but forgotten, his deed is not. In the early nineteenth century another sailor took credit for saving Decatur's life. That sailor, Reuben James, was still alive when Alexander Slidell Mackenzie wrote his biography of Decatur and, with little evidence other than James's testimony, accepted his story. In the 1850s a popular engraving showed James saving Decatur's life, and the name Reuben James entered navy lore. It was further immortalized in the twentieth century when the American merchant ship bearing the name was sunk by a German U-boat in 1941. "Daniel Frazer" of the *Enterprize* is on Preble's list of wounded, dated August 3, 1804; BW 4:362n.

24. The prayerbook is now in the Special Collections, Georgetown University Library, Washington, D.C. It was given to Georgetown by Mrs. Decatur. My account of the battle is drawn from Mackenzie, *Decatur*; from Edward Preble's report to the Secretary of the Navy, BW 4:293–308; from Cooper, *History of the Navy*, 1:248–51; and from McKee, *Preble*, 251–67.

25. Mackenzie, *Decatur*, 97.

26. McKee, *Preble*, 266.

27. Mackenzie, *Decatur*, 100.

28. Preble, Journal, August 8, 1804, BW 4:377.

Chapter 7

1. John Darby, Journal, August 9, 1804, BW 4:391.

2. McKee, *Gentlemanly and Honorable Profession*, 298.

3. BW 4:302n.

4. Midshipman Charles G. Ridgely, BW 4:508.

5. Robert Spence to his mother, Gibraltar, November 12, 1804, BW 4:350.

6. Ridgely, BW 4:508; names of crew in Edward Preble, "Names of Officers, Seamen, & Marines Killed & wounded," BW 4:309.

7. For this account, see Preble, Memorandum Book, September 10, 1804, BW 5:14.

8. Samuel Barron to Isaac Hull, USS *President* off Tripoli, September 13, 1804, BW 5:19–20.

9. William Eaton to Colonel [Timothy?] Dwight, Malta, September 20, 1804, BW 5:42–43.

10. Alexander Ball to Preble, Malta, September 20, 1804, BW 5:43.

11. Preble to Secretary of the Navy, USS *Constitution*, Malta Harbor, September 18, 1804, BW 4:308.

12. Preble to Decatur, *Constitution* off Tripoli, September 6, 1804, BW 4:522.

13. Preble to Decatur, Syracuse, September 24, 1804, BW 5:49.

14. Eaton, Journal, October 7, 1804, BW 5:78.

15. Preble to Secretary of the Navy, November 7, 1804, BW 5:127.

16. Tobias Lear to John Rodgers, Malta, October 16, 1804, BW 5:88.

17. Samuel Barron to Rodgers, *President*, Malta, October 26, 1804, BW 5:100; Preble, Memorandum Book, Malta, October 28, 1804, BW 5:104.

18. See Robert Denison, secretary to Samuel Barron, to Decatur, Malta, February 19, 1805, BW 5:361.

19. McKee, *Preble*, 309–10.

20. Spencer C. Tucker and Frank T. Reuter, *Injured Honor: The Chesapeake-Leopard Affair, June 22, 1807* (Annapolis: U.S. Naval Institute Press, 1996), 86.

21. George Davis to Decatur, Tunis, July 14, 1805, BW 6:181.

22. Eaton to Isaac Hull, Syracuse, July 26, 1805, BW 6:196.

23. Mackenzie, *Decatur*, 132.

24. Irving, *Journals and Notebooks*, 1:179–80.

25. Rodgers to Secretary of the navy, Tunis Bay, September 1, 1805, BW 6:261; Hamouda Pacha to Rodgers, Court of Tunis, August 5, 1805, BW 6:208.

26. Rodgers to Secretary of the navy, Tunis Bay, September 1, 1805, BW 6:261; Hamouda Pacha to Lear, Court of Tunis, August 7, 1805, BW 6:211.

27. Rodgers to Decatur, USS *Constitution*, Tunis Bay, September 4, 1805, BW 6:273; Lear to Secretary of State, USS *Constitution*, Tunis Bay, September 4, 1805, BW 6:273.

28. Hezekiah Loomis, Journal, Tuesday, September 24, 1805, BW 6:287.

29. Rodgers to Secretary of the Navy, USS *Constitution*, Livorno, October 30, 1805, BW 6:299.

Chapter 8

1. H. W. Burton, *The History of Norfolk, Virginia* (Norfolk: Norfolk Virginian Job Print, 1877), 5–6; William S. Forrest, *Historical and Descriptive Sketches of Norfolk and Vicinity* (Philadelphia: Lindsay and Blakiston, 1853), 106; Edward James, ed., *Lower Norfolk County, Virginia, Antiquary*, 5 vols. (Baltimore: Friedenwald Co., 1897), 2:29, 5:65.

2. Tayloe, *In Memoriam*, 158–61.

3. *Philadelphia Merchant: The Diary of Thomas P. Cope, 1800–1851*, ed. Eliza Cope Harrison (South Bend, Ind.: Gateway Editions, 1978), 191.

4. Ibid., 190.

5. Eaton to Preble, February 3, 1806, BW 6:360; Eaton to Preble, 20 February 1807, BW 6:507.

6. Cope, *Philadelphia Merchant*, 190.

7. Ibid., 191.

8. Decatur to Keith Spence, Tunis, January 9, 180[5], BW 4:346.

9. Richard Rush to Susan Decatur, May 22, 1846, quoted in Lewis, *Romantic Decatur*, 87.

10. Richard Rush to Charles Jared Ingersoll, London, June 4, 1820, Historical Society of Pennsylvania.

11. Eaton to Preble, Philadelphia, December 30, 1805, BW 6:328.

12. Lewis, *Romantic Decatur*, 85.

13. Mackenzie, *Decatur*, 136.

14. Benjamin Rush to John Adams, January 6, 1806, in *Letters of Benjamin Rush*, 2 vols., ed. L. H. Butterfield (Philadelphia: Published for the American Philosophical Society by Princeton University Press, 1951), 2:913.

15. Lewis, *Romantic Decatur*, 86.

16. Ibid.

17. Ibid.

18. Ibid., 87.

19. Ibid., 87; see also Mackenzie, *Decatur*, 138.

20. Decatur to Preble, quoted in Lewis, *Romantic Decatur,* 89.

21. Mackenzie, *Decatur*, 140–41.

22. Decatur to Secretary of the Navy, Newport, August 11, 1806, Captains' Letters, National Archives, Microfilm, M125, roll 6, no. 8; Decatur to Secretary of the Navy, Newport, September 1, 1806, roll 6, no. 17 (hereafter cited by reel and number).

23. Mackenzie, *Decatur*, 140–42; Decatur to Bainbridge, U.S. Frigate *Chesapeake*, June 27, 1808, Dreer Collection, Historical Society of Pennsylvania.

24. Decatur to Secretary of the Navy, Newport, August 11 and October 22, 1806, reel 6, nos. 8, 49.

25. Milton Lomask, *Aaron Burr*, vol. 2, *Conspiracy and Years of Exile, 1805–1836* (New York: Farrar Strauss & Giroux, 1982), 177–78.

26. Decatur to Secretary of the Navy, January 2, 1807, reel 7, no. 4.

27. Decatur to Secretary of the Navy, January 4, 1807, ibid.

Chapter 9

1. Quoted in Anthony Steel, "More Light on the *Chesapeake*," *Mariner's Mirror* 39, no. 4 (1953): 246.

2. Tucker and Reuter, *Injured Honor*, 62.

3. Ibid., 72–73.

4. Ibid., 71.

5. Captain Alexander Murray in Jay D. Smith, "Commodore James Barron: Guilty as Charged?" *U.S. Naval Institute Proceedings* 93 (November 1967), cited ibid., 88–89.

6. Eaton to Preble, September 22, 1806, BW 6:482; Tucker and Reuter, *Injured Honor*, 86–87.

7. Tucker and Reuter, *Injured Honor* 93, 175, 149; Cooper, *History of the Navy*, 2:13.

8. Tucker and Reuter, *Injured Honor*, 72; Steel, "More Light on the *Chesapeake*," 246.

9. Tucker and Reuter, *Injured Honor*, 72.

10. Ibid., 44–48, 55, 59.

11. Ibid., 75–76.

12. Ibid., 4; Cooper, *History of the Navy*, 2:14.

13. Tucker and Reuter, *Injured Honor*, 5.

14. Ibid., 6.

15. James Barron to Secretary of the Navy, June 23, 1807, BW 6:538.

16. Tucker and Reuter, *Injured Honor*, 7–8; Cooper *History of the Navy*, 2:17.

17. Tucker and Reuter, *Injured Honor*, 15.

18. Ibid., 16.

19. William Henry Allen to his father, late USS *Chesapeake*, Hampton Roads, June 24, 1807, *Huntington Library Quarterly* 1 (October 1937): 215–16 (hereafter *HLQ*).

20. Secretary Smith to Decatur, June 26, 1807, BW 6:541; Tucker and Reuter, *Injured Honor* 106.

21. Decatur to Secretary Smith, Norfolk, June 29, 1807, BW 6:543.

22. U.S. Frigate *Chesapeake*, Logbook, July 1, 1807, BW 6:543; Decatur to Secretary Smith, July 4, 1807, BW 6:544.

23. Decatur to Secretary Smith, July 4, 1807.

24. Norma Lois Peterson, *Littleton Waller Tazewell* (Charlottesville: University Press of Virginia, 1983) 50; Decatur to Secretary of the Navy, July 8, 1807, reel 8, no. 43.

25. Decatur to Secretary of the Navy, July 8, 1807, reel 8, no. 43, and deposition of John Cunningham, enclosed; Decatur to Secretary of the Navy, July 11, 1807, reel 8, no. 45.

26. Tucker and Reuter, *Injured Honor*, 107.

27. Decatur to Secretary of the Navy, July 8, 1807, reel 8, no. 43.

28. Decatur to Samuel Barron, July 12, 1807, extract in Decatur to Secretary of the Navy, July 12, 1807, reel 8, no. 46; Decatur to Secretary of the Navy, July 14, 1807, reel 8, no. 49.

29. Tucker and Reuter, *Injured Honor*, 109–10.

30. Decatur to Secretary of the Navy, August 5, 1807, reel 8, no. 77.

Chapter 10

1. Decatur to Secretary of the Navy, August 5, 1807, reel 8, no. 77.

2. Decatur to Secretary of the Navy, July 22, 1807, reel 8, no. 59. Sim tried to conquer his drinking problem. The following summer he was serving at the New Orleans station under David Porter, but by the next year he was drinking heavily again and was dismissed in December 1809. He returned home to Maryland, staying sober until 1811, when he was reinstated as a midshipman. But at the end of 1813 he was permitted to resign rather than face a court-martial for drunkenness and neglect of duty. McKee, *Gentlemanly and Honorable Profession*, 452–54.

3. Decatur to Isaac Hull, December 18, 1807, enclosed in Decatur to Smith, January 17, 1808, reel 10, no. 16; Decatur to Smith, May 24, 1808, reel 11, no. 78.

4. Decatur to Smith, February 12, 1808, reel 10, no. 50.

5. Decatur to Secretary of the Navy, August 27, 1807, reel 8, no. 82.

6. Peterson, *Tazewell*, 45–48.

7. William Ray, Elegy to Preble, September 7, 1807, in *The American Tars in Tripolitan Slavery* (1808), *Magazine of History*, extra no. 14 (1911): 293.

8. Allen to his father, USS *Chesapeake*, Newport Light, [August 1808], *HLQ*, 226; Decatur to Smith, October 21, 1807, reel 9, no. 30.

9. Decatur to Smith, November 1, 1807, reel 9, no. 38.

10. Decatur to Smith, November 19, 1807, reel 9, no. 49.

11. Paullin, "Dueling in the Old Navy," 1159; "Establishment of a Court of Honor," November 11, 1807, BW 6:578–79.

12. Decatur to Smith, December 17, 1807, reel 9, no. 83.

13. Allen to his father, May 19, 1808, *HLQ*, 225–26.

14. Allen to his father, January 15, 1808, *HLQ*, 221.

15. Decatur to Secretary of the Navy, January 6, 1808, reel 10, no. 6.

16. Steele, "More Light on the *Chesapeake*," 254–55.

17. Decatur to Secretary Hamilton, January 1808, enclosed in Decatur to Secretary of the Navy, January 14, 1808, reel 10, no. 12.

18. Steele, "More Light on the *Chesapeake*," 262.

19. Ibid.

20. Decatur to Secretary of the Navy, January 14, 1808, reel 10, no. 12; Decatur to Secretary of the Navy, February 12, 1808, reel 10, no. 50. For an extended discussion of foreign sailors in the U.S. Navy in 1808, see Christopher McKee, "Foreign Seamen in the United States Navy: A Census of 1808," *William and Mary Quarterly* 42, no. 3, 3d ser. (July 1985): 383–93; Steele, "More Light on the *Chesapeake*," 262.

21. Decatur to Secretary of the Navy, March 4, 1808, reel 10, no. 74.

22. Decatur to Secretary of the Navy, January 14, 1808, reel 10, no. 12; Decatur to Secretary of the Navy, April 13, 1808, reel 11, no. 24.

23. Allen to his father, September 30, 1808, *HLQ*, 228.

24. Decatur to Secretary of the Navy, August 26, 1808, reel 12, no. 85; Decatur to Secretary of the Navy, August 10, 1808, reel 12, no. 59.

25. Decatur to Secretary of the Navy, September 1, 1808, reel 12, no. 89.

26. Decatur to Secretary of the Navy, August 29, 1808, reel 12, no. 87.

27. Decatur to Secretary of the Navy, October 1, 1810, reel 20, no. 47; William P. Barton to Decatur, September 29, 1810, enclosed ibid.; Decatur to Secretary of the Navy, October 12, 1810, reel 20, no. 69; Decatur to Barton, March 30, 1810, Simon P. Gratz Collection, Historical Society of Pennsylvania;

28. Decatur to Secretary of the Navy, March 24, 1812, reel 23, no. 86.

29. Decatur to Secretary of the Navy, November 9, 1808, reel 13, no. 34.

30. Decatur to Secretary of the Navy, February 27, 1809, reel 14, no. 84.

Chapter 11

1. Mackenzie, *Decatur*, 155.

2. Wallace Hutcheon Jr., *Robert Fulton: Pioneer of Undersea Warfare* (Annapolis: Naval Institute Press, 1981), 103–4, 107.

3. John Rodgers to Secretary of the Navy, November 21, 1810, reel 20, no. 140.

4. Decatur to Secretary of the Navy, July 20, 1809, reel 16, no. 34.

5. Decatur to Secretary of the Navy, January 6, 1811, reel 21, no. 13; Decatur to Secretary of the Navy, February 5, 1811, reel 21, no. 63.

6. Decatur to Secretary of the Navy, February 5, 1811, reel 21, no. 63.

7. Decatur to Secretary of the Navy, July 14, 1810, reel 19, no. 84.

8. Decatur to Secretary of the Navy, June 7, 1811, reel 22, no. 7.

9. Decatur to Secretary of the Navy, June 10, 1811, reel 22, no. 17; Decatur to Secretary of the Navy, June 10, 1811, reel 22, no. 10.

10. Decatur to Secretary of the Navy, June 10, 1811, reel 22, no. 17.

11. Rodgers to Secretary of the Navy, July 9, 1811, reel 22, no. 59.

12. Rodgers to Secretary of the Navy, September 14, 1811, reel 22, no. 142.

13. Decatur to Secretary of the Navy, September 14, 1811, reel 22, no. 139.

Chapter 12

1. Mackenzie, *Decatur*, 165–66.

2. Tucker and Reuter, *Injured Honor*, 211; *A Curtail'd Memoir of the Incidents and Occurrences in the Life of John Surman Carden, Vice Admiral in the British Navy, Written by Himself* (Oxford: Clarendon Press, 1912), 271, 255; James T. De Kay, *Chronicles of the Frigate Macedonian, 1809–1922* (New York: W. W. Norton & Co., 1992).

3. Carden, *Memoir*, 265; Mackenzie, *Decatur*, 157–58.

4. Mackenzie, *Decatur*, 339.

5. Decatur to Secretary of the Navy, January 31, 1812, reel 23, no. 26.

6. Mackenzie, *Decatur*, 157–58.

7. Ibid., 158n.

8. Secretary of the Navy to Decatur, April 4, 1812, March 28, 1812–June 30, 1813, reel 10, nos. 7–8.

9. Decatur to Secretary of the Navy, Norfolk, March 24, 1812, reel 23, no. 86. The epitaph is inscribed in marble and granite, but can also be found in Rev. William White Bronson, A.M., *The Inscriptions in St. Peter's Church Yard, Philadelphia*, ed. Charles R. Hildeburn (Camden, N.J.: Sinnickson Chew, Printer, 1879), 263–69.

10. Secretary of the Navy to Decatur, May 21, 1812, reel 10, no. 42; Decatur to Secretary of the Navy, June 8, 1812, reel 24, no. 18.

11. Rodgers to Hamilton, Staten Island, June 5, 1812, reel 24, no. 13.

12. Decatur to Hamilton, Sandy Hook, June 20, 1812, reel 24, no. 45.

13. Rodgers to Hamilton, June 21, 1812, reel 24, no. 47.

14. Extract from Rodgers's journal in *The Naval Monument: containing official and other accounts of all the battles fought between the navies of the United States and Great Britain during the late war*, comp. Abel Bowen (Boston: A. Bowen, 1816), 210–11; Rodgers to Hamilton, Boston, September 1, 1812, ibid., 206–7.

15. Isaac Hull to Hamilton, August 31, 1812, ibid., 8–9.

16. Secretary of the Navy, circular letter to Rodgers, Bainbridge, and Decatur, October 2, 1812, reel 10, no. 167.

17. For this account, see S. Putnam Waldo, *The Life and Character of Stephen Decatur* (Hartford, 1821), 194; Mackenzie, *Decatur*, 173; *New England Palladium* (Boston), December 11, 1812.

18. Carden, *Memoir*, 263.

19. Samuel Leech, *Thirty Years from Home* (Boston, 1843), 136.

20. Ibid., 138.

21. Ibid., 142; Carden, *Memoir*, 265.

22. Lewis, *Romantic Decatur*, 275n33, citing John R. Spears, *The History of Our Navy from Its Origin to the Present Day, 1775–1897*, 5 vols. (New York: C. Scribner's Sons, 1897–99), 2:139. Samuel Leech, a boy on the *Macedonian*, described Decatur as later in the cruise toward North America dressed "in an old straw hat and a plain suit of clothes, which made him look more like a farmer than a naval commander."

Leech, *Thirty Years*, 161. Spears may have picked up this arresting image and imag-
ined Decatur wearing farmer's clothes into battle, which is unlikely.

23. Mackenzie, *Decatur*, 176; *New England Palladium*, December 11, 1812.
24. Decatur to Susan Decatur, quoted in Lewis, *Romantic Decatur*, 124.
25. Carden, *Memoirs*, 264.
26. Leech, *Thirty Years*, 147.
27. Mackenzie, *Decatur*, 179.
28. Carden, *Memoirs*, 265.
29. Decatur to Secretary of the Navy, October 30, 1812, in Bowen, *Naval Monument*, 22–23.
30. Ibid.
31. Mackenzie, *Decatur*, 178.
32. Decatur to Susan Decatur, December 4, 1804, in Lewis, *Romantic Decatur*,
124–25.
33. Ibid.

Chapter 13

1. For this account, see Samuel Mitchill, Washington, D.C., December 10, 1812;
"Dr. Mitchill's Letters from Washington, *Harper's New Monthly Magazine* (April
1879): 753; Mrs. B. H. Latrobe to Juliana Miller, December 14, 1812, in James
Barnes, *Naval Actions of the War of 1812* (New York: Harper & Brothers, 1896), 67–
69; Benjamin H. Latrobe to Henry S. B. Latrobe, Washington, D.C., December 9,
1812; and Benjamin H. Latrobe to Isaac Hazelhurst, Washington, D.C., December
13, 1812, in *The Correspondence and Miscellaneous Papers of Benjamin Henry Latrobe*, ed.
John C. Van Horne, vol. 3, *1811–1820* (New Haven: Yale University Press for the
Maryland Historical Society, 1988), 401–2, 404–5.
2. Bainbridge, private letter, at sea, January 24, 1813, in Bowen, *Naval Monument*, 221–22.
3. Rocellus S. Guernsey, *New York City and Vicinity During the War of 1812–15,
being a Military, Civic, and Financial Local History of That Period*, 2 vols. (New York:
Charles L. Woodward, Booksellers, 1889), 1:128, 144, 145.
4. Ibid., 145, 148–49.
5. Leech, *Thirty Years*, 153.
6. Ibid., 153, 155–60.
7. Washington Irving to Henry Brevoort, January 2, 1813, in *Complete Works of
Washington Irving: Letters*, vol. 1, *1802–1823*, ed. Ralph M. Aderman, Herbert L.
Kleinfeld, and Jenifer S. Banks (Boston: Twayne Publishers, 1978), 354–355.
8. Washington Irving to Peter Irving, New York, December 30, 1812, ibid., 351.
9. Guernsey, *New York City*, 1:151.
10. Ibid.
11. *Boston Patriot*, January 2, 1813; Guernsey, *New York City*, 1:151.
12. Elijah Shaw, *A Short Sketch of the Life of Elijah Shaw, Who served for twenty-one
years in the U.S. Navy, Taking an Active Part in Four Different Wars Between the United
States & Foreign Powers: . . . And in 1843 entered on Board the "Old Ship Zion" Under a
New Commander, being in the 73d year of his age*, 3d ed. (Rochester, N.Y.:E. Shepard,
Mammoth Printing House, 1845), 45; Leech, *Thirty Years*, 160.

13. Shaw, *Short Sketch*, 46;
14. Guernsey, *New York City*, 1:161.
15. Leech, *Thirty Years*, 160–61.
16. Guernsey, *New York City*, 1:162.
17. Ibid., 164; Benson J. Lossing, *A Pictorial Fieldbook of the War of 1812* (New York: Harper and Brothers, 1868), 457–58n; Shaw, *Short Sketch*, 46; Leech, *Thirty Years*, 161.
18. John Binns, *Recollections of the Life of John Binns* (Philadelphia, 1854), 225–26.
19. Leech, *Thirty Years*, 162.
20. McKee, *Gentlemanly and Honorable Profession*, 342.
21. Ibid., table 29, 490–91; table 33, 494.
22. Decatur to Secretary of the Navy, New York, February 10, 1813, reel 34, no. 104.
23. Leech, *Thirty Years*, 161–62.
24. [Washington Irving], "Commodore Stephen Decatur," *Analectic Magazine* 1 (January–June 1813): 465.

Chapter 14

1. Decatur, statement of May 6, 1813, in Hutcheon, *Robert Fulton*, 125. See also Hanson W. Baldwin, "Fulton and Decatur: An Unpublished Document," U.S. Naval Institute *Proceedings* 62 (February 1936): 235.
2. "Memorandum of an agreement . . . between Commodore Stephen Decatur . . . and Robert Fulton," May 8, 1813, in Baldwin, "Fulton and Decatur," 233.
3. Ibid., 232.
4. Ibid., 233.
5. Hutcheon, *Robert Fulton*, 125, 127.
6. Decatur to Secretary of the Navy, March 10, 1813, in *The Naval War of 1812: A Documentary History*, ed. William S. Dudley, vol. 2, *1813* (Washington, D.C.: Department of the Navy, Naval Historical Center, 1992), 51–52.
7. Ibid.
8. Lewis, *Romantic Decatur*, 134; Mackenzie, *Decatur*, 194; Decatur to Secretary of the Navy, New London, June 1813, in Dudley, *Naval War*, 136.
9. Mackenzie, *Decatur*, 195.
10. Carden, *Memoirs*, 271.
11. Samuel Griswold Goodrich, *Recollections of a Lifetime*, 2 vols. (New York: Miller, Orton, and Mulligan, 1856), 1:483.
12. Decatur to Secretary of the Navy, New London, June 18, 1813, reel 29, no. 85.
13. Goodrich, *Recollections of a Lifetime*, 1:483, 485.
14. H. B. Deering, Collector of Customs, Sag Harbor, to Decatur, June 6, 1813, contained in Decatur to Secretary of the Navy, June 6, 1813, reel 29, no. 21.
15. Decatur to Secretary of the Navy, July 2, 1813, reel 37, no. 123; Decatur to Secretary of the Navy, June 23, 1813, reel 29, no. 108.
16. Decatur to Secretary of the Navy, June 23, 1813, reel 29, no. 108; Lieutenant

Commander Douglas S. Jordan, "Stephen Decatur at New London: A Study in Strategic Frustration," *U.S. Naval Institute Proceedings* 93 (October 1967): 63.

17. Decatur to Secretary of the Navy, July 7, 1813, reel 29, no. 167; Decatur to Secretary of the Navy, July 14, 1813, reel 37, no. 163.

18. Captain T. M. Hardy to Admiral John B. Warren, *Ramillies,* June 26, 1813, in Dudley, *Naval War,* 162.

19. General Orders of Admiral Sir John B. Warren, R.N., San Domingo in the Chesapeake, July 19, 1813, ibid., 164.

20. Lewis, *Romantic Decatur,* 135; Fulton to Decatur, August 5, 1813, in Dudley, *Naval War,* 211.

21. Secretary of the Navy to Decatur, September 30, 1813, reel 11, no. 104; Decatur to Secretary of the Navy, October 6, 1813, reel 31, no. 130.

22. Binns, *Recollections,* 225.

23. Secretary of the Navy to Decatur, December 29, 1813, reel 11, no. 180.

24. Goodrich, *Recollections of a Lifetime,* 1:483, 485; Decatur to Secretary of the Navy, December 20, 1813, in Jordan, "Stephen Decatur at New London," 64.

25. Goodrich, *Recollections of a Lifetime,* 1:482–83.

26. Binns, *Recollections,* 225.

27. Mackenzie, *Decatur,* 201.

28. Ibid., 204.

29. Hardy to Decatur, January 18, 1814, enclosed in Decatur to Secretary of the Navy, January 19, 1814, reel 34, no. 48.

30. Stackpole to Decatur, *Statira* off New London, January 17, 1814, in Decatur to Secretary of the Navy, January 19, 1814, reel 34, no. 48.

31. Decatur to Hardy, January 19, 1814, reel 34, no. 50.

32. Jones to Decatur, March 14, 1814, reel 11, no. 241.

Chapter 15

1. Mackenzie, *Decatur,* 198.

2. Fulton to Decatur, August 5, 1813, in Dudley, *Naval War,* 210–11.

3. Hutcheon, *Robert Fulton,* 130.

4. Ibid., 130–32.

5. Bowen, *Naval Monument,* 60.

6. Lossing, *Pictorial Fieldbook,* 518–30.

7. Secretary of the Navy, Letters to Officers, reel 11, nos. 348–53; Lossing, *Pictorial Fieldbook,* 704–9; Theodore Roosevelt, *Naval War of 1812* (New York: Putnam, 1882), 178–95; Cooper, *History of the Navy,* 2:102–7; Decatur to Secretary of the Navy, March 30, 1814, reel 35, no. 91; Decatur to Secretary of the Navy, May 7, 1814, reel 36, no. 35.

8. William Biddle to his father, *Hornet,* Sunday, August 15, 1813, in Nicholas Biddle, Personal Letters, vol. 5, 1–10, Historical Society of Pennsylvania. For more on Biddle, see David F. Long, *Sailor-Diplomat: A Biography of Captain James Biddle, 1783–1848* (Boston: Northeastern University Press, 1983).

9. Simon Snyder to Stephen Decatur, February 11, 1814, Library Company of Philadelphia, Yi 2 7350 F; *Autobiography of Charles Biddle, Vice President of Supreme*

Executive Council of Pennsylvania, 1745–1821, ed. J. L. Biddle (Philadelphia: E. Claxton and Company, 1883), 349n.

10. Decatur to Jones, February 11, 1814, reel 34, no. 107
11. Decatur to Jones, March 18, 1814, reel 35, no. 50.
12. Ibid.; Mackenzie, *Decatur*, 205.
13. Decatur to Jones, Private, March 29, 1814, reel 35, no. 89.

Chapter 16

1. Jones to Decatur, July 16, 1814, reel 11, no. 379; September 24, 1814, reel 11, no. 423; on Porter, see August 11, 1814, reel 11, no. 400.
2. Decatur to Jones, August 2, 1814, reel 38, no. 57; Decatur to Jones, August 4, 1814, reel 38, no. 62; Decatur to Jones, August 8, 1814, reel 38, no. 75; Decatur to Jones, August 10, 1814, reel 38, no. 83; Chauncey to Jones, August 10, 1814, reel 38, no. 84.
3. Guernsey *New York City*, 2:217–18.
4. Decatur to Jones, November 16, 1814, reel 40, no. 135; Decatur to Jones, September 26, 1814, reel 39, no. 104; Mackenzie, *Decatur*, 209.
5. Decatur to Jones, September 22, 1814, reel 39, no. 87.
6. Lossing, *Pictorial Fieldbook*, 935n.
7. *Federal Republican* (Georgetown, Md.), January 20, 1815.
8. William Shaler to Jonathan Russell, USS *Guerriere* off the Azores, June 4, 1815, Shaler Papers, box 1, Correspondence, 1798–1818, Correspondence File, 1815–1818, Historical Society of Pennsylvania.
9. For this account, see Lossing, *Pictorial Fieldbook*, 887n.
10. Shaler to Russell, June 4, 1815.
11. Lossing, *Pictorial Fieldbook*, 878; account of battle from Lossing, and Roosevelt, *Naval War of 1812*, 376–399; Cooper, *History of the Navy*, 2:211–24.
12. Governor Daniel D. Tompkins, memorandum to Decatur, November 14, 1814, and Fulton, memorandum to Decatur, both in Decatur to Secretary of the Navy, November 16, 1814, reel 40, no. 135.

Chapter 17

1. Decatur to Secretary of the Navy, December 30, 1814, reel 41, no. 148; see also Benjamin Crowninshield to David Porter, January 19, 1815, Crowninshield Family Papers, MH 15, box 13, folder 6, Phillips Library, Salem, Mass.
2. Mackenzie, *Decatur*, 214; Shaw, *Short Sketch*, 48.
3. "Autobiography of Commodore George Nicholas Hollins," *Maryland Historical Magazine* 34, no. 3 (September 1939): 229
4. Ibid.
5. Mackenzie, *Decatur*, 218; Bowen, *Naval Monument*, 166.
6. Mackenzie, *Decatur*, 219.
7. Decatur to Secretary of the Navy, HBM Ship *Endymion*, January 18, 1815, in Bowen, *Naval Monument*, 162.
8. Hollins, "Autobiography," 229.
9. Ibid., 230.

10. Mackenzie, *Decatur,* 225.

11. Ibid., 226.

12. Decatur to Secretary of the Navy, January 18, 1815, in Bowen, *Naval Monument,* 164.

13. *Federal Republican,* January 30, 1815; Lewis, *Romantic Decatur,* 150–51; Mackenzie, *Decatur,* 228.

14. Ibid., 229, 231.

15. R. B. Randolph to *Commercial Advertiser* (New York), April 3, 1815, in Bowen, *Naval Monument* 171–72.

16. *Niles Weekly Register,* March 4, 1815, 426; Goodrich, *Recollections of a Lifetime,* 485.

Chapter 18

1. Decatur to Benjamin Crowninshield, March 20, 1815, Crowninshield Papers, box 13, folder 6.

2. Secretary of the Navy to Decatur, March 14, 1815, reel 12, no. 60; Alexander Murray to Secretary of the Navy, April 17, 1815, in Bowen, *Naval Monument* 175, 174.

3. Manuel Mordecai Noah, *Correspondence and Documents Relative to the Attempt to Negotiate for the Release of the American Captives at Algiers* (Washington, D.C., 1816), 98–99.

4. *Federal Republican,* February 21, and May 19, 1815.

5. Quoted in Pierre M. Irving, *The Life and Letters of Washington Irving,* 4 vols. (New York: G. P. Putnam, 1863), 1:326–28.

6. Susan Decatur to Crowninshield, February 25, 1815, Crowninshield Papers, box 13, folder 6.

7. Decatur to Crowninshield, March 20, 1815, ibid.

8. Irving, *Life and Letters of Washington Irving,* 1:327–28; Long, *Ready to Hazard,* 193.

9. Decatur to Benjamin Crowninshield, March 20, 1815, Crowninshield Papers, box 13, folder 6.

10. A. Spencer to Bainbridge, New York, April 5, 1815, reel 44, no. 25; Henry Dearborn to Crowninshield, April 10, 1815, Crowninshield Papers, box 13, folder 6.

11. Waldo, *Life and Character of Decatur,* 274.

12. Mackenzie, *Decatur,* 252; [James Kirke Paulding], "Account of Rais Hammida, The Late Algerine Admiral," *Analectic Magazine,* January 1816, 14.

13. Joseph Causten to James Causten, August 14, 1815, Causten Family Papers, box 2, folder 19, Special Collections, Georgetown University, Washington, D.C. I am indebted to Margherita Desy for bringing Causten's letters to my attention.

14. Charles Gordon to Joseph Nicholson, June 19, 1815, Collection of Mr. George Emery, Vice Admiral, U.S. Navy (Retired); Causten to James Causten, August 14, 1815, Causten Family Papers.

15. For this account, see Hollins, "Autobiography," 232.

16. Susan Decatur, *Documents Relative to the Claim of Mrs. Decatur,* 31.

17. Shaw, *Short Sketch,* 52.

18. Decatur and Shaler to Secretary of State, USS *Guerriere*, Bay of Algiers, July 4, 1815, in Bowen, *Naval Monument*, 305.

19. Ibid.

20. Waldo, *Life and Character of Stephen Decatur*, 278; see also "Naval History," *Richmond Enquirer*, March 27, 1816.

21. Mackenzie, *Decatur*, 267.

22. Decatur to Crowninshield, March 15, 1815, Crowninshield Papers. Mackenzie, *Decatur*, 271–72.

23. Shaler to Jonathan Russell, Algiers, September 26, 1815, Shaler Papers.

24. Quoted in Mackenzie, *Decatur*, 271n.

Chapter 19

1. James Monroe to Mordecai M. Noah, April 25, 1815, in Noah, *Correspondence and Documents*, 82.

2. Ibid., 117.

3. For this account, see M. M. Noah to Susan Decatur, New York, November 8, 1826, in Susan Decatur, *Documents Relative to the Claim of Mrs. Decatur*, 20.

4. Mackenzie, *Decatur*, 276.

5. Ibid., 279; Richard Jones to Stephen Cathalan, Tripoli, August 20, 1815, *Richmond Enquirer*, December 5, 1815.

6. *New York Herald*, November 22, 1815.

7. Washington Irving to Cadwallader Colden, Birmingham, July 29, 1815, in *Complete Works of Washington Irving: Letters*, 1:413; Irving to Henry Brevoort, Liverpool, August 19, 1815, ibid., 1:414–415.

8. Long, *Ready to Hazard*, 199, 201.

9. Shaler to Russell, September 26, 1815, Shaler Papers.

10. Bainbridge to Monroe, Bay of Tunis, September 6, 1815, ibid.

11. Mackenzie, *Decatur*, 285.

12. Ibid.

13. Ibid., 289.

14. Susan Decatur quoted in Long, *Ready to Hazard*, 204; Shaw, *Short Sketch*, 52–53.

15. *New York Herald*, November 15, 1815; *Richmond Enquirer*, November 22, 1815; *National Intelligencer*, report from New York, November 13, 20, 1815.

17. *New York Herald*, November 17, 1815.

18. *Richmond Enquirer*, November 15, 1815.

19. Crowninshield to Decatur, November 17, 1815, reel 12, no. 219; Crowninshield to Bainbridge, November 20, 1815, reel 12, no. 221; December 4, 1815, reel 12, no. 229

Chapter 20

1. *Richmond Enquirer*, November 18, 1815.

2. James Madison, Seventh Annual Message, December 5, 1815, in *Messages and Papers of the Presidents*, ed. James D. Richardson, 11 vols. (Washington, D.C.: Bureau of National Literature and Art, 1908), 1:562–63.

3. *Baltimore Patriot*, September 6 and 7, 1815.

4. *Niles Weekly Register*, August 17, 1816, 416; *Boston Patriot*, September 9, 1815; *Georgetown Federal Republican*, December 5, 1815.

5. *Daily National Intelligencer*, November 20, 1815.

6. Reprinted in *Daily National Intelligencer*, November 25, 1815.

7. *Baltimore Patriot*, November 18, 1815.

8. Ibid., September 2, 1815.

9. *Wilmington (Del.) Gazette*, quoted in *Federal Republican*, October 6, 1815.

10. *Federal Republican*, December 27, 1815.

11. *Baltimore Patriot*, December 19, 1815.

12. Mackenzie, *Decatur*, 292–93.

13. *Baltimore Patriot*, November 1, 1815.

14. *Daily National Intelligencer*, January 2, 1816.

15. Ibid., January 18, 1816.

16. "Yankee Tars," *Richmond Enquirer*, January 23, 1816.

17. *Daily National Intelligencer*, January 8, 1816.

18. For this account, see *American Beacon and Commerical Diary* (Norfolk), April 5, 1816.

19. *Niles Weekly Register*, April 20, 1816, 136.

20. John Quincy Adams to John Adams, August 1, 1816, quoted in Samuel Flagg Bemis, *John Quincy Adams and the Union* (New York: Alfred A. Knopf, 1956), 352.

21. John Quincy Adams, "War with Great Britain and Mexico" (1842), ibid.

22. *Niles Weekly Register*, August 17, 1816, 415.

Chapter 21

1. Decatur to Crowninshield, March 20, 1815, Crowninshield Papers, box 13, folder 6.

2. C. Edward Skeen, *1816: America Rising* (Lexington: University Press of Kentucky, 2003), 148–49.

3. Decatur to William Jones, January 26, 1813, John H. Dilks Jr. Papers, William Jones Section, Historical Society of Pennsylvania.

4. Journal of the Board of Naval Commissioners, vol. 1: 1818–1819, December 26, 1818, 411, National Archives.

5. Decatur, report on defenses of the Chesapeake, January 2, 1817, in Mackenzie, *Decatur*, 396.

6. Ibid., 390–91.

7. Ibid., 397.

8. Journal of the Board of Naval Commissioners, February 12, 1819, 1:436; November 12, 1819, 2:123.

9. Ibid., January 12, 1818, 1:219.

10. Ibid., August 11, 1817, 1:133; Mackenzie, *Decatur*, 296–97.

11. Journal of the Board of Naval Commissioners, February 10, 21, 1817.

12. Ibid., July 8, 1817, 1:105.

13. Ibid., May–October 1818, 1:267, 320, 331, 349, 354.

14. Ibid., February 6, 1819, and September 30, 1818, 1:432, 349.

15. Constance McLaughlin Green, *Washington: Village and Capital, 1800–1878* (Princeton: Princeton University Press, 1962), 4, 78–79.

16. Decatur to Benjamin Crowninshield, Norfolk, June 14, 1816, Crowninshield Papers, box 14, folder 2; Decatur to William Whamm, June 1816, Stauffer Collection, 32 vols., 14:1016, Historical Society of Pennsylvania.

17. See Edward W. James, ed. *Lower Norfolk County, Virginia, Antiquary,* vols. (Baltimore: Freidenwald Co., 1897), 2:29; Tayloe, *In Memoriam,* 159; Decatur to Crowninshield, August 2, 1816, Crowninshield Papers, box 14, folder 3; Mackenzie, *Decatur,* 343.

18. Richard Rush to Benjamin Rush, Paris, May 4, 1849, Richard Rush Papers, Historical Society of Pennsylvania.

19. Dolly Madison quoted in *Memoirs and Letters of Dolly Madison,* edited by her Grand-Niece (Boston: Houghton, Mifflin, & Co., 1886), 15. Skeen, *1816,* 212.

20. Rush to Decatur, March 15, 1818, National Archives, RG 45, Miscellaneous Letters to Commissioned Officers; Richard Rush to Charles Jared Ingersoll, London, June 4, 1820, Ingersoll Papers.

21. Rush to Ingersoll, June 4, 1820.

22. Richard Rush to James Rush, November 10, 1817; John Quincy Adams to Richard Rush, November 13, 1817; Richard Rush to James Monroe, November 15, 1817, Richard Rush Papers, microfilm, reel 2.

23. See Allgor, *Parlor Politics;* Green, *Washington,* 81.

24. William Irving to Washington Irving, October 24, 1818, in Irving, *Life and Letters of Washington Irving,* 1:408–9. On Paulding, see William I. Paulding, *Literary Life of James Kirke Paulding* (New York: Charles Scribner and Co., 1867), 69.

25. Benjamin Henry Latrobe to Robert Goodloe Harper, November 24, 1817, in *Correspondence and Miscellaneous Papers of Latrobe,* 3:969–70.

26. Benjamin Henry Latrobe, *The Journals of Benjamin Henry Latrobe, 1799–1820: from Philadelphia to New Orleans,* ed. Edward C. Carter II et al. (New Haven: Yale University Press for the Maryland Historical Society, 1980), 79–80.

27. See "Latrobe's America," *www.latrobesamerica.org,* for more on the architect and his vision. Work at the Decatur House itself has revealed that the room to the right of the entrance was originally the kitchen.

28. Decatur to Amos Binney, January 25, 1818, Houghton Library, Harvard University.

29. Benjamin Latrobe to John Latrobe, December 12, 1818, in *Correspondence and Miscellaneous Papers of Latrobe,* 3:1019.

30. Ibid.

31. Tayloe, *In Memoriam,* 158.

32. See Decatur to William P. C. Barton, April 28, 1809, Gratz Collection, case 5, box 31, Historical Society of Pennsylvania; Decatur to Barton, March 30, 1810, Gratz Autograph Collection, Historical Society of Pennylvania; Secretary Jones to Decatur, March 6, 1813, reel 10, no. 294.

33. Decatur to Barton, Washington, D.C., August 20, [1818 or 1819?], Gratz Collection, case 5, box 31.

34. For Lacock's account of this incident, see James Parton, *Life of Andrew Jackson,* 3 vols. (New York: Mason Brothers, 1860), 2:569–80; for Jackson's account, ibid., 2:571; Tayloe, *In Memoriam,* 164.

35. Tayloe, *In Memoriam,* 164.

Chapter 22

1. Decatur to Crowninshield, May 20, 1816, Crowninshield Papers, box 13, folder 6.

2. *Daily National Intelligencer*, December 29, 1815.

3. Decatur to Barron, Washington, D.C., October 31, 1819, *Niles Weekly Register*, April 8, 1820, 100.

4. Ibid.

5. Ibid.

6. Barron to Decatur, Hampton, June 12, 1819, *Niles Weekly Register*, April 8, 1820, 98.

7. Decatur to Barron, Washington, D.C., June 17, 1819, ibid.

8. Barron to Decatur, Hampton, June 25, 1819, ibid.

9. Decatur to Barron, Washington, D.C., June 29, 1819, ibid.

10. Long, *Ready to Hazard*, 229–30.

11. W. Carter to Decatur, Norfolk, August 24, 1819, *Niles Weekly Register*, April 8, 1820, 101.

12. Barron to Decatur, Hampton, October 23, 1819, ibid., 98–99.

13. Letters from the Board of Navy Commissioners, 1818–1819, 637, National Archives, RG 45; Stephen Decatur, Circular Letter to Commodore Alexander Murray, November 27, 1819, Historical Society of Pennsylvania; Priscilla Decatur Twiggs to ?, Washington, D.C., February 5, 1832, Miscellaneous Manuscripts, Historical Society of Pennsylvania.

14. Mackenzie, *Decatur*, 302n; John Quincy Adams to Richard Rush, February 10, 1820, Richard Rush Papers, reel 2, no. 3877.

15. For this account, see Decatur to Barron, Washington, D.C., October 31, 1819, *Niles Weekly Register*, April 8, 1820, 99–101.

16. For this account, see Barron to Decatur, Hampton, November 30, 1819, ibid., 102–4.

17. Paullin, "Dueling in the Old Navy," 1173.

18. Long, *Ready to Hazard*, 233–34.

19. Mackenzie, *Decatur*, 344–45.

20. Decatur to Barron, December 29, 1819, *Niles Weekly Register*, April 8, 1820, 105–6.

21. Ibid., Barron to Decatur, Norfolk, January 16, 1820, and Decatur to Barron, Washington, D.C., January 24, 1820, ibid., 106.

22. Ibid., 102–3.

Chapter 23

1. Long, *Ready to Hazard*, 237.

2. Ibid.

3. Tayloe, *In Memoriam*, 163.

4. Paullin, "Dueling in the Old Navy," 1183–84.

5. Long, *Nothing Too Daring: A Biography of Commodore David Porter, 1780–1843* (Annapolis, Md.: U.S. Naval Institute, 1970), 187.

6. Paul Barron Watson, *The Tragic Career of Commodore James Barron, U.S. Navy, 1769–1851* (New York: Coward-McCann, 1942), 79.

7. Long, *Nothing Too Daring*, 187.
8. Mackenzie, *Decatur*, 328–29.

Afterword

1. John Rodgers to Hezekiah Niles, March 25, 1820, Miscellaneous Letters Sent by the Board of Navy Commissioners, 10 vols., 2:107, National Archives.

2. *Niles Weekly Register*, March 25, 1820, 1.

3. Caesar A. Rodney to James Monroe, April 3, 1820, James Monroe Papers, Microfilm, series 1, reel 7, National Archives.

4. Paullin, "Duelling in the Old Navy," 1155–57.

5. Watson, *Tragic Career*, 82–84.

6. Tyrone Martin, *A Most Fortunate Ship: A Narrative History of "Old Ironsides,"* (Chester, Conn.: Globe Pequot Press, 1980).

7. David Curtis Skagg, "Aiming at the Truth: James Fenimore Cooper and the Battle of Lake Erie," *Journal of Military History* 59 (April 1995): 237–56.

8. Alexander Slidell Mackenzie to Jared Sparks, New York, June 21, 1844, Sparks Papers, Houghton Library, Harvard University.

9. Mackenzie to Sparks, December 13, 1844, ibid.

10. Mackenzie to Sparks, May 18, 1844, ibid.

11. Charles Carroll of Carrollton to Robert Goodloe Harper, Dongorhagen, June 3, 1820, Robert Goodloe Harper Family Papers, reel 4.

12. Anne Hollingsworth Wharton, *Social Life in the Early Republic* (Philadelphia: J. B. Lippincott Company, 1903), 189.

13. Tayloe, *In Memoriam*, 160–61.

14. The pamphlet was titled *Documents Relative to the Claim of Mrs. Decatur, with her Earnest Request that the Gentlemen of Congress will take the trouble to read them.*

15. Susan Decatur to Benjamin Crowninshield, December 28, 1827, Crowninshield Papers, box 15, folder 2.

16. Susan Decatur to Crowninshield, December 27 [n.d., 1824?], Crowninshield Papers, box 15, folder 1.

17. Susan Decatur to Crowninshield, n.d., Crowninshield Papers, box 15, folder 3.

18. Priscilla Decatur Twiggs letter, February 5, 1832, Miscellaneous Manuscripts, Decatur Family Papers, Historical Society of Pennsylvania.

19. Coleridge, "On the Law of Nations," 297.

20. The account of this second funeral is drawn from George Decatur Twiggs, Clipping Notebook, 1846, in Decatur Family Papers, Historical Society of Pennsylvania.

ACKNOWLEDGMENTS

ROBERT FOWKES started me on the trail of Stephen Decatur by asking if there was a good biography. As a teacher himself, he knows we can never anticipate where a question will lead. I thank him for setting the process in motion, and Paul Wright at the University of Massachusetts Press for patiently but persistently helping me finish it. Our longtime friendship has not only survived writing of the book; it has prospered.

The only surviving ship Decatur commanded is in Boston, and I thank the U.S. Navy for keeping Old Ironsides here. The staff at the USS *Constitution* Museum are almost an extended family. Burt Logan and Anne Grimes Rand have been generous in their assistance; Kate Lennon in the Samuel Eliot Morison Library has provided an elegant workspace and reference help. Sarah Watkins and Gary Forman have been able to answer offbeat questions on a moment's notice; Christopher White has kept me apprised of other Decatur scholars; and Harrie Slootbeek has generously shared his own insights into the Barbary Wars. Above all, I must thank Margherita Desy, who put me on the trail of many Decatur artifacts and works of maritime history, and corrected many of this landlubber's mistaken notions about life at sea.

In Philadelphia, the staff at the Historical Society of Pennsylvania made my exploration of Decatur's papers pleasant as well as efficient. In Washington, D.C., the staff at the National Archives and the Naval Historical Center have been extraordinary exemplars of public service. The Phillips Library at the Peabody Essex Museum, the Boston Athenaeum, and the Boston Public Library have been wonderful places to work. The Georgetown University Library has put its own Decatur letters on-line, which will make these special collections more widely available. The friendly and capable curators at the Stephen Decatur House in Washington make that elegant place what Stephen and Susan Decatur hoped it would be, a true treasure in our nation's capital. Thanks especially to Mary Doering and Marty Zell for insight into the Decaturs' brief life there, and to Sarah Taffer for tracking down illustrations.

Friends and family have generously assisted by listening and by reading. William M. Fowler and Bernard Bailyn have been generous with counsel; Rear Admiral George Emery (Retired) has read several versions of the manuscript and I hope will be satisfied with this one. Michael Crawford made astute suggestions about an early draft, and Dr. William J. Reid read successive drafts and urged me along with the project. William M. Bulger Jr., Hal Hansen, Anouar Majid, Louis P. Masur, Robert Rabil, Francis "Flyer" Santos, Doug Shidell, Svat Soucek, and Edward L. Widmer have offered their own comments and support; Dean Kenneth S. Greenberg at Suffolk University has kindly found ways to allow me to research and write while also teaching. Michael Shinagel at the Harvard Extension School has made it possible for faculty to engage student researchers, benefiting both students and faculty; through his generous support and Suzanne Spreadbury's able administration, I was able to find Cathy Perlmutter, a peerless scholar and researcher, who has combed early-nineteenth-century newspapers for news of Stephen Decatur.

I am deeply indebted to Carol Betsch, managing editor at the University of Massachusetts Press, for her thorough professionalism. I am grateful that she placed this book under the extraordinary eye of copy editor Amanda Heller, to whom both the reader and I owe an incalculable debt. Amanda Heller has a gift for the language; she should be given free rein over all written works. I would paraphrase our book's hero and say, "My copy editor, Right or Wrong!"—but Amanda, I think, is never wrong.

Peggy Gaudiano provided me a place to stay while doing research, and probably listened to more Decatur stories than she needed to. My wife, Phyllis, has endured much for the sake of Stephen Decatur. She and our two sons, John and Philip, continue to inspire me.

INDEX

ROBERT J. ALLISON received his A.L.B. from the Harvard University Extension School, and earned his A.M. in history and his Ph.D. in the history of American civilization from Harvard University. He teaches at the Harvard Extension School, where he won the Petra T. Shattuck Distinguished Teaching Award, and he is currently chair of the History Department at Suffolk University, where he has been on the faculty since 1992. In addition to *Stephen Decatur*, his books include *The Crescent Obscured: The United States and the Muslim World, 1776–1815* (1995) and *A Short History of Boston* (2004). He has also edited several volumes, including *The Interesting Narrative of Olaudah Equiano, or Gustavus Vassa, The African* (1995). Robert Allison lives in South Boston, Massachusetts, with his wife Phyllis and sons John Robert and Philip.